The Genius of
CHINESE
CHARACTERS

The Genius of Chinese Characters

ISBN-13: 978-988-8552-82-5

© 2020 ChinaNow

LANGUAGE / Chinese

EB133

All rights reserved. No part of this book may be reproduced in material form, by any means, whether graphic, electronic, mechanical or other, including photocopying or information storage, in whole or in part. May not be used to prepare other publications without written permission from the publisher except in the case of brief quotations embodied in critical articles or reviews. For information contact info@earnshawbooks.com

Published by Earnshaw Books Ltd. (Hong Kong)

EDITORIAL TEAM

EDITOR-IN-CHIEF
GRAHAM EARNSHAW

EXECUTIVE EDITOR
MARGARET SUN

EDITORS

CAMERON PAGE	YANG YIFEI
JULIA HUNG	ARIEL ZHAO
BIAN LIJUN	CHARLOTTE JIANG
JURNEE KELLEY	ADRIANNA MARSHALL
LAURA NAVARRO	REIKA SHIMOMURA
LEWIS VINT	SPENCER TILGHMAN
CUI YUE	CHIARA RONCALLO

CONSULTANTS
PROFESSOR LIU WOYU
SU PENG

DESIGN
JASON WONG
MAGIC WANG

CONTENTS

CHARACTERS LIST	viii
INTRODUCTION	ix
EXPLANATION	xii
CHARACTERS 1-250	1
RADICALS	251
INFORMATION SOURCES	255

CHARACTER LIST
1 to 250

一	1	口	33	個	65	關	97	服	129	喜	161	狗	193	已	225
七	2	可	34	和	66	裏	98	再	130	讀	162	漂	194	間	226
上	3	右	35	日	67	好	99	兒	131	館	163	椅	195	比	227
下	4	左	36	月	68	沒	100	住	132	歡	164	喂	196	手	228
不	5	吃	37	時	69	看	101	什	133	怎	165	蘋	197	表	229
中	6	名	38	期	70	點	102	書	134	杯	166	爲	198	兩	230
之	7	四	39	明	71	起	103	米	135	鐘	167	到	199	意	231
九	8	因	40	朋	72	星	104	師	136	呢	168	以	200	務	232
了	9	國	41	會	73	些	105	五	137	租	169	行	201	正	233
二	10	土	42	來	74	三	106	見	138	塊	170	就	202	房	234
人	11	在	43	家	75	很	107	熱	139	誰	171	新	203	問	235
今	12	外	44	生	76	商	108	買	140	嗎	172	經	204	門	236
他	13	多	45	們	77	麼	109	醫	141	叫	173	也	205	球	237
她	14	大	46	對	78	樣	110	愛	142	亮	174	場	206	題	238
你	15	天	47	能	79	那	111	校	143	哪	175	第	207	教	239
我	16	太	48	本	80	東	112	昨	144	媽	176	過	208	路	240
文	17	夫	49	學	81	西	113	站	145	爸	177	自	209	告	241
心	18	女	50	現	82	想	114	覺	146	坐	178	得	210	件	242
出	19	子	51	説	83	水	115	候	147	漢	179	報	211	運	243
入	20	字	52	作	84	影	116	飛	148	飯	180	進	212	給	244
八	21	安	53	電	85	話	117	錢	149	衣	181	動	213	常	245
公	22	完	54	前	86	視	118	歲	150	雨	182	還	214	每	246
六	23	客	55	開	87	果	119	請	151	冷	183	司	215	樂	247
力	24	小	56	京	88	老	120	識	152	姐	184	最	216	身	248
北	25	少	57	分	89	院	121	火	153	謝	185	所	217	別	249
十	26	山	58	高	90	認	122	聽	154	菜	186	但	218	張	250
千	27	川	59	都	91	打	123	興	155	零	187	長	219		
午	28	年	60	工	92	做	124	習	156	睡	188	員	220		
半	29	的	61	面	93	先	125	語	157	喝	189	次	221		
去	30	是	62	機	94	回	126	腦	158	茶	190	體	222		
又	31	有	63	同	95	系	127	店	159	猫	191	等	223		
友	32	這	64	車	96	氣	128	寫	160	桌	192	着	224		

INTRODUCTION

THIS BOOK IS CALLED *The Genius of Chinese Characters*, but the title itself deviates ever so slightly from the fundamental goal of the project, which is to highlight and celebrate the incredible breadth and depth of this writing system, historically and geographically. The characters were created in what is today China as part of Chinese culture, and they underpin its entire history, culture, philosophy and literature, as well as its political and social structures. But the impact of the characters extends well beyond the borders of China, over most of East Asia, just as English is used well beyond the British Isles. The objective of this series, which will cover a total of 3,000 characters, is to reflect on and celebrate these characters and their legacy.

The characters, known in Chinese as *hanzi* (漢字), form the only language in use in the world which is basically non-phonetic. It uses pictures to convey meaning, both in terms of the combination of pictograms into sentences, and also the combination of different picture parts to create the characters themselves. That is not to say that phonetics plays no role at all in the writing system — parts of many of the pictures have phonetic connotations, but they still form part of a larger picture.

The characters created and used throughout history in total number something like 50,000, although dictionaries mostly contain around 10,000 to 20,000. The modern Chinese language works on the basis of a core of around 3,000 characters, although educated people know more, perhaps up to 8,000. The number of strokes used to make up the characters varies from one stroke for the simplest, through to fifty-seven for the most complicated.

It has sometimes been said that the Chinese written language is not as efficient as strictly phonetic writing systems such as the one in which these words are based, the twenty-six letters of the English language. But there is another perspective, that the fundamentally pictorial Chinese language actually has advantages over phonetic writing systems. Certainly, scanning documents for characters is for many people much more effective than scanning for combinations of English letters.

The origins of the characters can be traced back into the mists of prehistory. They first appeared over 3,000 years ago on the so-called Oracle bones, scratchings on the bones of animals that were thrown into a fire to create cracks which were used as the basis for fortune telling pronouncements for the kings and tribal leaders of the lands that would eventually become China. Over the next millennium, these scratchings developed into a sophisticated writing system that are at the heart of Chinese civilization and the civilization of much of East Asia.

China, for almost all of this period, has been the dominant and most influential culture in East Asia. Surrounding societies, either willingly or unwillingly, to one degree or another, accepted the Chinese approach to culture, including the writing system. The most obvious example of the use of Chinese characters beyond the territorial boundaries of China is Japan, where the Japanese written language today consists of three different writing systems, two strictly phonetic and one composed of *hanzi*. The characters, known in Japanese as *kanji* — the Japanese pronunciation of the same two characters making up the Chinese *hanzi*, play a central role in the writing

THE GENIUS OF CHINESE CHARACTERS

system of Japan, even though Japanese grammar is fundamentally different from Chinese grammar. The *kanji* characters, as well as the vocabulary and concepts that they reflect, were borrowed from China starting more than a thousand years ago, and grafted on top of the Japanese linguistic base. The same process occurred with the Korean and Vietnamese languages without changing the fundamental grammatical structures of the languages.

In a strictly phonetic writing system, symbols are used to indicate sounds, and these sounds are combined to create groupings known as words. People read these groupings, sound the word in their mind, and create the image of what is being referred to by the collection of phonetic symbols. We look at C A and T and we sound it in our brains, then visualize the object associated with that sound (although it is true that with repetition, we also come to associate the visual combination of C, A and T with the animal). The Chinese written language, however, is fundamentally based on the pictorial nature of the characters. Characters can be viewed simply as a representation of meaning without necessarily associating each character with a sound. Also, the pronunciation of each character varies, sometimes dramatically, from one language and dialect to another. There is no absolute linkage between the meanings of Chinese characters and they way they are pronounced, and it would be theoretically possible to read Chinese without knowing how to pronounce a single word in any Chinese dialect.

But, as mentioned above, there is a phonetic element to many, though not all, *hanzi*. They are not random squiggles, and structurally many characters are composed of two parts—a "radical" indicating roughly the area of meaning to which the character belongs, and a "phonetic" which gives a hint as to the pronunciation.

When compiling this book, we were faced with the question of which character form to use as the standard, and we decided on the standard traditional Chinese character set, used for more than 2,000 years. In mainland China today, this has been replaced in recent decades by the simplified character set. The simplification of the writing system was widely debated starting in the 1920s, with some people arguing that the complexity of the written language was an obstacle to China's modernization. The current simplified character set was introduced in the 1950s, and has become the standard for communication in Chinese around the world. Some of the simplifications are only a moderate variation from their traditional equivalent. But there are some characters where the difference between the traditional and simplified forms is substantial.

Around a third of all commonly-used *hanzi* are simplified, which means that the majority are the same in both systems. It was felt that by simplifying the characters, reducing the number of strokes needed to write many of them, Chinese literacy rates would improve, and literacy levels in China today are very high. The downside is that people who learn only the simplified writing system have great trouble reading most written materials from across more than two thousand years of Chinese history.

A second set of more radically simplified characters was introduced in 1977 but withdrawn after a few years due to widespread opposition. Japan, too, has its own approach to the use of *hanzi* and has simplified some of them in its own way.

Each page of the book contains information on just one character, providing an overview of the meaning, origins and usage of that character. It is but a taste, and does not pretend to be completist. It is not a dictionary.

THE GENIUS OF CHINESE CHARACTERS

Looking at each page of the book, the starting point in the top-left corner is the traditional character, which would have been recognized, in almost all cases, by Confucius 2,500 years ago and by all the scholars and literate people through Chinese history down to the modern age. The second character, to the right, is the simplified version.

An objective of this book is to clarify that *hanzi* are not inextricably linked to the pronunciation of the Mandarin dialect. Mandarin is now the national language of China, and the Mandarin pronunciation is the most-used and the most-taught, but it is not the only way to pronounce these characters. Just as the Arabic numerals 1, 2 and 3 can be said in as many different ways as there are languages in the world, each language and dialect in the Chinese world and beyond has its own set of sounds and pronunciations for each character, and we have provided a sampling of these different sounds for the characters in this book. Alongside the standard Mandarin pronunciation, we provide that of Cantonese, as well as the Hokkien language of Xiamen, also used in Taiwan and many Chinese communities in Southeast Asia. These three were chosen because all three have had an impact internationally and have a much wider geographical spread than other Chinese languages and dialects. We could easily have added in others — such as Shanghainese and the Chongqing, Chengdu, and Shandong dialects — each of which is discrete from one another and from Mandarin. It is said, for example, that there are more than forty mutually unintelligible dialects in the province of Fujian alone, and each one of them would be able to pronounce the characters in the Chinese lexicon in their own slightly unique way.

The information provided for each character includes a hint of its etymology — that is, how the character developed, and information on meaning and character combinations to give a sense of the spectrum of usage. We also show examples of how the character has been written throughout history. But with all the elements on these pages, it is nor more than a hint of the cultural, historical and linguistic richness represented by each character. Each item on each page can be considered a springboard for further exploration.

What and what not to include? There were many compromises along the way, but while the result is subjective, it is not random. The aim was to choose the most representative and insightful meanings, combinations, fonts, pronunciations and sayings in the case of each word.

The purpose of *The Genius of Chinese Characters* is to celebrate this writing system, one that deserves to be studied more widely and deeply around the world in the years ahead as China's role in the world and the role of the Chinese language become ever more central to global affairs. We hope you find something interesting on every page.

Graham Earnshaw
October 2020

EXPLANATION

The format of each page of this book is fixed and standardized. Here is an explanation of each part of the matrix.

❶ Standard

The standard form of the character. Now sometimes called the "traditional" or "complex form". This is the version of the character as it has existed for generally the last 2,000 years and more.

❷ Simplified

The simplified form of the character. The simplified character set was introduced in the mainland in the 1950s and is now the standard for written communication in Chinese throughout most of the world. Not all characters have a simplified version—a few hundred only are significantly different from the standard form of the character. A larger number contain a simplification of a part of the character, to reduce the number of strokes, while retaining the general shape. About a third of characters included in this volume have simplified versions.

❸ Meaning

A summary of the most important meanings of the word.

❹ Stroke Number: Standard

The number of strokes for the Standard version of the character.

❺ Stroke Number: Simplified

The number of strokes for the Simplified version of the character.

❻ Etymology

Information on the origins and derivations of the character.

❼ Data

- **Radical**: Chinese characters are traditionally organized according to 214 "Radicals" – character components. The radicals were defined by the Kangxi dictionary published in 1716.
- **Strokes**: The number of strokes for each character: STANDARD | SIMPLIFIED
- **HSK**: HSK is the acronym for the standardized Mandarin oral language test administered by China's Ministry of Education. It stands for Hanyu Shuiping Kaoshi. There are six levels of materials, courses and tests, and the HSK number indicates the HSK level in which the character is introduced.
- **Frequency**: This number indicates the character's ranking on the list of the most frequently used words in modern Chinese.
- **Big 5**: Big 5 is a character encoding method for standard Chinese characters, mainly used in Taiwan and Hong Kong.
- **Unihan**: Unihan is part of Unicode, an IT coding system that encodes each character used for almost all the world's written languages. Unihan maps and assigns a unique code to each 漢字 character used in the Chinese, Japanese and Korean languages.
- **Kangxi Dictionary**: Created at the direction of the Kangxi Emperor of the Qing Dynasty in 1710, the Kangxi Dictionary was the standard

THE GENIUS OF CHINESE CHARACTERS

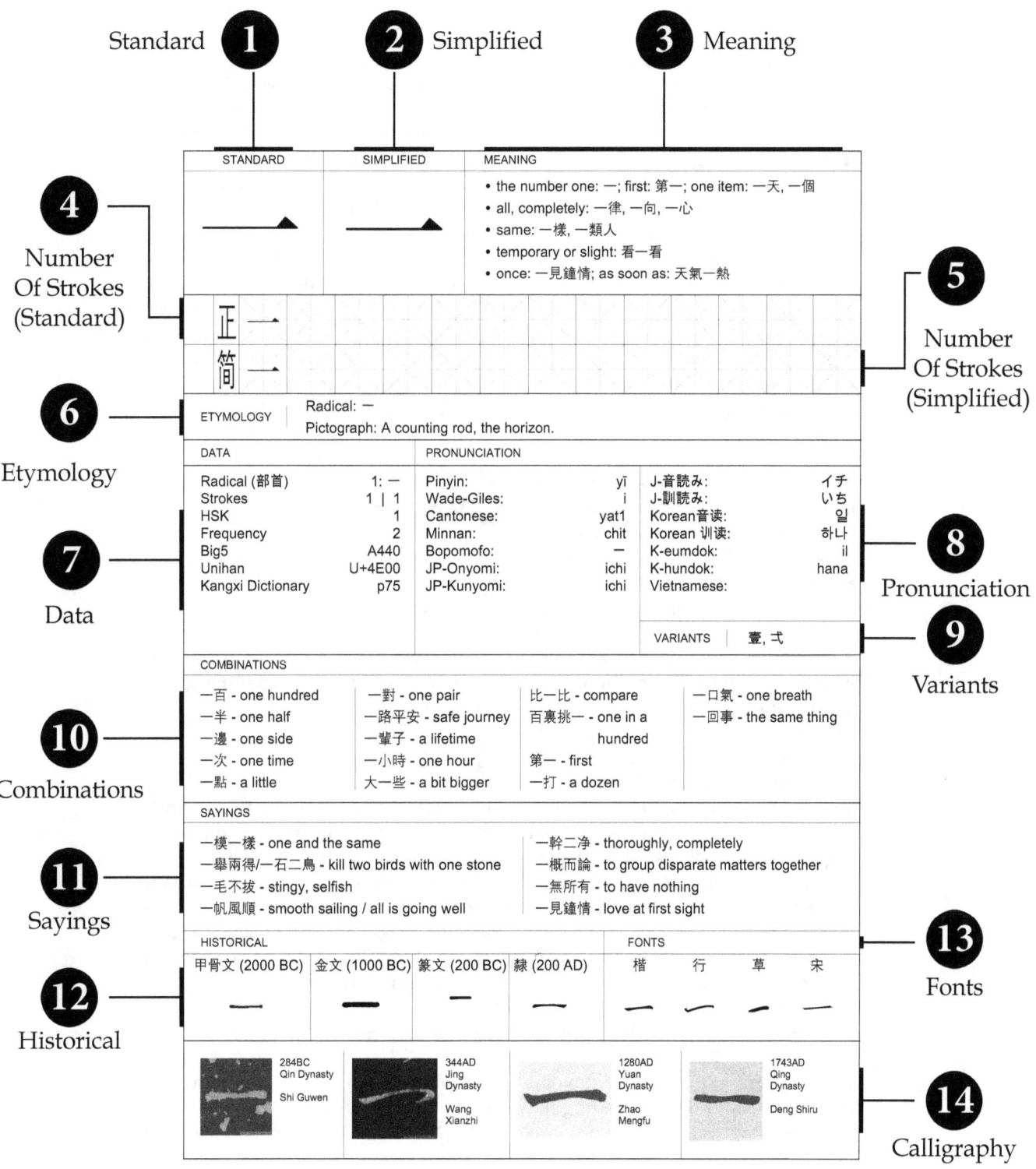

Chinese dictionary during the 18th and the 19th century. It contains 49,030 characters, ordered by 214 radicals. This indicates the page of the standard edition of the Kangxi Dictionary on which it appears.

❽ Pronunciation

- **Pinyin**: Pinyin is China's official romanization system used to transcribe Chinese characters. The phonetic transcriptions also include four diacritic elements used to signal tones.
- **Wade-Giles**: Developed by T.M. Wade and H.A. Giles in 1892, Wade-Giles was the dominant romanization system for the Mandarin language until the 1980s.
- **Cantonese**: The Cantonese language is one of the official languages of Hong Kong and Macau and is widely spoken in Chinese communities around the world.
- **Minnan**: The Minnan language is spoken in Taiwan, the southern region of Fujian province and also widely in Chinese communities in Southeast Asia.
- **Bopomofo**: The Mandarin Phonetic Symbols system, colloquially known as Bopomofo, was created in the 1910s and is still widely used in Taiwan.
- **JP-Onyomi**: The Japanese written language makes wide use of hanzi, called kanji in Japanese, and many characters have two pronunciations — one reading is derived from the Chinese pronunciation — Onyomi — and the second is derived from the pronunciation of the original Japanese word to which the character was attached — Kunyomi.
- **JP-Kunyomi**: The Kunyomi reading refers to the native, original pronunciation of the word in Japanese.
- **K-Eumdok**: The Korean language started using hanzi for the written form of the language from around 400 BC, called hanja in Korean. One reading is derived from the Chinese pronunciation — eumdok — and the second is derived from the pronunciation of the original korean word to which the character was attached — hundok.
- **K-Hundok**: The Hundok reading refers to the native, original pronunciation of the word in Korean.
- **Vietnamese**: The Vietnamese written language for many centuries used *hanzi* for the written form of the language, called Chu Nom in Vietnamese. It was abandoned in favor of a Western alphabet-based script in the 20th Century.

❾ Variants

Alternative forms of the character.

❿ Combinations

A selection of combinations containing the character, representing some of the most common words and phrases.

⓫ Sayings

The Chinese language contains a rich reservoir of idiomatic expressions and sayings, mostly made up of four characters, called *chengyu* (成語), which represent and contain much of the collected wisdom of Chinese culture. *Chengyu* are still extremely relevant in contemporary language.

⓬ Historical

Examples of the character as written in different historical periods.

- **甲骨文 (2000BC)**: From inscriptions found on Oracle Bones, tools of

divination which feature the earliest known use of *hanzi*.
- 金文 (**1000BC**): From inscriptions found on ancient bronze objects.
- 篆文 (**200BC**): From inscriptions using the calligraphic style known as "seal script"
- 隶 (**200AD**): From inscriptions on the official script of the Han dynasty.

⑬ Fonts

The character as written in common fonts for *hanzi*.
- 楷: Regular script
- 行: Running-hand script
- 草: Cursive script
- 宋: Standard "Song" font

⑭ Calligraphy

Examples of the character as found in pieces of calligraphy from famous scholars over the centuries.

THE GENIUS OF CHINESE CHARACTERS

STANDARD	SIMPLIFIED	MEANING
一	一	• the number one: 一; first: 第一; one item: 一天, 一個 • all, completely: 一律, 一向, 一心 • same: 一樣, 一類人 • temporary or slight: 看一看 • once: 一見鐘情; as soon as: 天氣一熱

正 一
简 一

ETYMOLOGY

Radical: 一
Pictograph: A counting rod, the horizon.

DATA		PRONUNCIATION			
Radical (部首)	1: 一	Pinyin:	yī	J-音読み:	イチ
Strokes	1 | 1	Wade-Giles:	i	J-訓読み:	いち
HSK	1	Cantonese:	yat1	Korean 音读:	일
Frequency	2	Minnan:	chit	Korean 训读:	하나
Big5	A440	Bopomofo:	ㄧ	K-eumdok:	il
Unihan	U+4E00	JP-Onyomi:	ichi	K-hundok:	hana
Kangxi Dictionary	p75	JP-Kunyomi:	ichi	Vietnamese:	

VARIANTS | 壹, 弌

COMBINATIONS

一百 - one hundred	一對 - one pair	比一比 - compare	一口氣 - one breath
一半 - one half	一路平安 - safe journey	百裏挑一 - one in a hundred	一回事 - the same thing
一邊 - one side	一輩子 - a lifetime		
一次 - one time	一小時 - one hour	第一 - first	
一點 - a little	大一些 - a bit bigger	一打 - a dozen	

SAYINGS

一模一樣 - one and the same
一舉兩得/一石二鳥 - kill two birds with one stone
一毛不拔 - stingy, selfish
一帆風順 - smooth sailing / all is going well

一幹二淨 - thoroughly, completely
一概而論 - to group disparate matters together
一無所有 - to have nothing
一見鐘情 - love at first sight

HISTORICAL | **FONTS**

甲骨文 (2000 BC)	金文 (1000 BC)	篆文 (200 BC)	隸 (200 AD)	楷	行	草	宋

284BC Qin Dynasty — Shi Guwen
344AD Jing Dynasty — Wang Xianzhi
1280AD Yuan Dynasty — Zhao Mengfu
1743AD Qing Dynasty — Deng Shiru

THE GENIUS OF CHINESE CHARACTERS

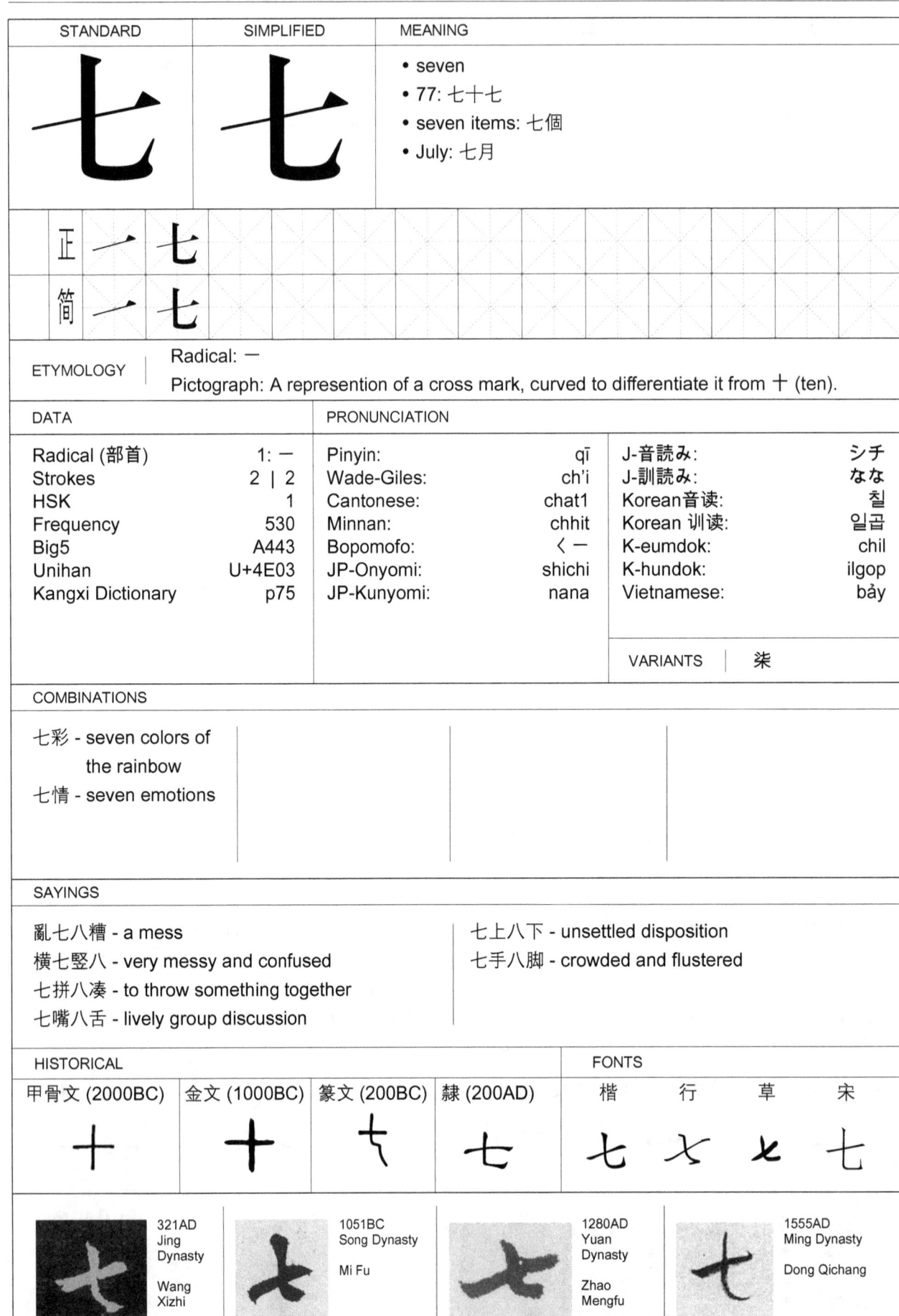

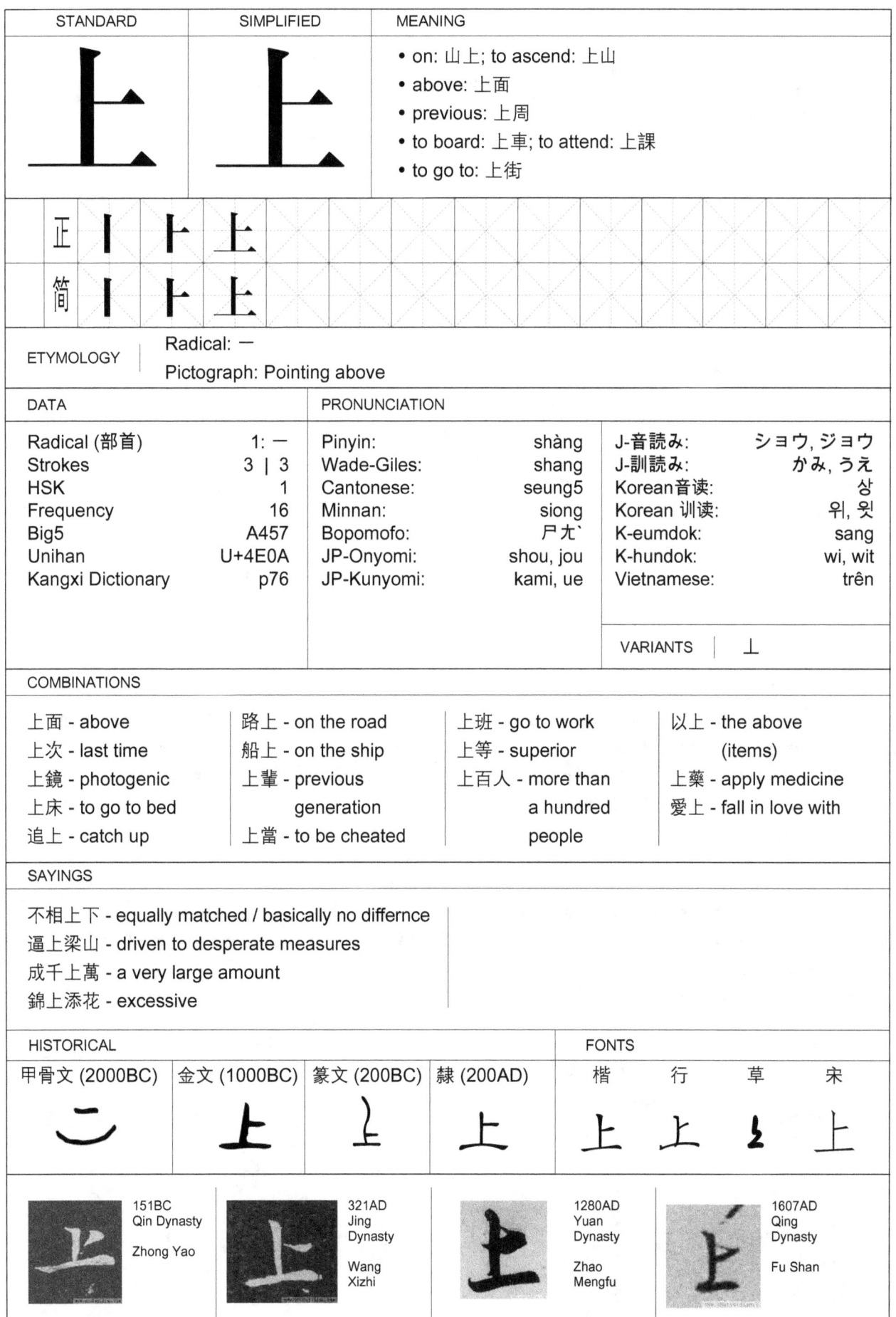

THE GENIUS OF Chinese CHARACTERS

STANDARD	SIMPLIFIED	MEANING
下	下	• beneath: 床下; a little: 看一下 • below: 下面; next: 下周; disembark: 下車 • to descend: 下山; leave work: 下班 • to issue: 下令; to make up mind: 下決心 • downwards: 坐下

正 一 丁 下
简 一 丁 下

ETYMOLOGY
Radical: 一
Pictograph: Pointing below

DATA

		PRONUNCIATION			
Radical (部首)	1: 一	Pinyin:	xià	J-音読み:	カ, ゲ
Strokes	3 | 3	Wade-Giles:	hsia	J-訓読み:	した, しも, くだ〜
HSK	1	Cantonese:	ha6	Korean 音读:	하
Frequency	42	Minnan:	e	Korean 训读:	아래
Big5	A455	Bopomofo:	ㄒㄧㄚˋ	K-eumdok:	ha
Unihan	U+4E0B	JP-Onyomi:	ka, ge	K-hundok:	arae
Kangxi Dictionary	P76	JP-Kunyomi:	shita, shimo, kuda~	Vietnamese:	dưới

VARIANTS | 丅

COMBINATIONS

桌下 - under the table	下班 - get off work	下周 - next week	想一下 - think about it
下馬 - get off the horse	坐下 - sit down	下課 - after class	下等 - inferior
下臺 - get off stage/step down	下次 - next time	樓下 - downstairs	下結論 - draw a conclusion
下棋 - play chess	下面 - below	下雨 - rain	
	下去 - go down	以下 - the following	

SAYINGS

不耻下問 - not ashamed to ask for help from subordinates
低三下四 - obsequious
下不爲例 - just this once

騎虎難下 - hard to stop halfway
對癥下藥 - suit the methods to the situation

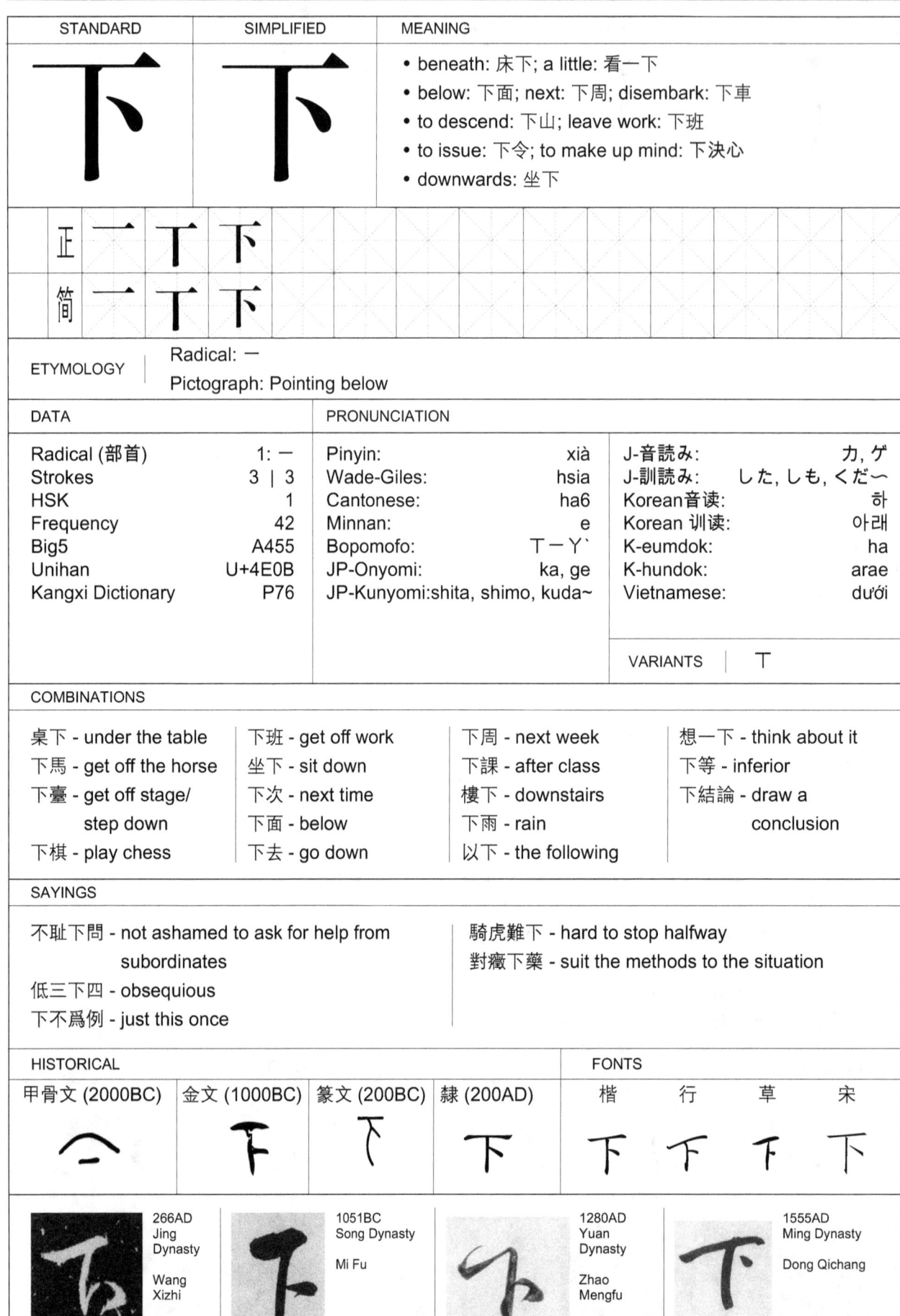

HISTORICAL
甲骨文 (2000BC) | 金文 (1000BC) | 篆文 (200BC) | 隸 (200AD)

FONTS
楷 行 草 宋

266AD Jing Dynasty Wang Xizhi
1051BC Song Dynasty Mi Fu
1280AD Yuan Dynasty Zhao Mengfu
1555AD Ming Dynasty Dong Qichang

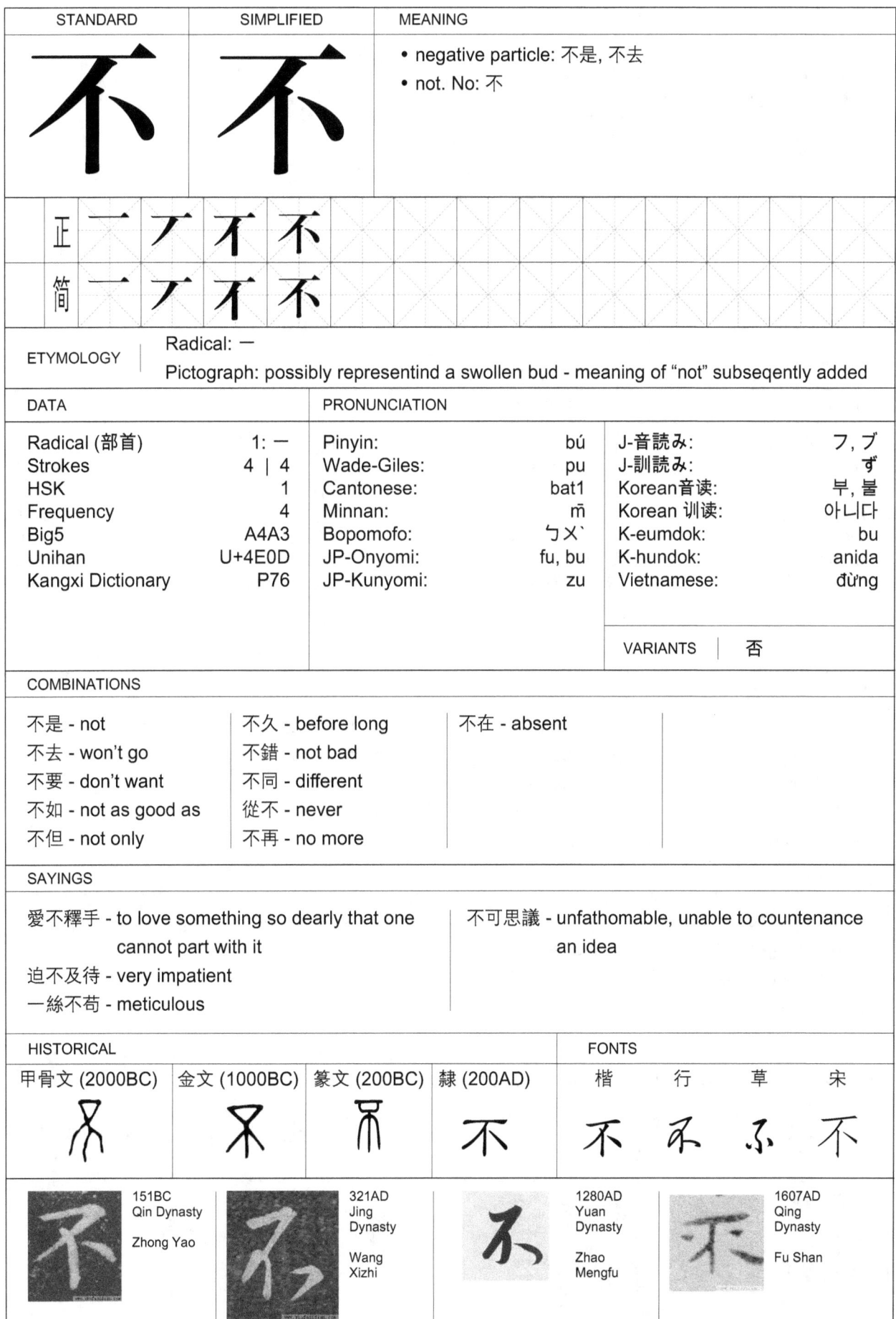

THE GENIUS OF CHINESE CHARACTERS

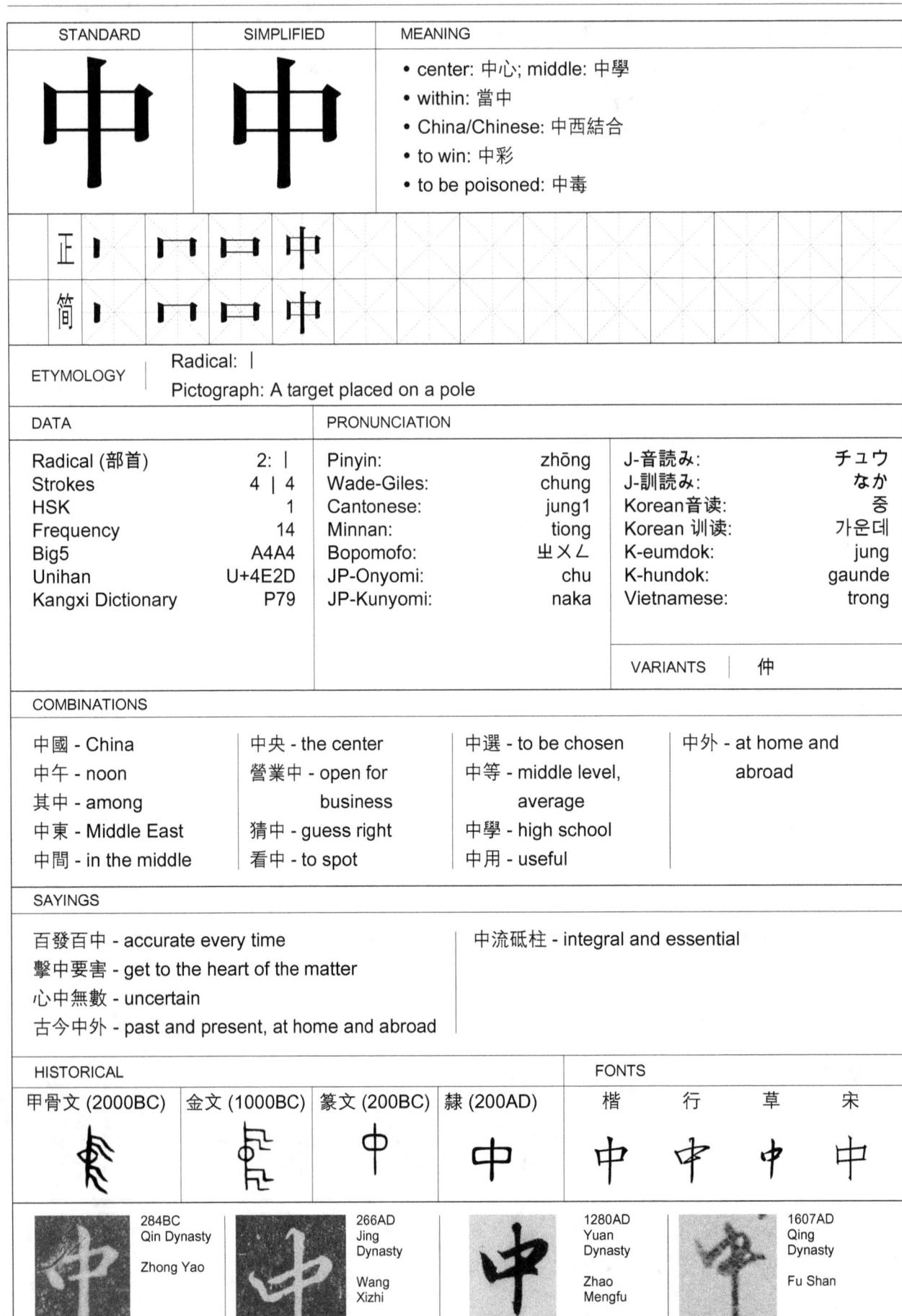

STANDARD	SIMPLIFIED	MEANING
中	中	• center: 中心; middle: 中學 • within: 當中 • China/Chinese: 中西結合 • to win: 中彩 • to be poisoned: 中毒

正: 丨 冂 口 中
简: 丨 冂 口 中

ETYMOLOGY
Radical: 丨
Pictograph: A target placed on a pole

DATA

Radical (部首)	2: 丨
Strokes	4 | 4
HSK	1
Frequency	14
Big5	A4A4
Unihan	U+4E2D
Kangxi Dictionary	P79

PRONUNCIATION

Pinyin:	zhōng	J-音読み:	チュウ
Wade-Giles:	chung	J-訓読み:	なか
Cantonese:	jung1	Korean 音读:	중
Minnan:	tiong	Korean 训读:	가운데
Bopomofo:	ㄓㄨㄥ	K-eumdok:	jung
JP-Onyomi:	chu	K-hundok:	gaunde
JP-Kunyomi:	naka	Vietnamese:	trong

VARIANTS | 仲

COMBINATIONS

中國 - China
中午 - noon
其中 - among
中東 - Middle East
中間 - in the middle

中央 - the center
營業中 - open for business
猜中 - guess right
看中 - to spot

中選 - to be chosen
中等 - middle level, average
中學 - high school
中用 - useful

中外 - at home and abroad

SAYINGS

百發百中 - accurate every time
擊中要害 - get to the heart of the matter
心中無數 - uncertain
古今中外 - past and present, at home and abroad

中流砥柱 - integral and essential

HISTORICAL

甲骨文 (2000BC) | 金文 (1000BC) | 篆文 (200BC) | 隸 (200AD)

FONTS

楷 行 草 宋

284BC Qin Dynasty — Zhong Yao
266AD Jing Dynasty — Wang Xizhi
1280AD Yuan Dynasty — Zhao Mengfu
1607AD Qing Dynasty — Fu Shan

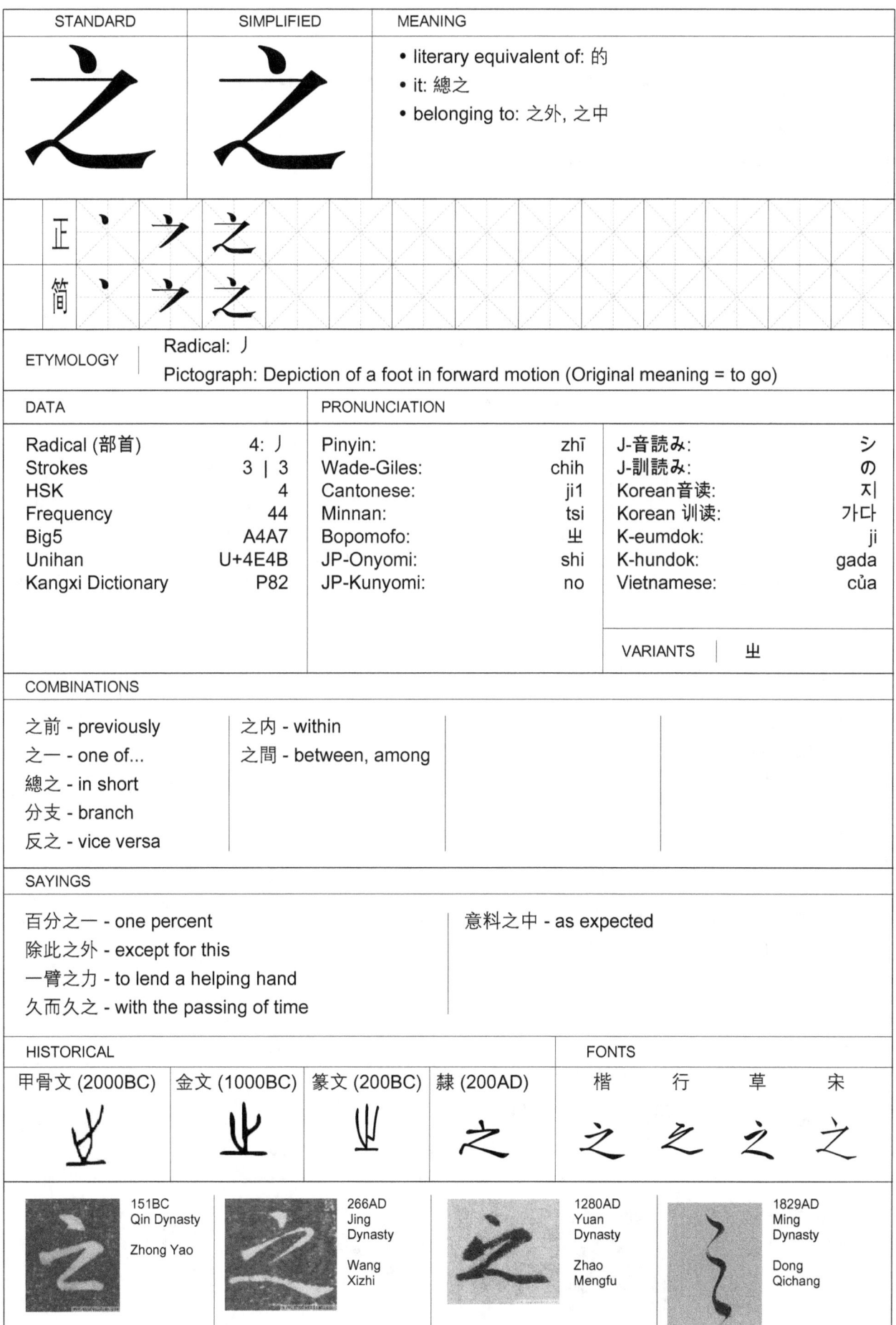

THE GENIUS OF CHINESE CHARACTERS

STANDARD	SIMPLIFIED	MEANING
九	九	• nine: 九 • ninety-nine: 九十九; nine (units): 九個 • September: 九月

正	丿	九
简	丿	九

ETYMOLOGY | Radical: 乙 Pictograph: An arm with hand outstretched, bumping against something and curving - meaning of 9 added later.

DATA

		PRONUNCIATION			
Radical (部首)	5: 乙	Pinyin:	jiǔ	J-音読み:	キュウ, ク
Strokes	2 | 2	Wade-Giles:	chiu	J-訓読み:	ここの
HSK	1	Cantonese:	gau2	Korean 音读:	구
Frequency	445	Minnan:	kíu	Korean 训读:	아홉
Big5	A445	Bopomofo:	ㄐ一ㄡˇ	K-eumdok:	gu
Unihan	U+4E5D	JP-Onyomi:	kyū, ku	K-hundok:	ahop
Kangxi Dictionary	P83	JP-Kunyomi:	kokono	Vietnamese:	chín

VARIANTS | 玖

COMBINATIONS

九重 - the sky
九天 - heaven
九泉 - hell, hades
九州 - Kyushu
九月 - September

SAYINGS

九戰九勝 - winning every time
九九歸一 - right after all

HISTORICAL

甲骨文 (2000BC)	金文 (1000BC)	篆文 (200BC)	隸 (200AD)

FONTS

楷　行　草　宋

151BC Qin Dynasty Zhong Yao
266AD Jing Dynasty Wang Xizhi
1280AD Yuan Dynasty Zhao Mengfu
1829AD Ming Dynasty Dong Qichang

THE GENIUS OF CHINESE CHARACTERS

STANDARD	SIMPLIFIED	MEANING
了	了	• completed action particle: 完了, 走了 • to understand: 了解 • to finish: 了事 • to settle: 了債

正 了 了

简 了 了

ETYMOLOGY | Radical: 亅
Pictograph: A depiction of a long object, rolled up.

DATA		PRONUNCIATION			
Radical (部首)	6: 亅	Pinyin:	le, liǎo	J-音読み:	リョウ
Strokes	2 | 2	Wade-Giles:	lê	J-訓読み:	お・わる
HSK	1	Cantonese:	liu5	Korean 音读:	료, 요
Frequency	5	Minnan:	liáu	Korean 训读:	마치다
Big5	A446	Bopomofo:	ㄌ一ㄠˇ	K-eumdok:	ryo
Unihan	U+4E86	JP-Onyomi:	ryō	K-hundok:	machida
Kangxi Dictionary	P85	JP-Kunyomi:	o·waru	Vietnamese:	tắt

VARIANTS | 瞭

COMBINATIONS

了斷 - call an end to sth.	了解 - understand	畢業了 - graduated	爲了 - for, in order to
了不得 - formidable	不得了 - great	做好了 - well done	
來不了 - can't come	了事 - Complete something, call an end to sth.	好了 - good	
了不起 - great		不了 - no	
		極了 - extremely	

SAYINGS

一目了然 - obvious at the first glance
草草了事 - to do something in a slapdash way
沒完沒了 - incessantly
不了了之 - end up with nothing definite

了如指掌 - to know something like the back of one's hand

HISTORICAL | **FONTS**

| 甲骨文 (2000BC) | 金文 (1000BC) | 篆文 (200BC) | 隸 (200AD) | 楷 | 行 | 草 | 宋 |

266AD Jing Dynasty Wang Xizhi

1051BC Song Dynasty Mi Fu

1037BC Song Dynasty Su Shi

1829AD Ming Dynasty Dong Qichang

9

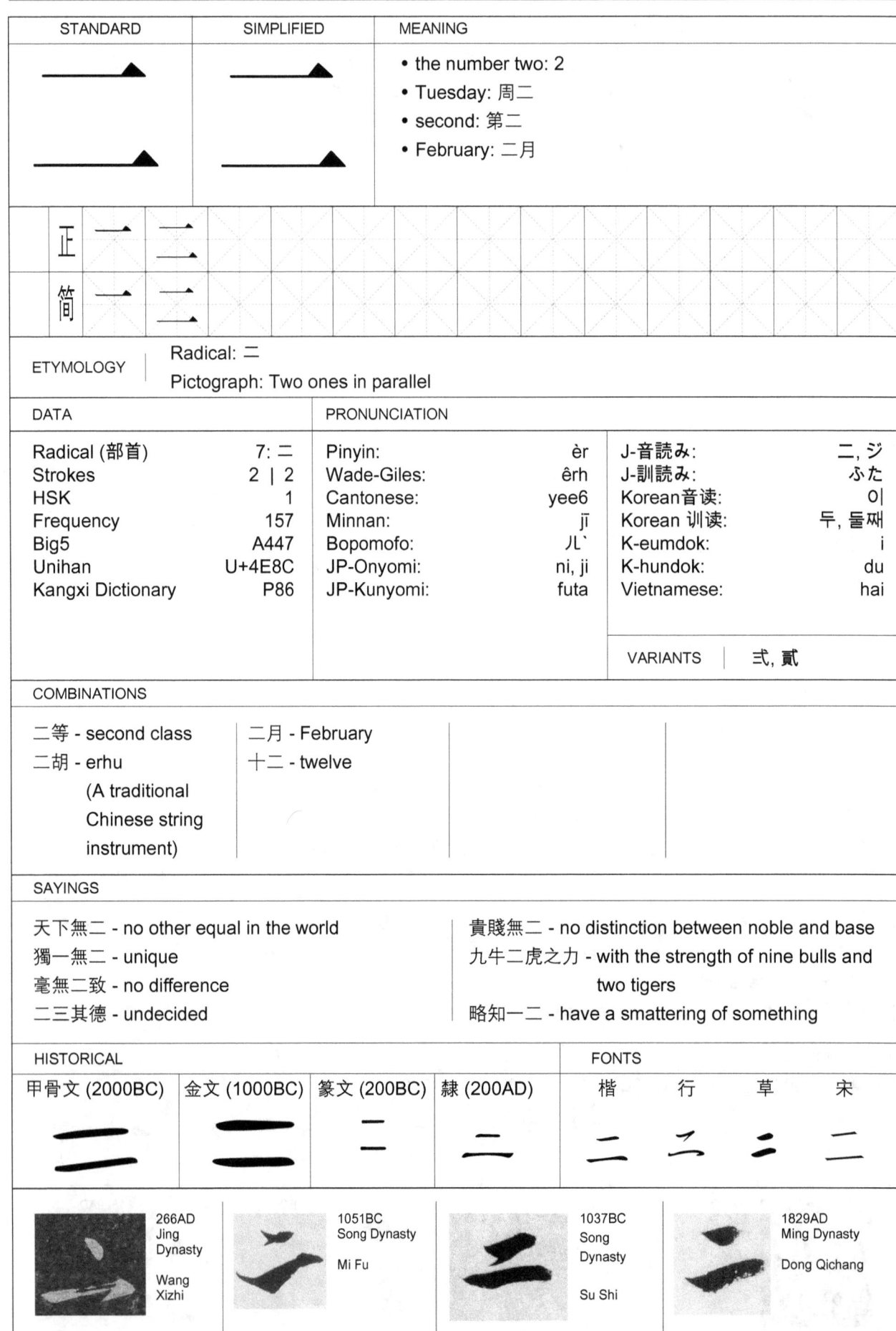

THE GENIUS OF CHINESE CHARACTERS

STANDARD	SIMPLIFIED	MEANING
人	人	• person: 人 • humanity: 人類 • other people: 人家

正 ノ 人
简 ノ 人

ETYMOLOGY	Radical: 人
	Pictograph: A human figure standing legs apart

DATA

		PRONUNCIATION			
Radical (部首)	9: 人	Pinyin:	rén	J-音読み:	ニン, ジン
Strokes	2 | 2	Wade-Giles:	jên	J-訓読み:	ひと
HSK	1	Cantonese:	yan4	Korean 音读:	인
Frequency	7	Minnan:	jîn	Korean 训读:	사람
Big5	A448	Bopomofo:	ㄖㄣˊ	K-eumdok:	in
Unihan	U+4EBA	JP-Onyomi:	nin, jin	K-hundok:	saram
Kangxi Dictionary	P91	JP-Kunyomi:	hito	Vietnamese:	mọi người

VARIANTS | 亻

COMBINATIONS

做人 - behave properly
法人 - legal person
人權 - human rights
人道 - humane
人格 - personality

人家 - other people
人人 - all without exception
人類 - human beings
男人 - man

女人 - woman
成年人 - adult
家人 - family member
工人 - worker

SAYINGS

人面獸心 - benign face but evil heart
人才輩出 - lots of talented people
人多手雜 - Too many cooks spoil the broth (soup)
人人自危 - everyone in danger

人雲亦雲 - follow others blindly
成人之美 - helping others virtuously
乘人之危 - take advantage of other's misfortune
人定勝天 - we are masters of our own fate

HISTORICAL

甲骨文 (2000BC)	金文 (1000BC)	(200BC)	隸 (200AD)

FONTS

楷 行 草 宋

266AD
Jing Dynasty
Wang Xizhi

778BC
Tang Dynasty
Liu Gongquan

1280AD
Yuan Dynasty
Zhao Mengfu

1829AD
Ming Dynasty
Dong Qichang

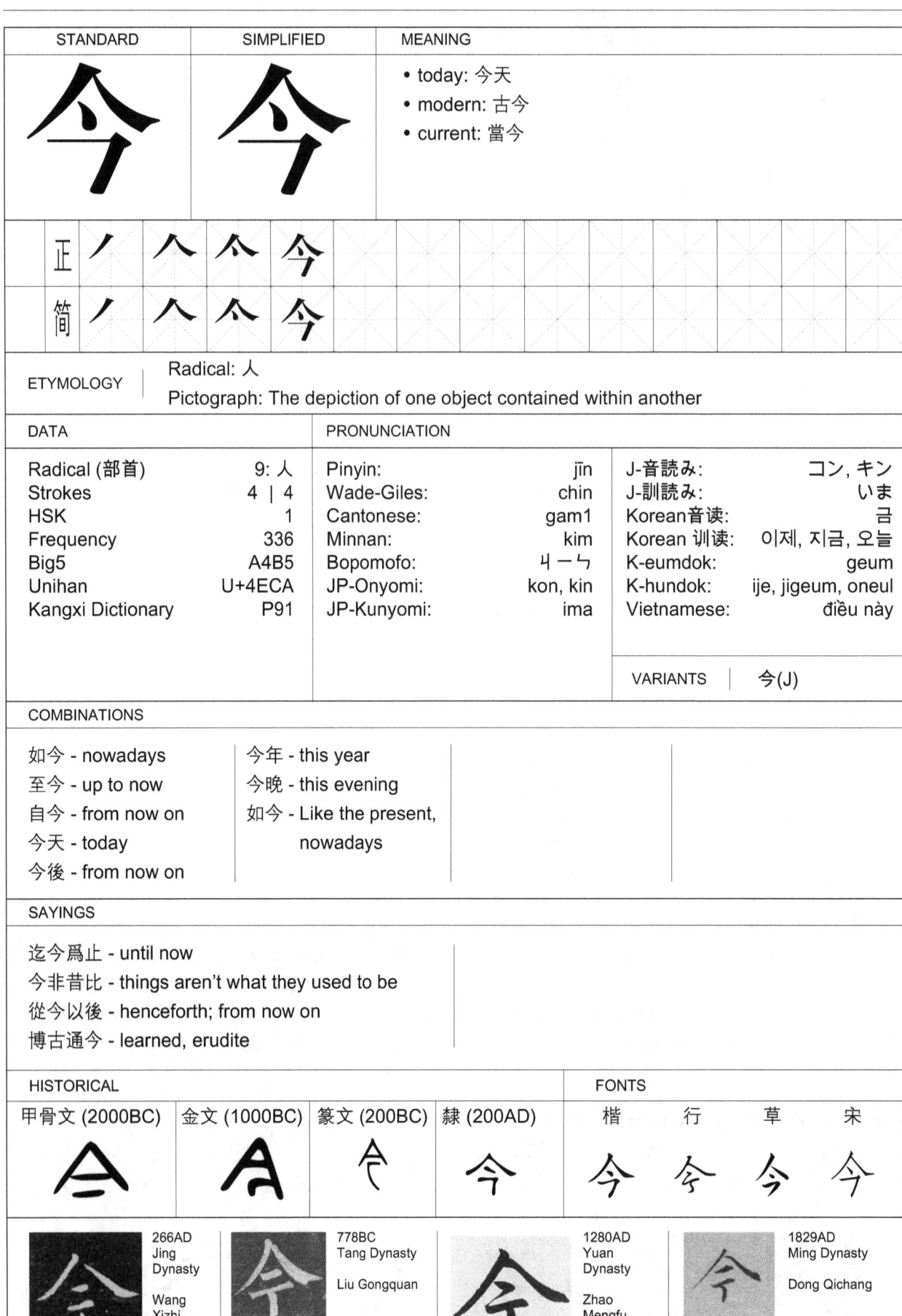

THE GENIUS OF CHINESE CHARACTERS

STANDARD	SIMPLIFIED	MEANING
他	他	• he; his; him: 他 • others: 其他 • other, another: 他國

正 ノ 亻 彳 仲 他
简 ノ 亻 彳 仲 他

ETYMOLOGY
Radical: 人 (people)
Pictograph: A variant form of 佗 - other

DATA

Radical (部首)	9: 人
Strokes	5 | 5
HSK	1
Frequency	10
Big5	A54C
Unihan	U+4ED6
Kangxi Dictionary	P92

PRONUNCIATION

Pinyin:	tā	J-音読み:	タ
Wade-Giles:	t'a	J-訓読み:	ほか
Cantonese:	ta1	Korean 音读:	타
Minnan:	tha	Korean 训读:	다르다, 남
Bopomofo:	ㄊㄚ	K-eumdok:	ta
JP-Onyomi:	ta	K-hundok:	dareuda, nam
JP-Kunyomi:	hoka	Vietnamese:	anh ta

VARIANTS | 它

COMBINATIONS

他的 - his
他們 - them, they
別管他 - ignore him
他媽的 - damn
他人 - other people

其他 - others
其他 - others
吉他 - guitar

SAYINGS

异國他鄉 - foreign lands and places, living as an expatriate
別無他法 - there is no alternative
利他主義 - altruism

HISTORICAL

甲骨文 (2000BC)	金文 (1000BC)	篆文 (200BC)	(200AD)
		他	他

FONTS

楷 行 草 宋
他 他 他 他

266AD Jing Dynasty - Wang Xizhi
778BC Tang Dynasty - Liu Gongquan
1280AD Yuan Dynasty - Zhao Mengfu
1829AD Ming Dynasty - Tang Yin

THE GENIUS OF CHINESE CHARACTERS

STANDARD	SIMPLIFIED	MEANING
她	她	• she: 她 • her • female

| 正 | ㄑ | 女 | 女 | 如 | 奼 | 她 |
| 简 | ㄑ | 女 | 女 | 如 | 奼 | 她 |

ETYMOLOGY
Radical: 女. (female)
Pictograph: Word created in 20th century. A variant form of 佗 - other.

DATA

Radical (部首)	38: 女
Strokes	6 | 6
HSK	1
Frequency	91
Big5	A66F
Unihan	U+5979
Kangxi Dictionary	P225

PRONUNCIATION

Pinyin:	tā
Wade-Giles:	t'a
Cantonese:	ta1
Minnan:	tha
Bopomofo:	ㄊㄚ
JP-Onyomi:	chi, ji
JP-Kunyomi:	aza·ru

J-音読み:	チ, ジ
J-訓読み:	あざ·る
Korean 音读:	저, 타
Korean 训读:	아가씨, 그녀
K-eumdok:	jeo, ta
K-hundok:	agassi, geunyeo
Vietnamese:	cô ấy đã

VARIANTS	姐

COMBINATIONS

她的 - her
她們 - them (females)

SAYINGS

This character is a creation of the feminist movement in the early 20th century, and has no traditional sayings attached to it

HISTORICAL

甲骨文 (2000BC)	金文 (1000BC)	篆文 (200BC)	隸 (200AD)
			她

FONTS

楷	行	草	宋
她	她	她	她

778BC Tang Dynasty Tang Xuanzong

778BC Tang Dynasty Liu Gongquan

778BC Tang Dynasty Chu suiliang

778BC Tang Dynasty Lu jian zhi

THE GENIUS OF Chinese Characters

STANDARD	SIMPLIFIED	MEANING
你	你	• you (colloquial and modern usage)

| 正 | 丿 | 亻 | 亻 | 伱 | 伱 | 你 | 你 |
| 简 | 丿 | 亻 | 亻 | 伱 | 伱 | 你 | 你 |

ETYMOLOGY
Radical: 人 (people)
Pictograph: The phoentic you 尔 with person radical 人 added

DATA

Radical (部首)	9: 人
Strokes	7 | 7
HSK	1
Frequency	32
Big5	A741
Unihan	U+4F60
Kangxi Dictionary	n/a

PRONUNCIATION

Pinyin:	nǐ	J-音読み:	ジ, ニ
Wade-Giles:	ni	J-訓読み:	なんじ
Cantonese:	nei5	Korean 音读:	니, 이
Minnan:	lí	Korean 训读:	너
Bopomofo:	ㄋㄧˇ	K-eumdok:	ni, i
JP-Onyomi:	ji, ni	K-hundok:	neo
JP-Kunyomi:	nanji	Vietnamese:	bạn

VARIANTS | 妳, 伱, 儞

COMBINATIONS

你們 - you plural
你好! - hello
你是誰? - who are you?
你的 - your/yours
你呢? - how about you?

給你 - give to you
麻煩你 - sorry for troubling you

SAYINGS

你死我活 - irreconcilable differences, lit. you die, I live
真有你的 - exclamation of surprise, 'you're really something!'

隨便你 - as you like, at your convenience
你爭我奪 - to fight or scramble fiercely for sth

HISTORICAL

甲骨文 (2000BC)	金文 (1000BC)	篆文 (200BC)	隸 (200AD)
			你
	266AD Jing Dynasty Wang Xizhi	778BC Tang Dynasty Liu Gongquan	

FONTS

楷 行 草 宋
你 你 你 你 你

1280AD Yuan Dynasty Zhao Mengfu

1829AD Ming Dynasty Tang Yin

THE GENIUS OF CHINESE CHARACTERS

STANDARD	SIMPLIFIED	MEANING
我	我	• I, my: 我的 • me, we: 我們 • our: 我們的 • our country: 我國

正	一	二	千	手	我	我	我
简	一	二	千	手	我	我	我

ETYMOLOGY
Radical: 戈
Pictograph: a sharp weapon - 戈。

DATA

		PRONUNCIATION			
Radical (部首)	62: 戈	Pinyin:	wǒ	J-音読み:	ガ
Strokes	7 | 7	Wade-Giles:	wo	J-訓読み:	われ, わ
HSK	1	Cantonese:	ngoh5	Korean 音读:	아
Frequency	9	Minnan:	góa	Korean 训读:	나
Big5	A7DA	Bopomofo:	ㄨㄛˇ	K-eumdok:	a
Unihan	U+6211	JP-Onyomi:	ga	K-hundok:	na
Kangxi Dictionary	P412	JP-Kunyomi:	ware, wa	Vietnamese:	tôi

VARIANTS

COMBINATIONS

我國 - my country
我軍 - our army
我們 - us
我的 - mine
自我 - self

你我 - you and I

SAYINGS

對我來説 - from my perspective
自我防衛 - self-defence
依然故我 - stuck in one's ways
爾虞我詐 - a dog-eat-dog arrangement

HISTORICAL

甲骨文 (2000BC)　　金文 (1000BC)　　篆文 (200BC)　　隸 (200AD)

FONTS

楷　　行　　草　　宋

266AD
Jing Dynasty
Wang Xizhi

778BC
Tang Dynasty
Liu Gongquan

1280AD
Yuan Dynasty
Zhao Mengfu

1829AD
Ming Dynasty
Dong Qichang

THE GENIUS OF Chinese CHARACTERS

STANDARD	SIMPLIFIED	MEANING
文	文	• writing: 文字 • language: 中文 • document: 公文 • literature: 文學 • culture: 文化

正: 丶 一 ナ 文
简: 丶 一 ナ 文

ETYMOLOGY

Radical: 文
Pictograph: Depiction of a pattern on earthenware, by extension, writing

DATA

		PRONUNCIATION			
Radical (部首)	67: 文	Pinyin:	wén	J-音読み:	ぶん, もん
Strokes	4 | 4	Wade-Giles:	wen	J-訓読み:	ふみ, あや
HSK	3	Cantonese:	man4	Korean 音读:	문
Frequency	148	Minnan:	bûn	Korean 训读:	글월
Big5	A4E5	Bopomofo:	ㄨㄣˊ	K-eumdok:	mun
Unihan	U+6587	JP-Onyomi:	bun, mon	K-hundok:	geul-wel
Kangxi Dictionary	P477	JP-Kunyomi:	fumi, aya	Vietnamese:	bản văn

VARIANTS: 彣, 玟, 玅, 紋

COMBINATIONS

- 作文 - composition
- 原文 - original text
- 英文 - English
- 日文 - Japanese
- 文法 - grammar
- 文章 - essay
- 文具 - stationery
- 文盲 - illiterate
- 文明 - civilization
- 文人 - writer
- 文雅 - refined
- 文化 - culture
- 文藝復興 - The Renaissance
- 文件 - document

SAYINGS

- 能文能武 - multi-capable
- 文質彬彬 - well-mannered
- 不立文字 - unwritten agreement, gentlemen's agreement
- 文過飾非 - cover up faults
- 分文不值 - worthless
- 咬文嚼字 - ruminate
- 文不加點 - well-written

HISTORICAL

甲骨文 (2000BC)	金文 (1000BC)	篆文 (200BC)	隸 (200AD)

FONTS

楷 行 草 宋

文 文 文 文

266AD
Jing Dynasty
Wang Xizhi

778BC
Tang Dynasty
Liu Gongquan

1280AD
Yuan Dynasty
Zhao Mengfu

1829AD
Ming Dynasty
Dong Qichang

THE GENIUS OF CHINESE CHARACTERS

STANDARD	SIMPLIFIED	MEANING
心	心	• heart: 心臟 • the mind: 心智; feelings: 心情 • love: 心愛 • peace of mind: 安心 • center: 地心

正 ㇀ 心 心 心
简 ㇀ 心 心 心

ETYMOLOGY
Radical: 心
Pictograph: a heart

DATA
Radical (部首)	61: 心	Pinyin: xīn	J-音読み: しん
Strokes	4 | 4	Wade-Giles: hsin	J-訓読み: こころ
HSK	3	Cantonese: sam1	Korean 音读: 심
Frequency	90	Minnan: sim	Korean 训读: 마음
Big5	A4DF	Bopomofo: ㄒㄧㄣ	K-eumdok: sim
Unihan	U+5FC3	JP-Onyomi: shin	K-hundok: maum
Kangxi Dictionary	p375	JP-Kunyomi: kokoro	Vietnamese: tim

VARIANTS | 忄

COMBINATIONS
心跳 - palpitations　　耐心 - patience　　死心 - given up all hope　　心願 - wish
專心 - concentrate on　良心 - conscience　心境 - state of mind　　放心 - set aside
決心 - determined　　誠心 - sincerity　　心裏 - in the mind　　　　　concerns
細心 - carefully　　　忠心 - loyal　　　　心思 - thinking
粗心 - careless　　　 熱心 - enthusiasm　心理學 - psychology

SAYINGS
三心二意 - undecided　　　　　　　　　心神不寧 - feel ill at ease
心心相印 - mutual affinity　　　　　　心力交瘁 - mentally exhausted
心猿意馬 - restless
力不從心 - ability fails to match ambition

HISTORICAL
甲骨文 (2000BC)　金文 (1000BC)　篆文 (200BC)　隸 (200AD)

FONTS
楷　行　草　宋

266AD Jing Dynasty Wang Xizhi
778BC Tang Dynasty Liu Gongquan
1280AD Yuan Dynasty Zhao Mengfu
1829AD Ming Dynasty Dong Qichang

THE GENIUS OF CHINESE CHARACTERS

STANDARD	SIMPLIFIED	MEANING
出	出	• to go out: 出去; to appear: 出現 • to produce: 出產; to occur: 出事 • come out: 出來; take out: 拿出 • come from: 出自廣東

正 ㄧ 凵 屮 出 出

简 ㄧ 凵 屮 出 出

ETYMOLOGY — Radical: 凵
Pictograph: Originally a foot 止 walking out of a pit

DATA		PRONUNCIATION			
Radical (部首)	17: 凵	Pinyin:	chū	J-音読み:	シュツ, スイ
Strokes	5 | 5	Wade-Giles:	ch'u	J-訓読み:	で・る, だ・す
HSK	1	Cantonese:	chut1	Korean 音读:	출
Frequency	28	Minnan:	chhut	Korean 训读:	나다, 나가다
Big5	A558	Bopomofo:	ㄔㄨ	K-eumdok:	chul
Unihan	U+51FA	JP-Onyomi:	shutsu, sui	K-hundok:	nada, nagada
Kangxi Dictionary	P135	JP-Kunyomi:	de·ru, da·su	Vietnamese:	ngoài

VARIANTS

COMBINATIONS

出自 - come from	出納 - cashier	送出去 - send out	出軌 - derailment,
出生 - birth	出租 - rent	說出來 - speak out	to have an affair
出事 - accident	指出 - point out	出國 - go abroad	出家 - Leave the
出口 - export	支出 - spend	出錢 - pay money	secular world,
出門 - go out	出兵 - send troops	出發 - departure	become a monk

SAYINGS

出入平安 - peace on all exits and entrances - new year's greeting
脫口而出 - escape from one's lips
推陳出新 - bring forth the new through the old

出爾反爾 - make a promise, then withdraw it
出其不意 - by surprise
神出鬼沒 - come and go like a shadow
足不出戶 - to stay indoors

HISTORICAL

甲骨文 (2000BC)	金文 (1000BC)	篆文 (200BC)	隸 (200AD)

FONTS

楷 行 草 宋

266AD
Jing Dynasty
Wang Xizhi

778BC
Tang Dynasty
Liu Gongquan

1280AD
Yuan Dynasty
Zhao Mengfu

1829AD
Ming Dynasty
Dong Qichang

THE GENIUS OF Chinese CHARACTERS

STANDARD	SIMPLIFIED	MEANING
入	入	• to enter: 進入 • join: 加入 • one of the four tones of Mandarin: 入聲

| 正 | ノ | 入 |
| 简 | ノ | 入 |

ETYMOLOGY
Radical: 入
Pictograph: a wedge-shaped object

DATA

		PRONUNCIATION			
Radical (部首)	11: 入	Pinyin:	rù	J-音読み:	ニュウ, ジュ
Strokes	2 | 2	Wade-Giles:	ju	J-訓読み:	い･る, はい･る
HSK	4	Cantonese:	yap6	Korean 音读:	입
Frequency	210	Minnan:	jip	Korean 训读:	들다, 들이다
Big5	A44A	Bopomofo:	ㄖㄨˋ	K-eumdok:	ip
Unihan	U+5165	JP-Onyomi:	nyū, ju	K-hundok:	deulda, deurida
Kangxi Dictionary	P125	JP-Kunyomi:	i·ru, hai·ru	Vietnamese:	đi vào

VARIANTS

COMBINATIONS

插入 - interrupt, penetrate	入黨 - become party member	入賬 - deposit into account	加入 - join in
入口 - entrance	入籍 - enter nationality	入境 - enter a country	介入 - intervene
出入 - in/out	入席 - take seat	入魔 - bewitched	入睡 - fall into sleep
入場 - enter the place	收入 - income	入院 - enter hospital	入侵 - invade

SAYINGS

病從口入 - part of 病從口入, 禍從口出, meaning sickness is caused by what we eat, and trouble is caused by what we say
不堪入耳 - offensive to the ear

長驅直入 - go straight to...
出生入死 - endure great danger
高聳入雲 - towering

HISTORICAL

甲骨文 (2000BC)	(1000BC)	篆文 (200BC)	隸 (200AD)

FONTS

楷　行　草　宋

266AD Jing Dynasty Wang Xizhi

778BC Tang Dynasty Liu Gongquan

1280AD Yuan Dynasty Zhao Mengfu

1829AD Ming Dynasty Dong Qichang

THE GENIUS OF CHINESE CHARACTERS

STANDARD	SIMPLIFIED	MEANING
八	八	• eight: 8 • all around, all sides: 八方 • August: 八月

正	ノ 八
简	ノ 八

ETYMOLOGY

Radical: 八

Pictograph: division; separation

DATA

Radical (部首)	12: 八	Pinyin:	bā	J-音読み:	ハチ
Strokes	2 | 2	Wade-Giles:	pa	J-訓読み:	や, よう
HSK	1	Cantonese:	baat3	Korean 音读:	팔
Frequency	451	Minnan:	pat	Korean 训读:	여덟
Big5	A44B	Bopomofo:	ㄅㄚ	K-eumdok:	pal
Unihan	U+516B	JP-Onyomi:	hachi	K-hundok:	yeodeol
Kangxi Dictionary	P126	JP-Kunyomi:	ya, you	Vietnamese:	tám

VARIANTS | 捌

COMBINATIONS

八字 - birthdate/time
八字胡 - moustache
八方 - 8 points of the compass
八度 - octave

八面周全 - pleasing all
八卦 - the Eight Trigrams
八角 - octagon

SAYINGS

四面八方 - from all sides
胡説八道 - talking nonsense
七零八落 - fragmented
五花八門 - multifarious

八方支援 - support from all sides
七嘴八舌 - mixed opinions

HISTORICAL

甲骨文 (2000BC)	金文 (1000BC)	篆文 (200BC)	隸 (200AD)
八	八	八	八

FONTS

楷	行	草	宋
八	八	八	八

266AD
Jing Dynasty
Wang Xizhi

778BC
Tang Dynasty
Liu Gongquan

1280AD
Yuan Dynasty
Zhao Mengfu

1829AD
Ming Dynasty
Dong Qichang

THE GENIUS OF CHINESE CHARACTERS

STANDARD	SIMPLIFIED	MEANING
公	公	• public affairs: 公務; attend to business: 辦公 • duke: 公爵; maternal grandfather: 外公 • fair and just: 公正; publicly owned: 公地 • male animal: 公牛; metric system: 公裏

| 正 | ノ | 八 | 公 | 公 |
| 簡 | ノ | 八 | 公 | 公 |

ETYMOLOGY
Radical: 八
Pictograph: Originally a space created by dividing things, becoming public

DATA

		PRONUNCIATION			
Radical (部首)	12: 八	Pinyin:	gōng	J-音読み:	コウ, ク
Strokes	4 | 4	Wade-Giles:	kung	J-訓読み:	おおやけ
HSK	2	Cantonese:	gung1	Korean 音读:	공
Frequency	115	Minnan:	kang	Korean 训读:	공평하다
Big5	A4BD	Bopomofo:	ㄍㄨㄥ	K-eumdok:	gong
Unihan	U+516C	JP-Onyomi:	kou, ku	K-hundok:	gongpyeonghada
Kangxi Dictionary	P126	JP-Kunyomi:	ooyake	Vietnamese:	công cộng

VARIANTS | 公

COMBINATIONS

公社 - commune
公司 - company
公平 - equal, fair
公共 - public
公園 - park

公務/公事 - official business
公公 - father in-law of the bride
辦公 - conduct business

外公 - maternal-grandfather
公安 - public security
公安局 - police station
公布 - publicly announce

公衆 - general public
公開 - public and open
公里 - kilometer
公路 - highway
公墓 - cemetery

SAYINGS

大公無私 - selfless
公之于衆 - make known to the public
花花公子 - playboy
克己奉公 - self-sacrifice for public good

開誠布公 - to be honest
例行公事 - routine business
公公道道 - just, fair
公用事業 - public utilities

HISTORICAL

甲骨文 (2000BC)	金文 (1000BC)	篆文 (200BC)	隸 (200AD)

FONTS

楷　行　草　宋

266AD
Jing Dynasty
Wang Xizhi

778BC
Tang Dynasty
Liu Gongquan

1280AD
Yuan Dynasty
Zhao Mengfu

1829AD
Ming Dynasty
Dong Qichang

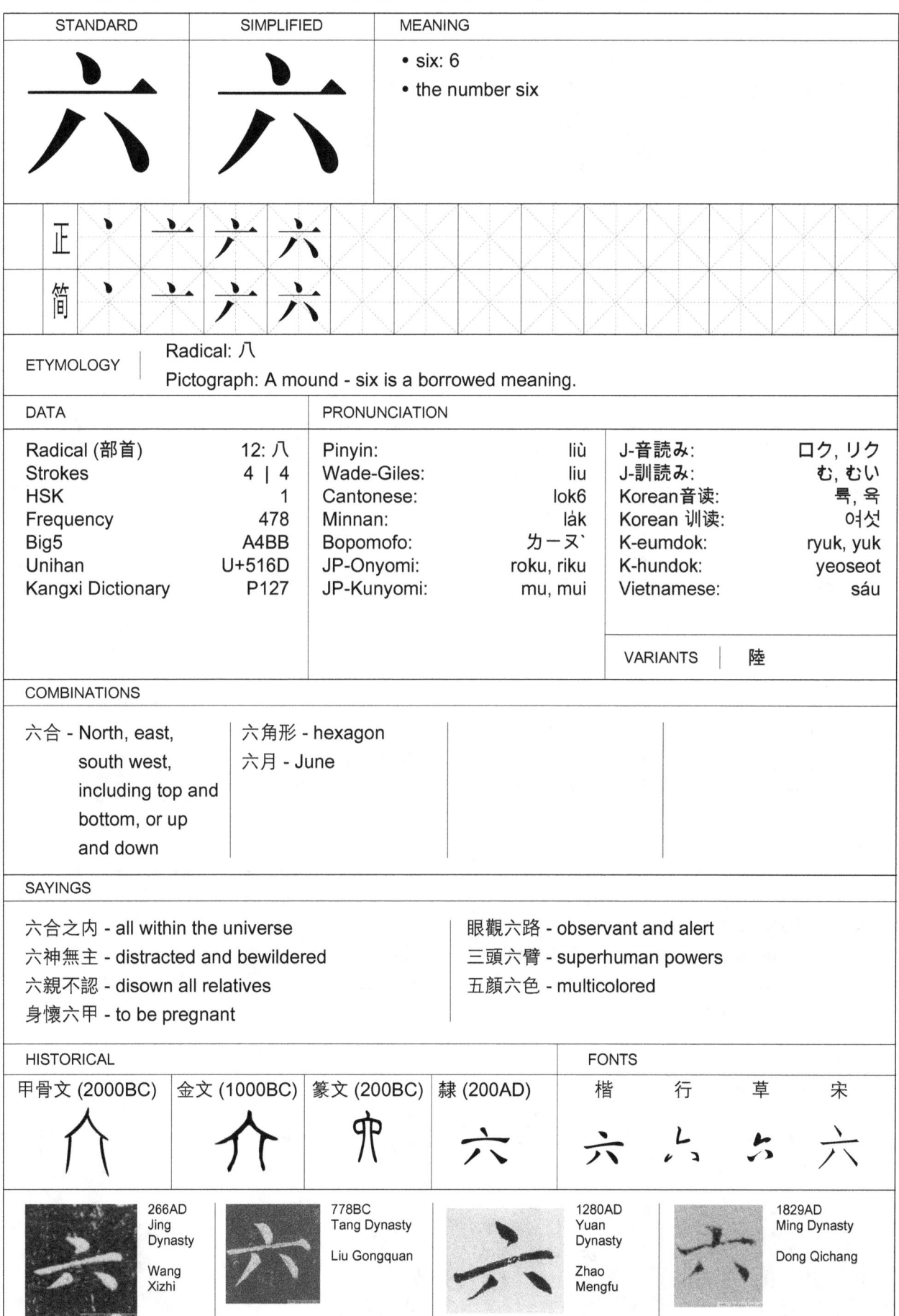

THE GENIUS OF CHINESE CHARACTERS

STANDARD	SIMPLIFIED	MEANING
力	力	• strength: 力量 • power: 勢力 • force: 水力/電力 • capability: 力氣

正 ㇕ 力
简 ㇕ 力

ETYMOLOGY
Radical: 力
Pictograph: An arm curved to indicate muscle flexing

DATA

		PRONUNCIATION			
Radical (部首)	19: 力	Pinyin:	lì	J-音読み:	リョク, リキ
Strokes	2 | 2	Wade-Giles:	li	J-訓読み:	ちから
HSK	3	Cantonese:	lik6	Korean 音读:	력
Frequency	106	Minnan:	lėk	Korean 训读:	힘
Big5	A44F	Bopomofo:	ㄌㄧˋ	K-eumdok:	ryeok
Unihan	U+529B	JP-Onyomi:	ryoku, riki	K-hundok:	him
Kangxi Dictionary	P146	JP-Kunyomi:	chikara	Vietnamese:	lực lượng

VARIANTS | 仂

COMBINATIONS

精力 - mental energy
毅力 - perseverance
魅力 - charm
智力 - intelligence
才力 - talent

影響力 - influence
勢力 - force
人力 - manpower
動力 - power
電力 - electricity

力量 - strength
無力 - weak

SAYINGS

盡力而爲 - to do one's utmost
力不從心 - unable to achieve the heart's desires
力之所及 - what is within ones power to do
竭盡全力 - make every effort

精疲力竭 - exhausted
據理力争 - argue on the basis of reason
力可拔山 - strong enough to lift a mountain
力求上進 - to do better

HISTORICAL

甲骨文 (2000BC)	金文 (1000BC)	篆文 (200BC)	隸 (200AD)

FONTS

楷 行 草 宋

266AD Jing Dynasty Wang Xizhi

778BC Tang Dynasty Liu Gongquan

1280AD Yuan Dynasty Zhao Mengfu

1829AD Ming Dynasty Dong Qichang

THE GENIUS OF CHINESE CHARACTERS

STANDARD	SIMPLIFIED	MEANING
北	北	• north: 北方 • northern, northward: 北面

正 丨 十 才 北ˊ 北
简 丨 十 才 北ˊ 北

ETYMOLOGY
Radical: 匕
Pictograph: Two persons back-to-back

DATA

Radical (部首)	21: 匕
Strokes	5 | 5
HSK	1
Frequency	315
Big5	A55F
Unihan	U+5317
Kangxi Dictionary	P152

PRONUNCIATION

Pinyin:	běi
Wade-Giles:	pei
Cantonese:	bak1
Minnan:	pak
Bopomofo:	ㄅㄟˇ
JP-Onyomi:	hoku
JP-Kunyomi:	kita
J-音読み:	ホク
J-訓読み:	きた
Korean 音读:	북
Korean 训读:	북쪽
K-eumdok:	buk
K-hundok:	bukjjok
Vietnamese:	bắc

VARIANTS 背

COMBINATIONS

- 北面 - north side
- 北方 - the north
- 北斗 - the Big Dipper
- 北京 - Beijing
- 北極 - North Pole
- 北美 - North America
- 北半球 - northern hemisphere

SAYINGS

- 天南海北 - regardless of wherever
- 北面稱臣 - swear allegiance
- 大江南北 - on both sides of the Yangtze
- 南轅北轍 - self-defeating
- 南來北往 - busy traffic of people or vehicles
- 南徵北戰 - to campaign all across the country

HISTORICAL

甲骨文 (2000BC)	金文 (1000BC)	篆文 (200BC)	隸 (200AD)

FONTS

楷　行　草　宋

- 266AD Jing Dynasty — Wang Xizhi
- 778BC Tang Dynasty — Yan Zhenqing
- 1280AD Yuan Dynasty — Zhao Mengfu
- 1829AD Ming Dynasty — Dong Qichang

THE GENIUS OF CHINESE CHARACTERS

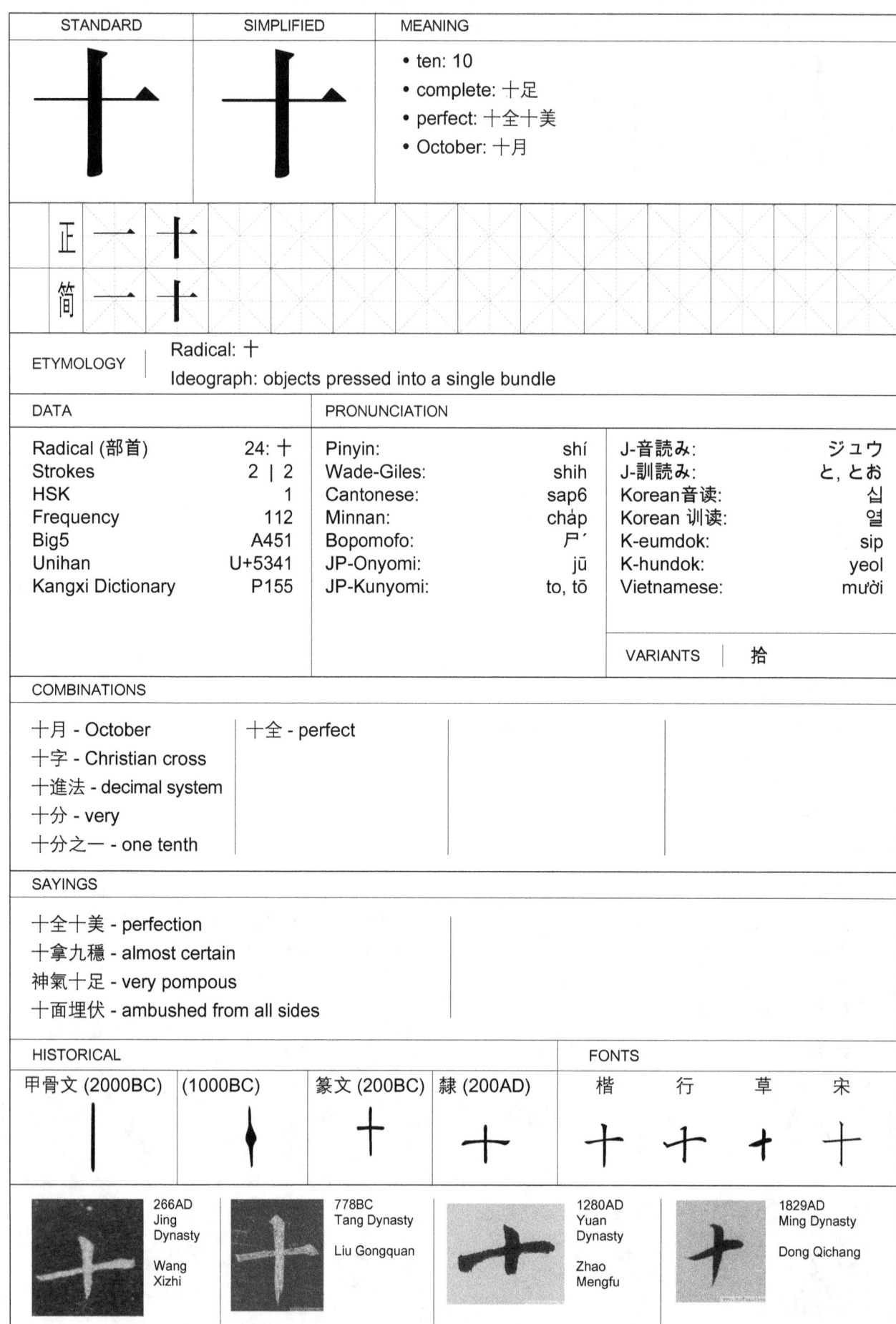

THE GENIUS OF CHINESE CHARACTERS

STANDARD	SIMPLIFIED	MEANING
千	千	• thousand • a cheater (Cantonese): 老千 • many • music of bells and drums • numerous

| 正 | 一 | 二 | 千 |
| 简 | 一 | 二 | 千 |

ETYMOLOGY

Radical: 十

Pictograph: The word 人 (people) with an extra line added.

DATA		PRONUNCIATION			
Radical (部首)	24: 十	Pinyin:	qiān	J-音読み:	セン
Strokes	3 | 3	Wade-Giles:	ch'ien	J-訓読み:	ち
HSK	2	Cantonese:	chin1	Korean 音读:	천
Frequency	599	Minnan:	chheng	Korean 训读:	일천
Big5	A464	Bopomofo:	ㄑㄧㄢ	K-eumdok:	cheon
Unihan	U+5343	JP-Onyomi:	sen	K-hundok:	ilcheon
Kangxi Dictionary	P155	JP-Kunyomi:	chi	Vietnamese:	ngàn

| | | VARIANTS | 仟 |

COMBINATIONS

千萬 - be sure to
千裏馬 - good horse
千克 - kilogram
千米 - kilometer
秋千 - swing

SAYINGS

千篇一律 - all the same
千思萬想 - to think about over and over
千千萬萬 - many
成千上萬 - myriads

感慨萬千 - filled with mixed feelings
各有千秋 - each has advantages
大千世界 - the big wide world
氣象萬千 - grand and majestic

HISTORICAL

甲骨文 (2000BC)	(1000BC)	(200BC)	隸 (200AD)

FONTS

| 楷 | 行 | 草 | 宋 |

| 266AD
Jing Dynasty
Wang Xizhi | 778BC
Tang Dynasty
Liu Gongquan | 1280AD
Yuan Dynasty
Zhao Mengfu | 1829AD
Ming Dynasty
Dong Qichang |

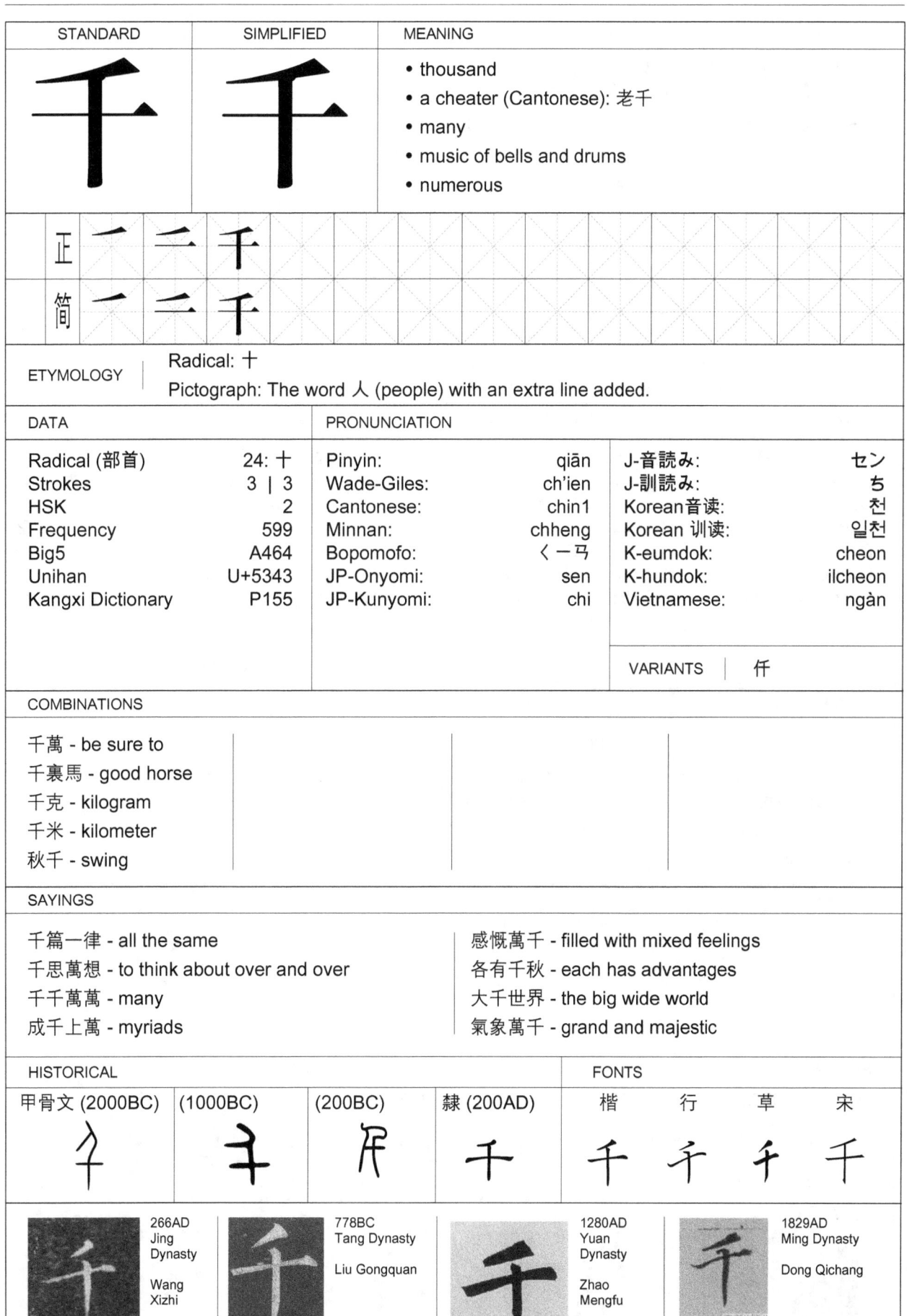

THE GENIUS OF CHINESE CHARACTERS

STANDARD	SIMPLIFIED	MEANING
午	午	• noon: 中午 • 11 a.m.-1 p.m: 午時 • 7th earthly branch • 7th terrestrial branch

正 ノ 乞 仁 午
简 ノ 乞 仁 午

ETYMOLOGY

Radical: 十
Pictograph: a square-headed mallet

DATA

		PRONUNCIATION			
Radical (部首)	24: 十	Pinyin:	wǔ	J-音読み:	ゴ
Strokes	4 | 4	Wade-Giles:	wu	J-訓読み:	うま, ひる
HSK	1	Cantonese:	ng5	Korean音读:	오
Frequency	1004	Minnan:	tàu	Korean 训读:	정오
Big5	A4C8	Bopomofo:	ㄨˇ	K-eumdok:	o
Unihan	U+5348	JP-Onyomi:	go	K-hundok:	jeongo
Kangxi Dictionary	P156	JP-Kunyomi:	uma, hiru	Vietnamese:	không bật

VARIANTS

COMBINATIONS

午前 - a.m.　　　　正午 - noon
午後 - p.m.　　　　午睡 - afternoon nap
上午 - morning　　端午節 - The Dragon
下午 - afternoon　　　　　　Boat Festival
午夜 - midnight

SAYINGS

n/a

HISTORICAL

甲骨文 (2000BC)	金文 (1000BC)	篆文 (200BC)	隸 (200AD)

FONTS

楷　行　草　宋

266AD Jing Dynasty — Wang Xizhi
778BC Tang Dynasty — Yan Zhenqing
1051BC Song Dynasty — Mi Fu
1607AD Qing Dynasty — Fu Shan

THE GENIUS OF Chinese CHARACTERS

STANDARD	SIMPLIFIED	MEANING
半	半	• half • (after a number) and a half • incomplete • semi-

| 正 | 丶 | 丷 | 丷 | 半 | 半 |
| 简 | 丶 | 丷 | 丷 | 半 | 半 |

ETYMOLOGY

Radical: 十
Pictograph: splitting an obect in two

DATA

Radical (部首)	24: 十
Strokes	5 | 5
HSK	3
Frequency	513
Big5	A562
Unihan	U+534A
Kangxi Dictionary	P156

PRONUNCIATION

Pinyin:	bàn
Wade-Giles:	pan
Cantonese:	boon3
Minnan:	pòaⁿ
Bopomofo:	ㄅㄢˋ
JP-Onyomi:	han
JP-Kunyomi:	naka·ba

J-音読み:	ハン
J-訓読み:	なか·ば
Korean 音读:	반
Korean 训读:	절반
K-eumdok:	ban
K-hundok:	jeolban
Vietnamese:	một nửa

VARIANTS

COMBINATIONS

大半 - mostly
半夜 - midnight
多半 - mostly
半途 - midway
半島 - peninsula

半徑 - radius

SAYINGS

半身不遂 - semi-paralysis
半壁江山 - half a country
半斤八兩 - two of a kind
三更半夜 - in the middle of the night

事半功倍 - half the effort, double the result
一官半職 - official appointment
半信半疑 - half-believe
半途而廢 - leave unfinished

HISTORICAL

甲骨文 (2000BC)	金文 (1000BC)	篆文 (200BC)	隸 (200AD)
		半	半

FONTS

楷	行	草	宋
半	半	半	半

266AD
Jing Dynasty
Wang Xizhi

778BC
Tang Dynasty
Yan Zhenqing

1280AD
Yuan Dynasty
Zhao Mengfu

1829AD
Ming Dynasty
Dong Qichang

THE GENIUS OF CHINESE CHARACTERS

STANDARD	SIMPLIFIED	MEANING
去	去	• to go: 去過 • to enter: 進去 • to go or not？: 去不去 • last year: 去年 • fourth tone in Mandarin: 去聲

| 正 | 一 | 十 | 土 | 去 | 去 |
| 简 | 一 | 十 | 土 | 去 | 去 |

ETYMOLOGY
Radical: 厶
Pictograph: A mouth behind a person, originally indicating turning one's back on another

DATA

Radical (部首)	28: 厶
Strokes	5 | 5
HSK	1
Frequency	64
Big5	A568
Unihan	U+53BB
Kangxi Dictionary	P156

PRONUNCIATION

Pinyin:	qù
Wade-Giles:	ch'ü
Cantonese:	hui3
Minnan:	khì
Bopomofo:	ㄑㄩˋ
JP-Onyomi:	kyo, ko
JP-Kunyomi:	sa·ru, nozo·ku

J-音読み:	キヨ, コ
J-訓読み:	さ・る, のぞ・く
Korean 音读:	거
Korean 训读:	가다
K-eumdok:	geo
K-hundok:	gada
Vietnamese:	đi với

VARIANTS	厺, 厽

COMBINATIONS

去路 - way out	去不了 - unable to go
去世 - to die	失去 - lose
進去 - to go in	回去 - go back
去年 - last year	出去 - go out
去職 - to leave office	去掉 - remove

SAYINGS

大勢已去 - on the decline	不如過去 - not as good as the past
大江東去 - things are on the decline	説來説去 - reiterate
翻來覆去 - reiterate, toss and turn	拂袖而去 - turn on one's heel
何去何從 - which path to follow	不知去向 - disappear without a trace

HISTORICAL

甲骨文 (2000BC)	金文 (1000BC)	篆文 (200BC)	隸 (200AD)

FONTS

楷	行	草	宋

266AD
Jing Dynasty
Wang Xizhi

778BC
Tang Dynasty
Yan Zhenqing

1280AD
Yuan Dynasty
Zhao Mengfu

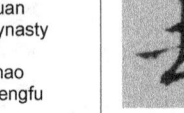
1829AD
Ming Dynasty
Dong Qichang

THE GENIUS OF CHINESE CHARACTERS

STANDARD	SIMPLIFIED	MEANING
又	又	• again • also • (once) again • both... and... (often used in rebuke)

正 ㇇ 又
简 ㇇ 又

ETYMOLOGY Radical: 又
Pictograph: A person's arm contracted in surrounding or protecting an object

DATA		PRONUNCIATION			
Radical (部首)	29: 又	Pinyin:	yòu	J-音読み:	ユウ, ウ
Strokes	2 | 2	Wade-Giles:	you	J-訓読み:	また, ふたた·び
HSK	3	Cantonese:	yau6	Korean 音读:	우
Frequency	126	Minnan:	iū	Korean 训读:	또, 다시
Big5	A453	Bopomofo:	ーㄡˋ	K-eumdok:	u
Unihan	U+53C8	JP-Onyomi:	yū,u	K-hundok:	tto, dasi
Kangxi Dictionary	P164	JP-Kunyomi:	mata, futata·bi	Vietnamese:	cũng thế

VARIANTS | 叹, 右

COMBINATIONS

又來了 - you again!
又聾又啞 - both deaf and mute
又冷又下雨 - both cold and rainy

SAYINGS

欲言又止 - bite one's lip
又作別論 - another thing
一波未平一波又起 - troubles coming one after another

柳暗花明又一村 - every cloud has a silver lining. there's a way out
賠了夫人又折兵 - pay a double penalty
玄之又玄 - mystery of mysteries

HISTORICAL

甲骨文 (2000BC)	金文 (1000BC)	篆文 (200BC)	隸 (200AD)
		㇋	又

FONTS

楷	行	草	宋
又	又	又	又

266AD Jing Dynasty Wang Xizhi

778BC Tang Dynasty Yan Zhenqing

1280AD Yuan Dynasty Zhao Mengfu

1829AD Ming Dynasty Dong Qichang

THE GENIUS OF CHINESE CHARACTERS

STANDARD	SIMPLIFIED	MEANING
友	友	• friend: 朋友 • companion: 酒友 • schoolfriends/alumni: 校友

正	一	𠂇	方	友
简	一	𠂇	方	友

ETYMOLOGY
Radical: 又
Pictograph: Two hands working together.

DATA

Radical (部首)	29: 又
Strokes	4 | 4
HSK	1
Frequency	594
Big5	A4CD
Unihan	U+53CB
Kangxi Dictionary	P165

PRONUNCIATION

Pinyin:	yǒu	J-音読み:	ユウ
Wade-Giles:	you	J-訓読み:	とも
Cantonese:	yau5	Korean 音读:	우
Minnan:	iú	Korean 训读:	벗
Bopomofo:	ㄧㄡˇ	K-eumdok:	u
JP-Onyomi:	yū	K-hundok:	beot
JP-Kunyomi:	tomo	Vietnamese:	bạn bè

VARIANTS | 㕛

COMBINATIONS

朋友 - friends
親友 - relatives and friends
交友 - make friends
酒友 - wine friends
老友 - old friends
好友 - good friends
友好 - friendly
友人 - friends
友誼 - friendship

SAYINGS

狐朋狗友 - bad friends
良師益友 - good teachers and helpful friends
歲寒三友 - referring to the pine, the bamboo, and the plum blossom
賣友求榮 - betray friends for personal gain
兄友弟恭 - show brotherly respect and love
至親好友 - close family and friends

HISTORICAL

甲骨文 (2000BC)	金文 (1000BC)	篆文 (200BC)	隸 (200AD)

FONTS

楷 行 草 宋

266AD Jing Dynasty Wang Xizhi
778BC Tang Dynasty Liu Gongquan
1280AD Yuan Dynasty Zhao Mengfu
1829AD Ming Dynasty Dong Qichang

THE GENIUS OF CHINESE CHARACTERS

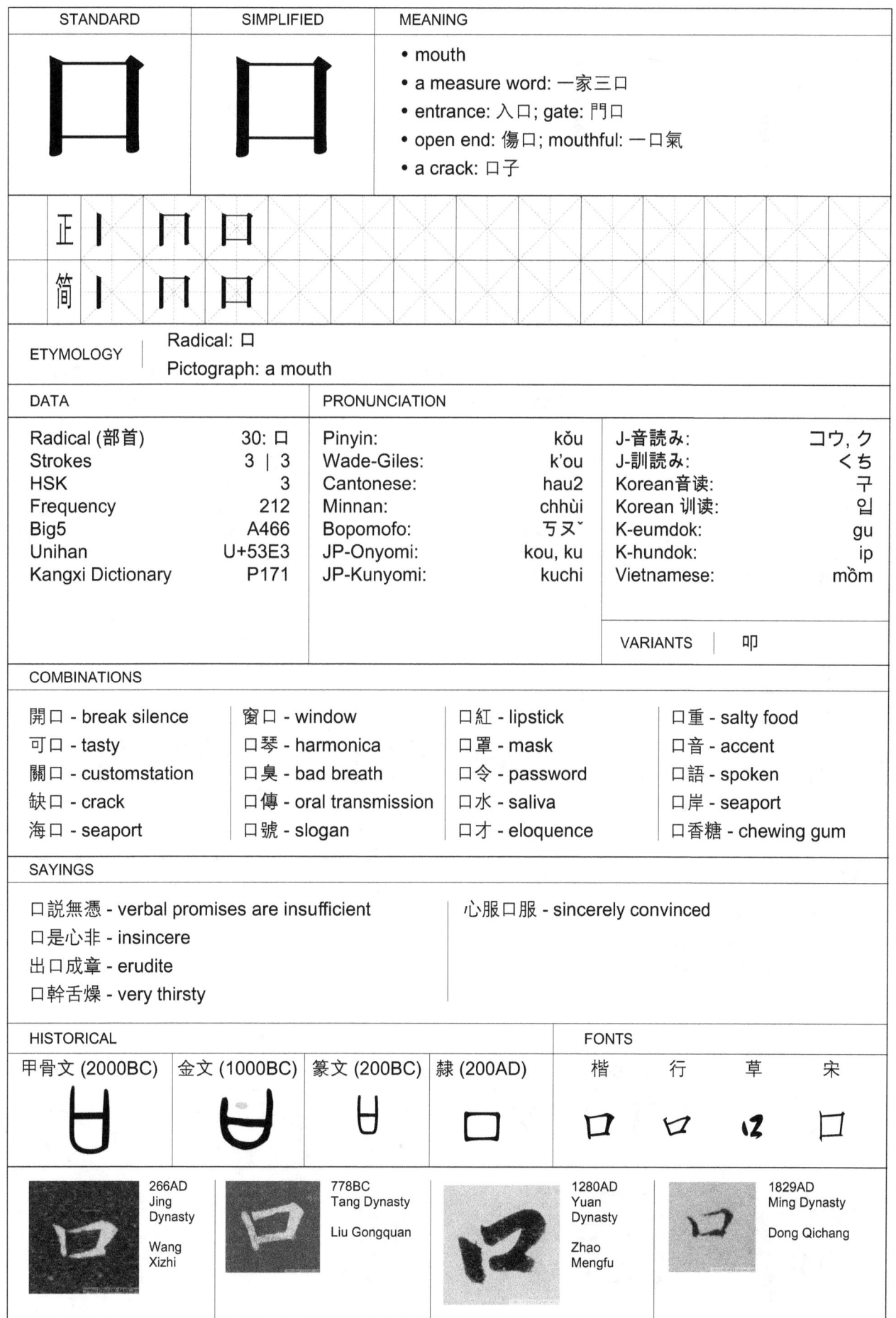

STANDARD	SIMPLIFIED	MEANING
口	口	• mouth • a measure word: 一家三口 • entrance: 入口; gate: 門口 • open end: 傷口; mouthful: 一口氣 • a crack: 口子

正 丨 冂 口
简 丨 冂 口

ETYMOLOGY
Radical: 口
Pictograph: a mouth

DATA
Radical (部首)	30: 口
Strokes	3 | 3
HSK	3
Frequency	212
Big5	A466
Unihan	U+53E3
Kangxi Dictionary	P171

PRONUNCIATION
Pinyin:	kǒu
Wade-Giles:	k'ou
Cantonese:	hau2
Minnan:	chhùi
Bopomofo:	ㄎㄡˇ
JP-Onyomi:	kou, ku
JP-Kunyomi:	kuchi

J-音読み:	コウ, ク
J-訓読み:	くち
Korean 音读:	구
Korean 训读:	입
K-eumdok:	gu
K-hundok:	ip
Vietnamese:	mồm

VARIANTS | 叩

COMBINATIONS

開口 - break silence	窗口 - window	口紅 - lipstick	口重 - salty food
可口 - tasty	口琴 - harmonica	口罩 - mask	口音 - accent
關口 - customstation	口臭 - bad breath	口令 - password	口語 - spoken
缺口 - crack	口傳 - oral transmission	口水 - saliva	口岸 - seaport
海口 - seaport	口號 - slogan	口才 - eloquence	口香糖 - chewing gum

SAYINGS

口説無憑 - verbal promises are insufficient
口是心非 - insincere
出口成章 - erudite
口幹舌燥 - very thirsty

心服口服 - sincerely convinced

HISTORICAL

甲骨文 (2000BC)	金文 (1000BC)	篆文 (200BC)	隸 (200AD)

FONTS

楷　行　草　宋

266AD Jing Dynasty Wang Xizhi	778BC Tang Dynasty Liu Gongquan	1280AD Yuan Dynasty Zhao Mengfu	1829AD Ming Dynasty Dong Qichang

THE GENIUS OF CHINESE CHARACTERS

STANDARD	SIMPLIFIED	MEANING
可	可	• can: 可以 • may, able to: 可行 • particle used for emphasis: 可不是嗎 • ...able: 可愛; but: 可是 • possible: 可吃

正	一	丆	丆	可	可				
简	一	丆	丆	可	可				

ETYMOLOGY

Radical: 口

Pictograph: Shouting with hands cupped, making it possible to be heard at a distance.

DATA

Radical (部首)	30: 口
Strokes	5 | 5
HSK	2
Frequency	30
Big5	A569
Unihan	U+53EF
Kangxi Dictionary	P172

PRONUNCIATION

Pinyin:	kě
Wade-Giles:	k'ê
Cantonese:	hoh2
Minnan:	khó
Bopomofo:	ㄎㄜˇ
JP-Onyomi:	ka, koku
JP-Kunyomi:	yo·i, be·shi

J-音読み:	カ, コク
J-訓読み:	よ・い, べ・し
Korean 音读:	가
Korean 训读:	옳다
K-eumdok:	ga
K-hundok:	olta
Vietnamese:	có thể

VARIANTS	歌, 契

COMBINATIONS

可以 - can/yes	可不是嗎 - isn't it so?	可愛 - cute	可憐 - pitiful
不可以 - can't/no	可行 - feasible	可恥 - shameful	可怕 - terrible
可大可小 - can be expanded or shrunk	可吃 - tasty	可靠 - reliable	可疑 - suspicious
	可敬 - worthy of respect	可可 - cocoa	
	可是 - but	可口 - delicious	

SAYINGS

可有可無 - optional

可大可小 - flexible in size

無可奈何 - feel helpless

不可思議 - unbelievable

HISTORICAL

甲骨文 (2000BC) | 金文 (1000BC) | 篆文 (200BC) | 隸 (200AD)

FONTS

楷 行 草 宋

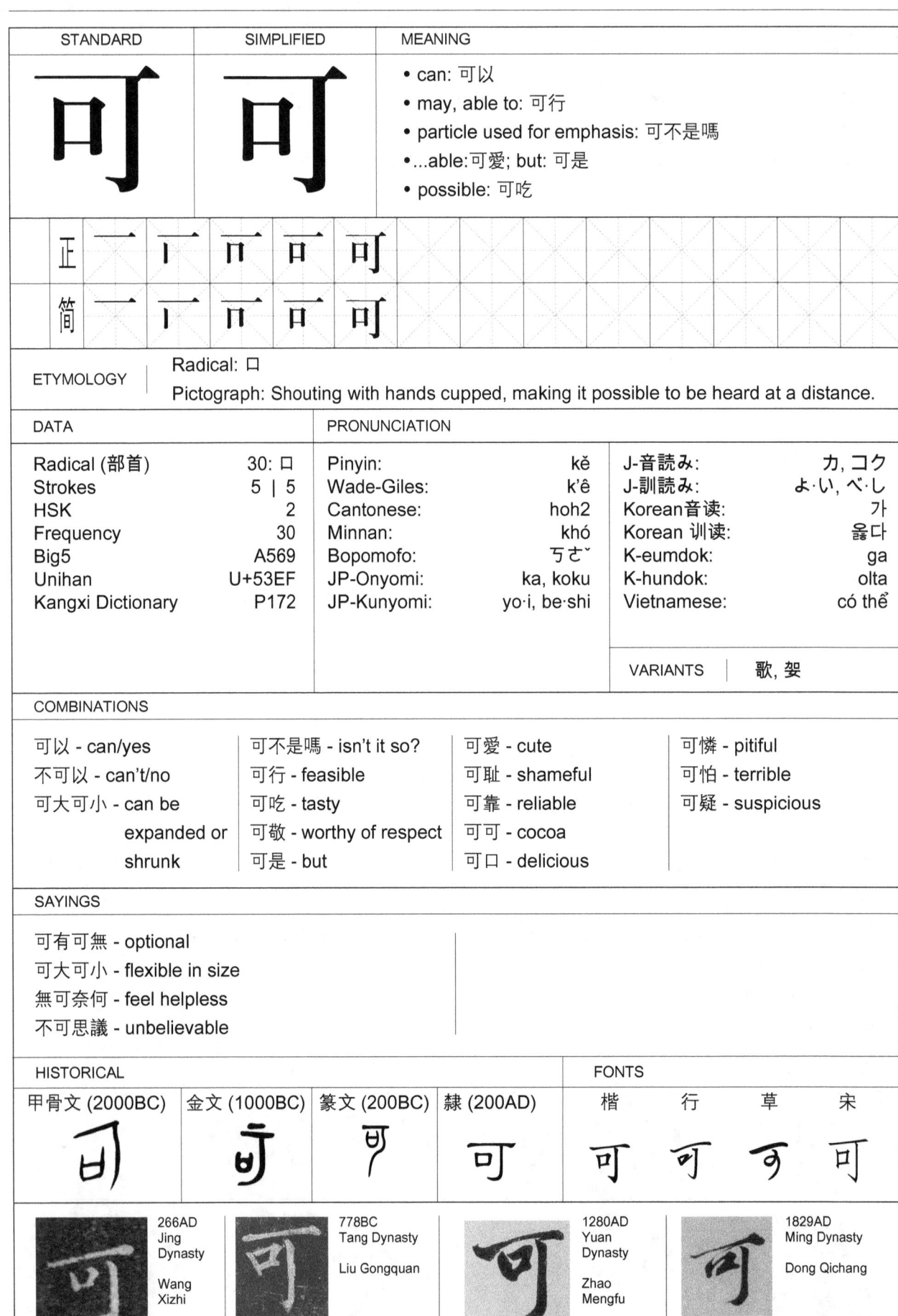

266AD Jing Dynasty Wang Xizhi

778BC Tang Dynasty Liu Gongquan

1280AD Yuan Dynasty Zhao Mengfu

1829AD Ming Dynasty Dong Qichang

THE GENIUS OF Chinese CHARACTERS

STANDARD	SIMPLIFIED	MEANING
右	右	• right: 右面 • right-wing: 右翼 • west

正 一 ナ オ 右 右
简 一 ナ オ 右 右

ETYMOLOGY Radical: 口
Pictograph: Right arm protecting an object.

DATA

Radical (部首)	30: 口
Strokes	5 | 5
HSK	2
Frequency	783
Big5	A56B
Unihan	U+53F3
Kangxi Dictionary	P173

PRONUNCIATION

Pinyin:	yòu
Wade-Giles:	you
Cantonese:	yau4
Minnan:	iū
Bopomofo:	ㄧㄡˋ
JP-Onyomi:	u, yū
JP-Kunyomi:	migi

J-音読み:	ウ, ユウ
J-訓読み:	みぎ
Korean 音读:	우
Korean 训读:	오른쪽
K-eumdok:	u
K-hundok:	oreunjjok
Vietnamese:	đúng

VARIANTS | 佑

COMBINATIONS

右面 - right side
右邊 - right
右手 - right hand
左右 - approximately

SAYINGS

左思右想 - turn sth. over in one's mind
左宜右有 - talented and capable

HISTORICAL

甲骨文 (2000BC) | 金文 (1000BC) | 篆文 (200BC) | 隸 (200AD)

FONTS

楷 行 草 宋

266AD Jing Dynasty Wang Xizhi
778BC Tang Dynasty Liu Gongquan
1280AD Yuan Dynasty Zhao Mengfu
1829AD Ming Dynasty Dong Qichang

THE GENIUS OF CHINESE CHARACTERS

STANDARD	SIMPLIFIED	MEANING
左	左	• left: 左右, 左邊 • east; unorthodox: 左道 • politically left wing: 左翼

正	一	ナ	ナ	左	左	
简	一	ナ	ナ	左	左	

ETYMOLOGY

Radical: 口

Pictograph: The left hand aligned to assist the right hand with work.

DATA

Radical (部首)	30: 口
Strokes	5 | 5
HSK	2
Frequency	782
Big5	A5AA
Unihan	U+5DE6
Kangxi Dictionary	P325

PRONUNCIATION

Pinyin:	zuǒ
Wade-Giles:	tso
Cantonese:	joh2
Minnan:	chó
Bopomofo:	ㄗㄨㄛˇ
JP-Onyomi:	sa
JP-Kunyomi:	hidari

J-音読み:	サ
J-訓読み:	ひだり
Korean 音读:	좌
Korean 训读:	왼쪽
K-eumdok:	jwa
K-hundok:	oenjjok
Vietnamese:	trái

VARIANTS	佐

COMBINATIONS

左邊 - left side
左側 - leftside
左右 - approximately

SAYINGS

左思右想 - turn over in one's mind
左宜右有 - talented and capable
意見相左 - cannot see eye to eye

HISTORICAL

甲骨文 (2000BC)	金文 (1000BC)	篆文 (200BC)	隸 (200AD)

FONTS

楷　行　草　宋

266AD Jing Dynasty Wang Xizhi

778BC Tang Dynasty Liu Gongquan

1280AD Yuan Dynasty Zhao Mengfu

1829AD Ming Dynasty Dong Qichang

THE GENIUS OF CHINESE CHARACTERS

STANDARD	SIMPLIFIED	MEANING
吃	吃	• to eat: 吃飯 • to drink: 吃酒 • take fright: 吃驚 • to bear: 吃不消 • to endure: 吃苦

正 丨 冂 口 叮 吒 吃
简 丨 冂 口 叮 吒 吃

ETYMOLOGY

Radical: 口 (mouth)
phonetic = 乞 (beggar)

DATA

Radical (部首)	30: 口
Strokes	6 | 6
HSK	1
Frequency	475
Big5	A659
Unihan	U+5403
Kangxi Dictionary	P174

PRONUNCIATION

Pinyin:	chī
Wade-Giles:	ch'ih
Cantonese:	hek3
Minnan:	chia̍h
Bopomofo:	ㄔ
JP-Onyomi:	kitsu
JP-Kunyomi:	domo·ru

J-音読み:	キツ
J-訓読み:	ども・る
Korean 音读:	흘
Korean 训读:	말을 더듬다
K-eumdok:	heul
K-hundok:	mareul deodeumda
Vietnamese:	ăn

VARIANTS	乞

COMBINATIONS

吃豆腐 - make a pass at a girl
吃素 - vegetarian
吃飯 - eat
吃醋 - jealous

吃虧 - to suffer losses
吃力 - have difficulty in
吃喝玩樂 - having a great time
吃苦 - bear hardship

SAYINGS

沒吃沒穿 - very poor
吃喝不盡 - enough to live on for life
大吃一驚 - be surprised at, be startled at
省吃儉用 - save money on food and necessities

HISTORICAL

甲骨文 (2000BC)	金文 (1000BC)	篆文 (200BC)	隸 (200AD)
			吃

FONTS

楷	行	草	宋
吃	吃	吃	吃

THE GENIUS OF CHINESE CHARACTERS

STANDARD	SIMPLIFIED	MEANING
名	名	• name: 人名/地名 • measure word for persons: 一名犯人 • place (e.g. among winners): 第一名 • reputation: 名譽

正 ノ ク タ 夕 名 名
简 ノ ク タ 夕 名 名

ETYMOLOGY
Radical: 口
Pictograph: To identify oneself 口 in the dark evening 夕.

DATA
Radical (部首)　　30: 口
Strokes　　6 | 6
HSK　　1
Frequency　　203
Big5　　A657
Unihan　　U+540D
Kangxi Dictionary　　P175

PRONUNCIATION
Pinyin: míng
Wade-Giles: ming
Cantonese: ming4
Minnan: miâ
Bopomofo: ㄇㄧㄥˊ
JP-Onyomi: mei, myou
JP-Kunyomi: na

J-音読み: メイ, ミョウ
J-訓読み: な
Korean 音读: 명
Korean 训读: 이름
K-eumdok: myeong
K-hundok: ireum
Vietnamese: tên

VARIANTS | 铭, 詺

COMBINATIONS
人名 - a person's name
地名 - a place's name
筆名 - pen name
名產 - famous products
名氣 - reputation

名單 - namelist
名片 - namecard
名人 - celebrity
名師 - famous teacher
名譽 - reputation

出名 - become famous
著名 - be famous
名稱 - name
　　　(people or
　　　 objects)

SAYINGS
久仰大名 - have heard of your great reputation
名滿天下 - famous
名不符實 - hollow reputation
莫名其妙 - puzzled

名勝古迹 - scenic spots and historical sites
名正言順 - be right and proper

HISTORICAL
甲骨文 (2000BC)　　金文 (1000BC)　　篆文 (200BC)　　隸 (200AD)

FONTS
楷　行　草　宋

266AD Jing Dynasty Wang Xizhi
778BC Tang Dynasty Liu Gongquan
1280AD Yuan Dynasty Zhao Mengfu
1829AD Ming Dynasty Dong Qichang

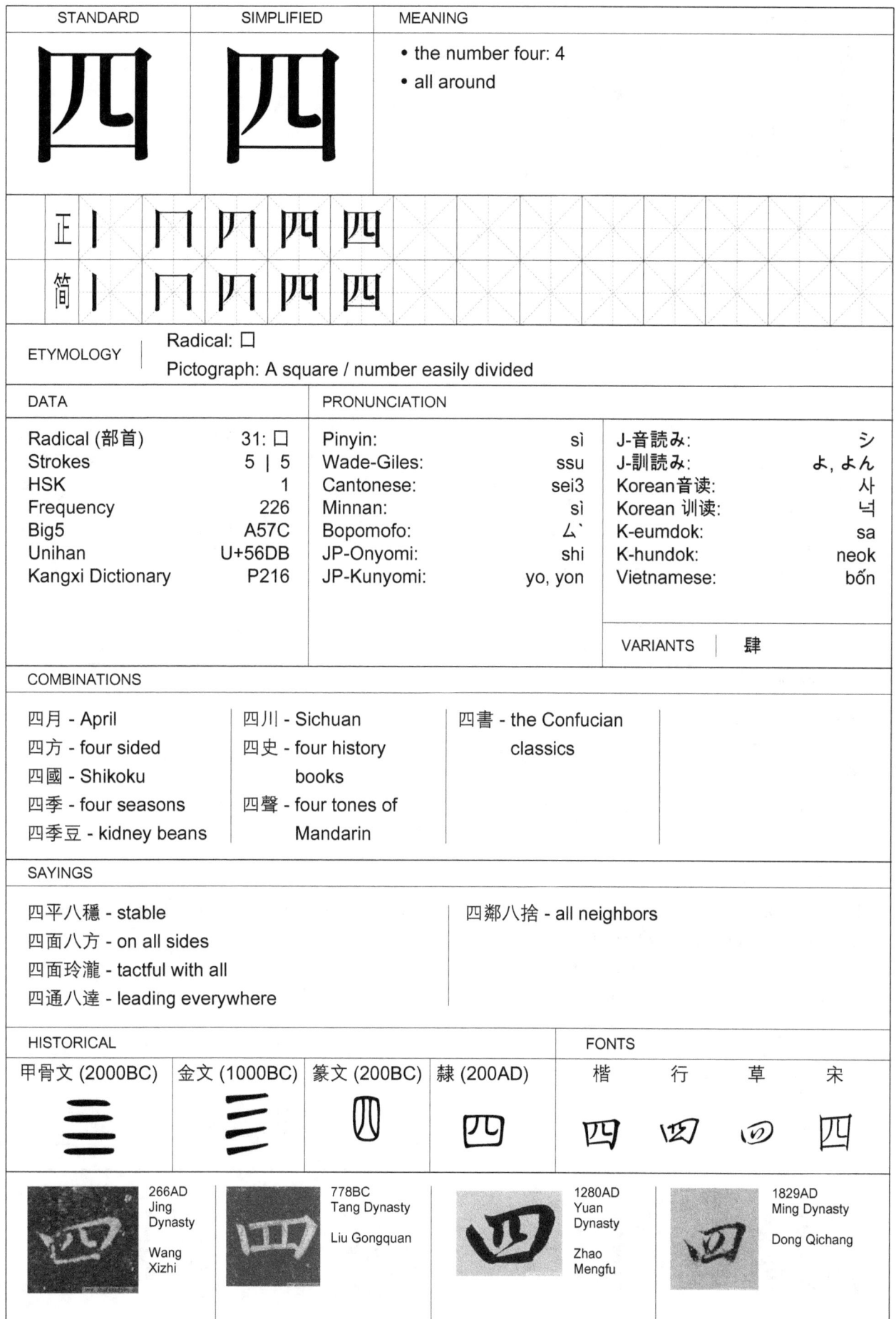

THE GENIUS OF CHINESE CHARACTERS

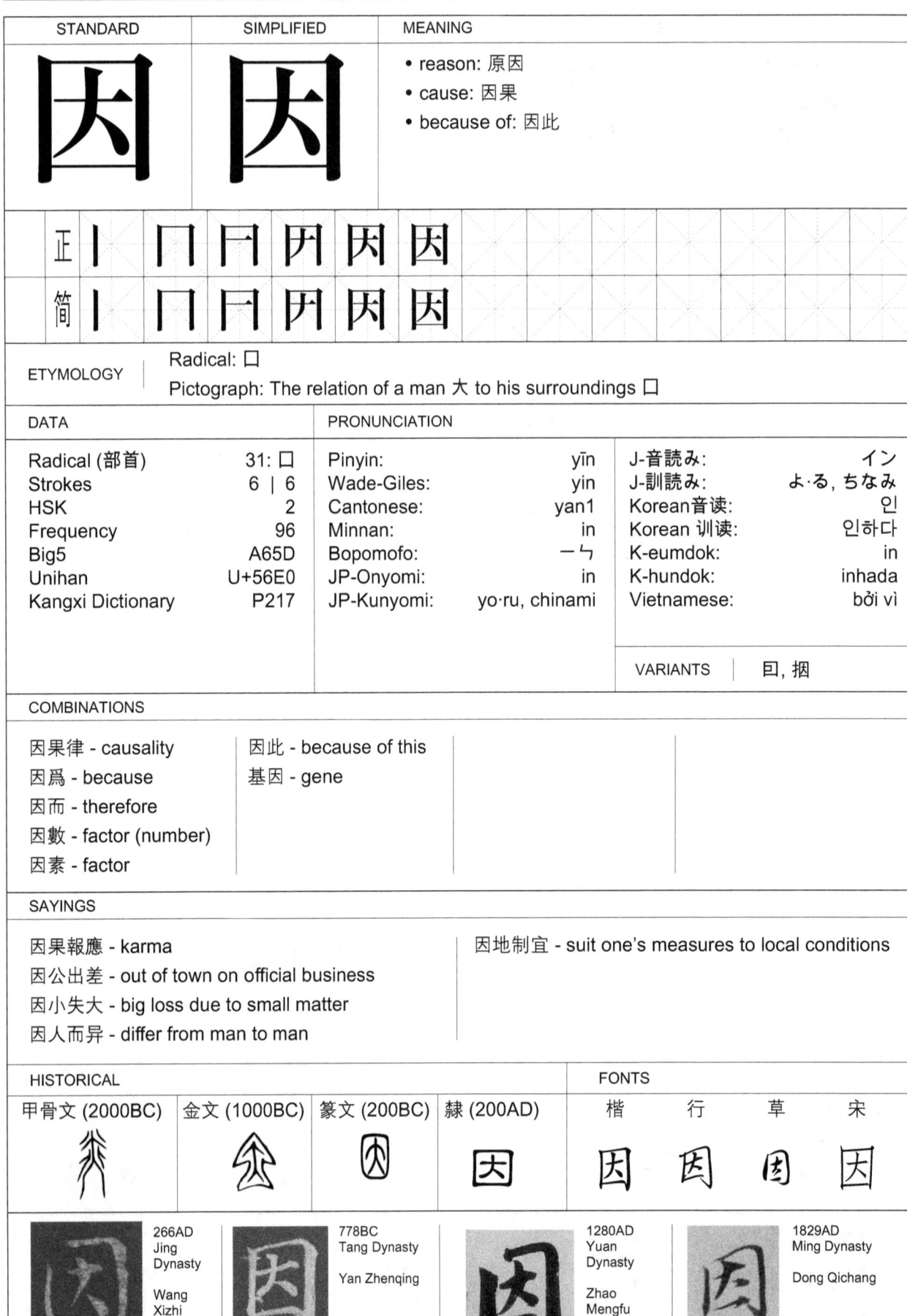

THE GENIUS OF CHINESE CHARACTERS

STANDARD	SIMPLIFIED	MEANING
國	国	• country, nation: 國家 • state: 國有

正	丨	冂	冂	冃	冋	同	戓	或	國	國	
简	丨	冂	冂	冃	用	国	国	国			

ETYMOLOGY

Radical: 囗
Pictograph: An enclosed region 域

DATA

Radical (部首)	31: 囗
Strokes	11 | 8
HSK	1
Frequency	20
Big5	B0EA
Unihan	U+56FD
Kangxi Dictionary	P219

PRONUNCIATION

Pinyin:	guó	J-音読み:	コク
Wade-Giles:	kuo	J-訓読み:	くに
Cantonese:	gwok3	Korean 音读:	국
Minnan:	kok	Korean 训读:	나라
Bopomofo:	ㄍㄨㄛˊ	K-eumdok:	guk
JP-Onyomi:	koku	K-hundok:	nara
JP-Kunyomi:	kuni	Vietnamese:	quốc gia

VARIANTS	国(J)

COMBINATIONS

國內 - domestic	國旗 - national flag	國歌 - national anthem	國家 - national
國外 - abroad	國情 - national conditions	國畫 - Chinese painting	國際 - international
國立 - state (institution)		國貨 - national goods	國土 - national territory
國寶 - national treasure	國防 - national defense	國魂 - national soul	國王 - king
國慶 - national day	國父 - national father	國債 - national debt	

SAYINGS

國家機密 - state secrets
愛國如家 - to love country as family

HISTORICAL

甲骨文 (2000BC)	金文 (1000BC)	篆文 (200BC)	隸 (200AD)

FONTS

楷 行 草 宋

266AD Jing Dynasty Wang Xizhi
778BC Tang Dynasty Yan Zhenqing
1280AD Yuan Dynasty Zhao Mengfu
1829AD Ming Dynasty Dong Qichang

THE GENIUS OF CHINESE CHARACTERS

STANDARD	SIMPLIFIED	MEANING
土	土	• territory: 土地 • earth: 泥土 • Turkey/Turkish: 土耳其 • items made of earth: 土瓶 • local: 土產

正 一 十 土
简 一 十 土

ETYMOLOGY
Radical: 土
Pictograph: the altar of the soil – or an object rising from the ground

DATA		PRONUNCIATION			
Radical (部首)	32: 土	Pinyin:	tǔ	J-音読み:	ド, ト
Strokes	3 | 3	Wade-Giles:	t'u	J-訓読み:	つち
HSK	5	Cantonese:	to2	Korean 音读:	토
Frequency	515	Minnan:	thô	Korean 训读:	흙
Big5	A467	Bopomofo:	ㄊㄨˇ	K-eumdok:	to
Unihan	U+571F	JP-Onyomi:	do, to	K-hundok:	heuk
Kangxi Dictionary	P223	JP-Kunyomi:	tsuchi	Vietnamese:	trái đất

VARIANTS | 圡

COMBINATIONS

國土 - national territory	土豪 - rich but rude	土包子 - bumpkin
土地 - land	土氣 - rustic/uncouth	土豆 - potatoes
黃土 - loess	土匪 - bandits	土話 - local dialect
沙土 - sand	土星 - saturn	土耳其 - Turkey
土產 - local product	土色 - brown	

SAYINGS

土牛木馬 - useless persons
土地改革 - land reform

HISTORICAL

甲骨文 (2000BC)	金文 (1000BC)	篆文 (200BC)	隸 (200AD)

FONTS

楷　行　草　宋

266AD Jing Dynasty Wang Xizhi
778BC Tang Dynasty Liu Gongquan
1280AD Yuan Dynasty Zhao Mengfu
1829AD Ming Dynasty Dong Qichang

THE GENIUS OF CHINESE CHARACTERS

STANDARD	SIMPLIFIED	MEANING
在	在	• exist: 存在 • to be at: 在家 • ongoing action: 在做

正 一 ナ オ 右 在 在
简 一 ナ オ 右 在 在

ETYMOLOGY | Radical: 土
Pictograph: A pile of earth to cut off the flow of a river.

DATA

		PRONUNCIATION			
Radical (部首)	32: 土	Pinyin:	zài	J-音読み:	ザイ
Strokes	6 | 6	Wade-Giles:	tsai	J-訓読み:	あ・る
HSK	1	Cantonese:	joi6	Korean 音读:	재
Frequency	6	Minnan:	chāi	Korean 训读:	있다
Big5	A662	Bopomofo:	ㄗㄞˋ	K-eumdok:	jae
Unihan	U+5728	JP-Onyomi:	zai	K-hundok:	itda
Kangxi Dictionary	P223	JP-Kunyomi:	a·ru	Vietnamese:	trong

VARIANTS | 扗

COMBINATIONS

存在 - existence
在不在 - presence
在世 - living
在這裏 - here
在做 - doing

在學 - studying
在夢中 - in a dream
在乎 - to be concerned about
在內 - in

在意 - care
實在 - actually, really
正在 - in process of
潛在 - potential

SAYINGS

在官言官 - official position
在劫難逃 - inescapable
大權在握 - great power is within grasp
高高在上 - superior

懷恨在心 - to bear a grudge
不在話下 - be no difficulty
大有人在 - there are lots of people who
近在咫尺 - close at hand

HISTORICAL

甲骨文 (2000BC) | 金文 (1000BC) | 篆文 (200BC) | 隸 (200AD)

FONTS

楷 行 草 宋

266AD Jing Dynasty Wang Xizhi
778BC Tang Dynasty Liu Gongquan
1280AD Yuan Dynasty Zhao Mengfu
1829AD Ming Dynasty Dong Qichang

THE GENIUS OF CHINESE CHARACTERS

STANDARD	SIMPLIFIED	MEANING
外	外	• outside: 外面 • external: 境外 • foreign: 國外 • in addition: 以外 • maternal grandmother: 外婆

正 ノ ク タ 列 外
简 ノ ク タ 列 外

ETYMOLOGY

Radical: 夕
Pictograph: Divination 卜 with the moon.

DATA

Radical (部首)	36: 夕
Strokes	5 | 5
HSK	2
Frequency	131
Big5	A57E
Unihan	U+5916
Kangxi Dictionary	P246

PRONUNCIATION

Pinyin:	wài	J-音読み:	ガイ, ゲ
Wade-Giles:	wai	J-訓読み:	そと, ほか
Cantonese:	ngoi6	Korean 音读:	외
Minnan:	gōa	Korean 训读:	바깥
Bopomofo:	ㄨㄞˋ	K-eumdok:	oe
JP-Onyomi:	gai, ge	K-hundok:	bakkat
JP-Kunyomi:	soto, hoka	Vietnamese:	bên ngoài

VARIANTS

COMBINATIONS

世外 - beyond the world	外傷 - external injury	(in a contract)	grandfather
例外 - exception	外國 - foreign	外觀 - external	外匯 - foreign
意外 - accident	外幣 - foreign currency	appearance	exchange
圈外 - out-of circle	外賓 - foreign guest	外國 - foreign country	外債 - foreign debt
外表 - appearance	外方 - foreign party	外公 - maternal-	外出 - to go out

SAYINGS

超然物外 - beyond material things
古今中外 - ancient & modern, Chinese & foreign
馳名中外 - well known both at home and abroad
海外奇談 - strange stories from overseas

裏應外合 - collaborate within and outside
拒之門外 - to shut out
拒人于千裏之外 - very arrogant
不足爲外人道 - no need to let others know

HISTORICAL

甲骨文 (2000BC)	金文 (1000BC)	篆文 (200BC)	隸 (200AD)
Y	外	外	外

FONTS

楷	行	草	宋
外	外	外	外

266AD Jing Dynasty Wang Xizhi
778BC Tang Dynasty Liu Gongquan
1280AD Yuan Dynasty Zhao Mengfu
1829AD Ming Dynasty Dong Qichang

THE GENIUS OF CHINESE CHARACTERS

STANDARD	SIMPLIFIED	MEANING
多	多	• many, much: 很多; multi: 多方面 • how many (of degree): 多少 • over; (expressing degree) how: 多開心! • excessive: 多了; too many/too much: 太多 • one more: 多一个

正 ノ ク タ 夕 多 多
简 ノ ク タ 夕 多 多

ETYMOLOGY

Radical: 夕
Pictograph: Originally meaning two nights 夕; later a multiplicity of anything

DATA

Radical (部首)	36: 夕
Strokes	6 | 6
HSK	1
Frequency	61
Big5	A668
Unihan	U+591A
Kangxi Dictionary	P246

PRONUNCIATION

Pinyin:	duō	J-音読み:	夕
Wade-Giles:	to	J-訓読み:	おお・い
Cantonese:	doh1	Korean 音读:	다
Minnan:	to	Korean 训读:	많다
Bopomofo:	ㄉㄨㄛ	K-eumdok:	da
JP-Onyomi:	ta	K-hundok:	manta
JP-Kunyomi:	ō·i	Vietnamese:	nhiều

VARIANTS | 夛

COMBINATIONS

多餘 - redundant
多于 - more than
很多 - many
多次 - many times
好多了 - much better

多久 - how long
多少 - how much
多麼 - how (as in, how beautiful!)
多半 - mostly

多多 - a lot
多神教 - polytheism
多謝 - thank you
多年朋友 - friends for many years

多數 - the majority
多少錢 - how much money
最多 - the most, maximum

SAYINGS

變化多端 - changeable
多才多藝 - versatile
夜長夢多 - delay brings more trouble
多此一舉 - superfluous

人多手雜 - too many cooks spoil the broth
多聞多見 - experienced

HISTORICAL

甲骨文 (2000BC)	金文 (1000BC)	篆文 (200BC)	隸 (200AD)
		多	多

FONTS

楷 行 草 宋

266AD Jing Dynasty Wang Xizhi
778BC Tang Dynasty Yan Zhenqing
1280AD Yuan Dynasty Zhao Mengfu
1829AD Ming Dynasty Dong Qichang

THE GENIUS OF CHINESE CHARACTERS

STANDARD	SIMPLIFIED	MEANING
大	大	• big: 大門 • doctor: 大夫 • great: 偉大 • honored: 大名 • generally: 大概

正 一 ナ 大
简 一 ナ 大

ETYMOLOGY

Radical: 大

Pictograph: a man 人 with outstretched arms

DATA

		PRONUNCIATION			
Radical (部首)	37: 大	Pinyin:	dà	J-音読み:	ダイ, タイ
Strokes	3 | 3	Wade-Giles:	ta	J-訓読み:	おお, おお·きい
HSK	1	Cantonese:	daai6	Korean 音读:	대
Frequency	17	Minnan:	tāi	Korean 训读:	크다
Big5	A46A	Bopomofo:	ㄉㄚˋ	K-eumdok:	dae
Unihan	U+5927	JP-Onyomi:	dai, tai	K-hundok:	keuda
Kangxi Dictionary	P248	JP-Kunyomi:	ō, ō·kī	Vietnamese:	lớn

VARIANTS | 亣

COMBINATIONS

大門 - gate	大概 - probably	大便 - stool	大綱 - outline
大陸 - continent	大前天 - the day before yesterday	大腸 - large intestine	大話 - exaggeration
大樓 - building		大膽 - bold	大會 - convention
大清 - Qing	大後年 - the year after next	大豆 - soybean	大眾 - mass
大事 - major events		大方 - generous	大局 - the big picture

SAYINGS

粗心大意 - careless
不識大體 - ignorance
長篇大論 - long-winded
春回大地 - spring returns to earth

博大精深 - broad and profound
勃然大怒 - burn with anger
大大咧咧 - not serious, shallow
真相大白 - facts now clear

HISTORICAL

甲骨文 (2000BC)	金文 (1000BC)	篆文 (200BC)	隸 (200AD)

FONTS

楷　行　草　宋

266AD Jing Dynasty Wang Xizhi

778BC Tang Dynasty Liu Gongquan

1280AD Yuan Dynasty Zhao Mengfu

1829AD Ming Dynasty Dong Qichang

THE GENIUS OF CHINESE CHARACTERS

STANDARD	SIMPLIFIED	MEANING
天	天	• sky: 天空 • day: 每天 • heaven: 天堂 • weather: 天氣

正 一 二 丅 天
简 一 二 丅 天

ETYMOLOGY | Radical: 大
Pictograph: A line above a person's head to represent the horizon.

DATA		PRONUNCIATION			
Radical (部首)	37: 大	Pinyin:	tiān	J-音読み:	テン
Strokes	4 | 4	Wade-Giles:	t'ien	J-訓読み:	あま, あめ
HSK	1	Cantonese:	tin1	Korean 音读:	천
Frequency	78	Minnan:	thian	Korean 训读:	하늘
Big5	A4D1	Bopomofo:	ㄊㄧㄢ	K-eumdok:	cheon
Unihan	U+5929	JP-Onyomi:	ten	K-hundok:	haneul
Kangxi Dictionary	P248	JP-Kunyomi:	ama, ame	Vietnamese:	ngày

VARIANTS | 兲, 天(J)

COMBINATIONS

天空 - sky
天下 - world
天然 - natural
天性 - nature
天堂 - heaven

天啊 - oh
今天 - today
明天 - tomorrow
每天 - every day
春天 - spring

陰天 - cloudy
天命 - mandate of heaven
後天 - the day after tomorrow

SAYINGS

一手遮天 - hide truth from the masses
天朗氣清 - the sky is clear and bright
天花亂墜 - exaggerations
天南海北 - all over the country

別有洞天 - hidden but beautiful
不見天日 - oppressed
天長地久 - forever, a long time
天公地道 - equitable

HISTORICAL

甲骨文 (2000BC) | 金文 (1000BC) | 篆文 (200BC) | 隸 (200AD)

FONTS

楷 行 草 宋

266AD Jing Dynasty Wang Xizhi

778BC Tang Dynasty Liu Gongquan

1280AD Yuan Dynasty Zhao Mengfu

1829AD Ming Dynasty Dong Qichang

THE GENIUS OF CHINESE CHARACTERS

STANDARD	SIMPLIFIED	MEANING
太	太	• too (much): 太多 • grand: 太師

正	一	ナ	大	太	
简	一	ナ	大	太	

ETYMOLOGY: Radical: 大 Pictograph: A variant of 大 with a dot 、 for emphasis, acquiring the meaning of "extremely", "too"

DATA

		PRONUNCIATION			
Radical (部首)	37: 大	Pinyin:	tài	J-音読み:	タイ, タ
Strokes	4 | 4	Wade-Giles:	t'ai	J-訓読み:	ふと・い/る
HSK	1	Cantonese:	taai3	Korean 音读:	태
Frequency	240	Minnan:	thài	Korean 训读:	심하다
Big5	A4D3	Bopomofo:	ㄊㄞˋ	K-eumdok:	tae
Unihan	U+592A	JP-Onyomi:	ta, tai	K-hundok:	simhada
Kangxi Dictionary	P248	JP-Kunyomi:	futo·i/ru	Vietnamese:	quá

VARIANTS	泰, 夳

COMBINATIONS

太子 - Prince
太好 - too good
太后 - queen mother
太監 - eunuch
太極拳 - Tai Chi

太空 - space
太太 - Mrs.
太陽 - sun
太不像話 - too unreasonable

太平 - Taiping

SAYINGS

粉飾太平 - false peace
欺人太甚 - bullying
太平盛世 - time of peace
太歲頭上動土 - provoke the almighty

太公釣魚 - setting a trap for someone
花花公子 - playboy

HISTORICAL

甲骨文 (2000BC)	金文 (1000BC)	篆文 (200BC)	隸 (200AD)

FONTS

楷　行　草　宋

| 266AD Jing Dynasty Wang Xizhi | 778BC Tang Dynasty Liu Gongquan | 1280AD Yuan Dynasty Zhao Mengfu | 1829AD Ming Dynasty Dong Qichang |

THE GENIUS OF CHINESE CHARACTERS

STANDARD	SIMPLIFIED	MEANING
夫	夫	• man: 農夫 • husband: 夫妻

| 正 | 一 | 二 | 夫 | 夫 |
| 简 | 一 | 二 | 夫 | 夫 |

ETYMOLOGY	Radical: 大
	Pictograph: A man 人 with hairpins 一 showing he is of a certain age

DATA

Radical (部首)	37: 大
Strokes	4 | 4
HSK	2
Frequency	377
Big5	A4D2
Unihan	U+592B
Kangxi Dictionary	P248

PRONUNCIATION

Pinyin:	fū	J-音読み:	フ, フウ, ブ
Wade-Giles:	fu	J-訓読み:	おっと
Cantonese:	fu1	Korean 音读:	부
Minnan:	hu	Korean 训读:	지아비, 남편
Bopomofo:	ㄈㄨ	K-eumdok:	bu
JP-Onyomi:	fu, fū, bu	K-hundok:	jiabi, nampyeon
JP-Kunyomi:	otto	Vietnamese:	người chồng

VARIANTS	伕

COMBINATIONS

農夫 - farmer
馬夫 - stable hand
丈夫 - husband
夫婦 - couple
夫人 - wife

夫子 - master
夫妻 - husband and wife

SAYINGS

相夫教子 - assisting husband and educating son is a woman's duty
凡夫俗子 - mortal men
千夫所指 - universally condemned

匹夫之勇 - brute courage
匹夫有責 - expect everyone to do his duty
婦唱夫隨 - harmony between husband and wife

HISTORICAL

甲骨文 (2000BC)	金文 (1000BC)	篆文 (200BC)	隸 (200AD)

FONTS

楷 行 草 宋

266AD Jing Dynasty Wang Xizhi

778BC Tang Dynasty Liu Gongquan

1280AD Yuan Dynasty Zhao Mengfu

1829AD Ming Dynasty Dong Qichang

THE GENIUS OF CHINESE CHARACTERS

STANDARD	SIMPLIFIED	MEANING
女	女	• woman • female • feminine • girl

| 正 | く | 女 | 女 |
| 简 | く | 女 | 女 |

ETYMOLOGY

Radical: 女
Pictograph: A depiction of a woman

DATA

		PRONUNCIATION			
Radical (部首)	38: 女	Pinyin:	nǚ	J-音読み:	ジョ, ニョ
Strokes	3 | 3	Wade-Giles:	nü	J-訓読み:	おんな, め
HSK	1	Cantonese:	nui5	Korean 音读:	녀
Frequency	224	Minnan:	lú	Korean 训读:	여자
Big5	A46B	Bopomofo:	ㄋㄩˇ	K-eumdok:	nyeo
Unihan	U+5973	JP-Onyomi:	jo, nyo	K-hundok:	yeoja
Kangxi Dictionary	P254	JP-Kunyomi:	on'na, me	Vietnamese:	giống cái

| VARIANTS | 汝 |

COMBINATIONS

女司機 - female driver	女兒 - daughter	女僕 - maid
女朋友 - girlfriend	子女 - child	女人 - woman
處女 - virgin	孫女 - granddaughter	女性 - female
美女 - beauty	女婿 - son-in-law	巫女 - witch
少女 - girl	女孩 - girl	

SAYINGS

兒女情長 - immersed in love
天花散女 - angels scattering flowers
男耕女織 - chinese version of 'Adam delved and Eve span'
郎才女貌 - a perfect match
九天仙女 - stunning beauty
男女有別 - distinctions between men and women
男女老少 - everyone

HISTORICAL

甲骨文 (2000BC)	金文 (1000BC)	篆文 (200BC)	隸 (200AD)

FONTS

| 楷 | 行 | 草 | 宋 |

266AD Jing Dynasty Wang Xizhi
778BC Tang Dynasty Yan Zhenqing
1280AD Yuan Dynasty Zhao Mengfu
1829AD Ming Dynasty Dong Qichang

THE GENIUS OF CHINESE CHARACTERS

STANDARD	SIMPLIFIED	MEANING
子	子	• children: 子女; father and son: 父子 • 11 p.m.-1 a.m.: 子時 • 1st earthly branch; midnight: 子夜 • seed: 種子 • small thing; noun suffix-.

ETYMOLOGY — Radical: 子
Pictograph: A child with head and arms visible and legs swaddled

DATA

Radical (部首)	39: 子		
Strokes	3 | 3		
HSK	1		
Frequency	37		
Big5	A46C		
Unihan	U+5B50		
Kangxi Dictionary	P277		

PRONUNCIATION

Pinyin:	zǐ	J-音読み:	シ, ス
Wade-Giles:	tzu	J-訓読み:	こ, ね, み
Cantonese:	ji2	Korean 音读:	자
Minnan:	chí	Korean 训读:	아들
Bopomofo:	ㄗˇ	K-eumdok:	ja
JP-Onyomi:	shi, su	K-hundok:	adeul
JP-Kunyomi:	ko, ne, mi	Vietnamese:	đứa trẻ

VARIANTS | 仔

COMBINATIONS

桌子 - table	太子 - prince	男子 - man	子宮 - uterus
猴子 - monkey	王子 - prince	女子 - woman	子母 - mother and son
孩子 - child	孟子 - Mencius	丸子 - pill or sphere	子時 - midnight
種子 - seed	天子 - emperor	子彈 - bullet	子夜 - midnight
魚子 - roe	妻子 - wife	子弟 - young children	

SAYINGS

赤子之心 - innocence
不肖子孫 - unworthy descendants
父慈子孝 - when a father is kind the son will be filial
君子之交 - gentlemanly friendship

不入虎穴, 焉得虎子 - how can you catch tiger cubs without entering the tiger's lair? nothing ventured, nothing gained

HISTORICAL

甲骨文 (2000BC)	金文 (1000BC)	篆文 (200BC)	隸 (200AD)

FONTS

楷 行 草 宋

266AD Jing Dynasty — Wang Xizhi
778BC Tang Dynasty — Liu Gongquan
1280AD Yuan Dynasty — Zhao Mengfu
1829AD Ming Dynasty — Dong Qichang

THE GENIUS OF CHINESE CHARACTERS

STANDARD	SIMPLIFIED	MEANING
字	字	• word: 字典

正: 丶 丷 宀 宀 字 字
简: 丶 丷 宀 宀 字 字

ETYMOLOGY

Radical: 子
Pictograph: A roof 宀 under which children 子 are raised.

DATA

Radical (部首)	39: 子
Strokes	6 | 6
HSK	1
Frequency	393
Big5	A672
Unihan	U+5B57
Kangxi Dictionary	P277

PRONUNCIATION

Pinyin:	zì
Wade-Giles:	tzu
Cantonese:	ji6
Minnan:	jī
Bopomofo:	ㄗˋ
JP-Onyomi:	ji
JP-Kunyomi:	aza, azana

J-音読み:	ジ
J-訓読み:	あざ, あざな
Korean 音读:	자
Korean 训读:	글자
K-eumdok:	ja
K-hundok:	geulja
Vietnamese:	tự

VARIANTS

COMBINATIONS

字母 - letter
字句 - sentences
字條 - notes
字典 - dictionaries
寫字 - writing

別字 - typos
認字 - recognition
字號 - type size
字迹 - handwriting
字幕 - subtitles

字體 - fonts

SAYINGS

咬文嚼字 - overfastidious in wording
不立文字 - unwritten agreement, gentlemen's agreement
待字閨中 - not yet betrothed

祇字不提 - keep silent about
一字千金 - writing of enormous value
字裏行間 - read between the lines

HISTORICAL

甲骨文 (2000BC)	金文 (1000BC)	篆文 (200BC)	隸 (200AD)

FONTS

楷 行 草 宋

266AD Jing Dynasty Wang Xizhi

778BC Tang Dynasty Yan Zhenqing

1280AD Yuan Dynasty Zhao Mengfu

1829AD Ming Dynasty Dong Qichang

THE GENIUS OF CHINESE CHARACTERS

STANDARD	SIMPLIFIED	MEANING
安	安	• quiet: 安静 • peace: 安寧 • to calm: 安神 • content: 安樂 • to pacify: 安定

| 正 | 丶 | 丷 | 宀 | 宊 | 安 | 安 |
| 简 | 丶 | 丷 | 宀 | 宊 | 安 | 安 |

ETYMOLOGY

Radical: 宀

Pictograph: When the woman 女 is under the roof 宀, in the house, then all is well

DATA

Radical (部首)	40: 宀
Strokes	6 | 6
HSK	3
Frequency	232
Big5	A677
Unihan	U+5B89
Kangxi Dictionary	P282

PRONUNCIATION

Pinyin:	ān
Wade-Giles:	an
Cantonese:	on1
Minnan:	an
Bopomofo:	ㄢ
JP-Onyomi:	an
JP-Kunyomi:	yasu·i/raka

J-音読み:	アン
J-訓読み:	やす·い/らか
Korean 音读:	안
Korean 训读:	편안
K-eumdok:	an
K-hundok:	pyeonan
Vietnamese:	an

VARIANTS	侒

COMBINATIONS

安裝 - to install	安全 - safety	安家 - to settle down	安排 - arrangement
安置 - placement	安定 - stability	安静 - quiet	安穩 - stability
安心 - peace of mind	安邊 - pacify the border	安裝 - installation	公安 - public security
安居 - settle down	安頓 - to place securely	安眠藥 - sleeping pills	平安 - safety
安民 - pacify the people	安放 - settle down	安寧 - tranquility	

SAYINGS

安邦治國 - peacefully manage state affairs
安分守己 - abide by the law
安家立業 - set up a home and establish a business

安之若素 - regard with equanimity
安土重遷 - unwilling to move from home
一路平安 - have a good trip

HISTORICAL

甲骨文 (2000BC)	金文 (1000BC)	篆文 (200BC)	隸 (200AD)

FONTS

楷	行	草	宋

266AD
Jing Dynasty
Wang Xizhi

778BC
Tang Dynasty
Liu Gongquan

1280AD
Yuan Dynasty
Zhao Mengfu

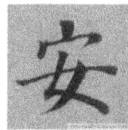
1829AD
Ming Dynasty
Dong Qichang

THE GENIUS OF CHINESE CHARACTERS

STANDARD	SIMPLIFIED	MEANING
完	完	• complete: 完畢 • to finish: 完成 • whole: 完全 • finished: 完美

正 ` 丶 宀 宁 宀 宁 完
简 ` 丶 宀 宁 宀 宁 完

ETYMOLOGY

Radical: 宀
Pictograph: Putting on a roof 宀 =completion

DATA

		PRONUNCIATION			
Radical (部首)	40: 宀	Pinyin:	wán	J-音読み:	カン
Strokes	7 | 7	Wade-Giles:	wan	J-訓読み:	まっと・うする
HSK	2	Cantonese:	yuen4	Korean 音读:	완
Frequency	301	Minnan:	ôan	Korean 训读:	완전하다
Big5	A7B9	Bopomofo:	ㄨㄢˊ	K-eumdok:	wan
Unihan	U+5B8C	JP-Onyomi:	kan	K-hundok:	wanjeonhada
Kangxi Dictionary	P282	JP-Kunyomi:	matto·usuru	Vietnamese:	hoàn thành

| VARIANTS | 院 |

COMBINATIONS

完了 - finished
完成 - to complete
完工 - to complete work
完蛋 - done for
完全 - completely

完美 - perfect
完畢 - completed
完整 - complete, whole
完勝 - a complete victory

完善 - perfect

SAYINGS

體無完膚 - beaten completely, to be criticized
沒完沒了 - endless
完美無缺 - perfection
人無完人 - no one is perfect

完璧歸趙 - to return something intact, whole

HISTORICAL

甲骨文 (2000BC)	金文 (1000BC)	篆文 (200BC)	隸 (200AD)
		宍	完

FONTS

楷	行	草	宋
完	完	完	完

266AD Jing Dynasty Wang Xizhi

1280AD Yuan Dynasty Zhao Mengfu

1280AD Yuan Dynasty Zhao Mengfu

1829AD Ming Dynasty Han Daoheng

THE GENIUS OF Chinese CHARACTERS

STANDARD	SIMPLIFIED	MEANING
客	客	• guest: 客人 • customer: 顧客 • visitor: 來客

| 正 | 丶 | 丶 | 宀 | 宀 | 夗 | 安 | 客 | 客 | 客 |
| 简 | 丶 | 丶 | 宀 | 宀 | 夗 | 安 | 客 | 客 | 客 |

ETYMOLOGY Radical: 宀
Pictograph: come to a stop 各 in a house 宀 = guest

DATA
Radical (部首)   40: 宀
Strokes   9 | 9
HSK   1
Frequency   583
Big5   ABC8
Unihan   U+5BA2
Kangxi Dictionary P284

PRONUNCIATION
Pinyin: kè
Wade-Giles: k'ê
Cantonese: haak3
Minnan: kheh
Bopomofo: ㄎㄜˋ
JP-Onyomi: kyaku, kaku
JP-Kunyomi: maroudo

J-音読み: キャク, カク
J-訓読み: まろうど
Korean 音读: 객
Korean 训读: 손님, 나그네
K-eumdok: gaek
K-hundok: sonnim, nageune
Vietnamese: khách hàng

VARIANTS 㾮

COMBINATIONS
來客 - guest
請客 - invite guests
旅客 - traveler
刺客 - assassin
客廳 - living room

客房 - hotel room
客車 - passenger car
客氣 - polite
客船 - passenger boat
客觀 - objective

客棧 - inn
客人 - visitor

SAYINGS
不速之客 - uninvited guest
賓客盈門 - full house, many visitors
客死他鄉 - die abroad
反客爲主 - gain the initiative

杜門謝客 - live in seclusion
客座教授 - visiting professor
不要客氣 - don't be so polite, don't stand on
           ceremony, feel at home

HISTORICAL
甲骨文 (2000BC)   金文 (1000BC)   篆文 (200BC)   隸 (200AD)

FONTS
楷   行   草   宋
客   客   客   客

778BC
Tang Dynasty
Ouyang Xun

778BC
Tang Dynasty
Yan Zhenqing

1280AD
Yuan Dynasty
Zhao Mengfu

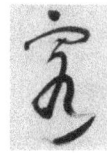
1829AD
Ming Dynasty
Dong Qichang

THE GENIUS OF CHINESE CHARACTERS

STANDARD	SIMPLIFIED	MEANING
小	小	• small: 小小 • young: 年紀小; tiny: 小型 • insignificant: 小意思; minor: 小弟

| 正 | 亅 | 亅 | 小 |
| 简 | 亅 | 亅 | 小 |

ETYMOLOGY
Radical: 小
Pictograph: small wood shavings, tiny things.

DATA

Radical (部首)	42: 小
Strokes	3 | 3
HSK	1
Frequency	83
Big5	A470
Unihan	U+5C0F
Kangxi Dictionary	P296

PRONUNCIATION

Pinyin:	xiǎo
Wade-Giles:	hsiao
Cantonese:	siu2
Minnan:	sió
Bopomofo:	ㄒㄧㄠˇ
JP-Onyomi:	shō
JP-Kunyomi:	chī·sai, ko

J-音読み:	ショウ
J-訓読み:	ちい·さい, こ
Korean 音读:	소
Korean 训读:	작다
K-eumdok:	so
K-hundok:	jakda
Vietnamese:	nhỏ

VARIANTS

COMBINATIONS

小巷 - alley	小腸 - intestines	小姐 - unmarried girl	小説 - novel
小指 - small finger	小氣 - petty	小康 - relatively well off	小食 - snack
小孩 - child	小醜 - clown	小麥 - wheat	小偷 - thief
小看 - despise	小吃 - snacks	小寫 - small letters	矮小 - short, small, undersized
小便 - urinate	小賬 - tip	小心 - careful	

SAYINGS

不拘小節 - not concerned with trivial matters
大材小用 - wasting talent
膽小怕事 - overcautious
雕蟲小技 - insignificant skills

膽小如鼠 - as timid as a mouse
兩小無猜 - innocence of childhood friends
小題大作 - much ado about nothing

HISTORICAL

甲骨文 (2000BC)	金文 (1000BC)	篆文 (200BC)	隸 (200AD)

FONTS

楷 行 草 宋

266AD Jing Dynasty Wang Xizhi
778BC Tang Dynasty Liu Gongquan
1280AD Yuan Dynasty Zhao Mengfu
1829AD Ming Dynasty Dong Qichang

THE GENIUS OF CHINESE CHARACTERS

STANDARD	SIMPLIFIED	MEANING
少	少	• few: 很少; young: 少時 • lacking: 缺少; less: 少了 • don't: 少說話; missing: 東西少了

正 丨 丿 小 少
简 丨 丿 小 少

ETYMOLOGY — Radical: 小
Pictograph: Four small pieces, possibly grains of sand, indicative of few in number.

DATA

		PRONUNCIATION			
Radical (部首)	42: 小	Pinyin:	shǎo	J-音読み:	ショウ
Strokes	4 | 4	Wade-Giles:	shao	J-訓読み:	すこ·し
HSK	1	Cantonese:	siu3	Korean 音读:	소
Frequency	233	Minnan:	chió	Korean 训读:	적다
Big5	A4D6	Bopomofo:	ㄕㄠˇ	K-eumdok:	so
Unihan	U+5C11	JP-Onyomi:	shō	K-hundok:	jeokda
Kangxi Dictionary	P296	JP-Kunyomi:	suko·shi	Vietnamese:	ít hơn

VARIANTS

COMBINATIONS

東西少了 - something is missing
少不了 - can't do without
少見 - rarely seen
少少 - a little
至少 - at least
缺少 - lacking
多少 - how much
少數 - minority
少有 - rare
少年 - young people

SAYINGS

少見多怪 - provincials who are easily awed
僧多粥少 - not enough to go around
少年老成 - young but experienced
凶多吉少 - ominous
少不經事 - young and inexperienced
少言寡語 - short on words
少管閒事 - don't meddle

HISTORICAL

(2000BC)	金文 (1000BC)	篆文 (200BC)	隸 (200AD)
	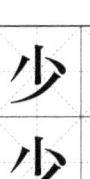	⺍	少

FONTS

楷 行 草 宋
少 少 少 少

266AD
Jing Dynasty
Wang Xizhi

778BC
Tang Dynasty
Liu Gongquan

1280AD
Yuan Dynasty
Zhao Mengfu

1829AD
Ming Dynasty
Dong Qichang

THE GENIUS OF CHINESE CHARACTERS

STANDARD	SIMPLIFIED	MEANING
山	山	• hill: 上山 • mountain: 高山

正 丨 止 山
简 丨 止 山

ETYMOLOGY

Radical: 山
Pictograph: a mountain range

DATA

Radical (部首)	46: 山
Strokes	3 | 3
HSK	3
Frequency	259
Big5	A473
Unihan	U+5C71
Kangxi Dictionary	P307

PRONUNCIATION

Pinyin:	shān
Wade-Giles:	shan
Cantonese:	saan1
Minnan:	soa^n
Bopomofo:	ㄕㄢ
JP-Onyomi:	san, sen
JP-Kunyomi:	yama
J-音読み:	サン, セン
J-訓読み:	やま
Korean 音读:	산
Korean 训读:	메
K-eumdok:	san
K-hundok:	me
Vietnamese:	núi

VARIANTS

COMBINATIONS

上山 - uphill
山水 - landscape
山河 - river
山崩 - landslide
山丘 - hillock
山地 - mountainous country
山洞 - mountain cave
山東 - Shandong Province
山峰 - peak
山歌 - folk song
山根 - foothills
山谷 - valley
山楂 - hawberry
山脊 - ridge
山口 - mountain pass
山嶺 - mountain range
山坡 - slope
山西 - Shanxi Province

SAYINGS

萬水千山 - trials of a long journey
山崩地裂 - drastic changes
山長水遠 - the road is long and difficult
不識泰山 - cannot recognize greatness
安如泰山 - solid as a rock
山高水長 - lasting forever
半壁江山 - half of national territory, refers to parts lost from invasion

HISTORICAL

甲骨文 (2000BC)
金文 (1000BC)
篆文 (200BC)
(200AD)

FONTS

楷 行 草 宋

266AD Jing Dynasty Wang Xizhi
778BC Tang Dynasty Liu Gongquan
1280AD Yuan Dynasty Zhao Mengfu
1829AD Ming Dynasty Dong Qichang

THE GENIUS OF CHINESE CHARACTERS

STANDARD	SIMPLIFIED	MEANING
川	川	• river: 高山大川 • Sichuan: 四川

正 ノ 丿 川
简 ノ 丿 川

ETYMOLOGY | Radical: 川
Pictograph: Depiction of a river course.

DATA
Radical (部首)   47: 川
Strokes   3 | 3
HSK   6
Frequency   1109
Big5   A474
Unihan   U+5DDD
Kangxi Dictionary   P323

PRONUNCIATION
Pinyin: chuān
Wade-Giles: ch'uan
Cantonese: chuen1
Minnan: chhoan
Bopomofo: ㄔㄨㄢ
JP-Onyomi: sen
JP-Kunyomi: kawa

J-音読み: セン
J-訓読み: かわ
Korean 音读: 천
Korean 训读: 내
K-eumdok: cheon
K-hundok: nae
Vietnamese: luân

VARIANTS | 巛

COMBINATIONS
山川 - mountains
四川 - Sichuan
川流 - river current
冰川 - glacier

SAYINGS
川流不息 - continuous flow
海納百川 - sea embraces all rivers, containing many things
一馬平川 - boundless plain

山川表裏 - dangers of natural barriers like mountains and rivers
跋涉山川 - make a difficult journey

HISTORICAL
甲骨文 (2000BC)   金文 (1000BC)   (200BC)   隸 (200AD)

FONTS
楷   行   草   宋

266AD Jing Dynasty — Wang Xizhi
778BC Tang Dynasty — Liu Gongquan
1280AD Yuan Dynasty — Zhao Mengfu
1829AD Ming Dynasty — Wang Chong

THE GENIUS OF Chinese CHARACTERS

STANDARD	SIMPLIFIED	MEANING
年	年	• year: 今年 • annual: 年薪 • new years: 新年 • person's age: 老年

正 ノ 厂 匚 匚 匚 年
简 ノ 厂 匚 匚 匚 年

ETYMOLOGY
Radical: 干
Pictograph: Based on grain/rice -禾.

DATA

		PRONUNCIATION			
Radical (部首)	51: 干	Pinyin:	nián	J-音読み:	ネン
Strokes	6 | 6	Wade-Giles:	nien	J-訓読み:	とし
HSK	1	Cantonese:	nin4	Korean 音读:	년
Frequency	45	Minnan:	nî	Korean 训读:	해
Big5	A67E	Bopomofo:	ㄋㄧㄢˊ	K-eumdok:	nyeon
Unihan	U+5E74	JP-Onyomi:	nen	K-hundok:	hae
Kangxi Dictionary	P340	JP-Kunyomi:	toshi	Vietnamese:	năm

VARIANTS | 秊, 季

COMBINATIONS

今年 - this year	過年 - new year	年級 - class or grade	年齡 - age
年年 - every year	年夜 - new year's eve	年代 - era	流年 - course of one's life
年末 - end of the year	童年 - childhood	年底 - end of year	
往年 - years gone by	老年 - old age	年度 - annual	
新年 - new year	年輕 - youth	年假 - annual leave	

SAYINGS

年年有餘 - may you have more than you wish for
長年累月 - year after year
年輕力壯 - young and strong
流年不利 - an unlucky year

延年益壽 - prolong life
多年往事 - matters of long ago
忘年之交 - old friends

HISTORICAL

甲骨文 (2000BC)	金文 (1000BC)	篆文 (200BC)	隸 (200AD)

FONTS

楷 行 草 宋

266AD Jing Dynasty Wang Xizhi

778BC Tang Dynasty Liu Gongquan

1280AD Yuan Dynasty Zhao Mengfu

1829AD Ming Dynasty Dong Qichang

THE GENIUS OF Chinese Characters

STANDARD	SIMPLIFIED	MEANING
的	的	• adjectival possessive suffix: 我的 • really and truly: 的確 • aim: 目的

正: ′ 丨 𠂉 𠂉 白 白 的 的 的
简: ′ 丨 𠂉 𠂉 白 白 的 的 的

ETYMOLOGY — Radical: 白 Pictograph: During Yuan Dynasty (1271-1368), 的 replaced 底 (similiar pronunciation) as a possessive particle.

DATA

		PRONUNCIATION			
Radical (部首)	106: 白	Pinyin:	de / di	J-音読み:	テキ
Strokes	8 | 8	Wade-Giles:	tê	J-訓読み:	まと
HSK	1	Cantonese:	dik1	Korean 音读:	적
Frequency	1	Minnan:	ê	Korean 训读:	과녁
Big5	AABA	Bopomofo:	ㄉㄜ˙/ㄉㄧ˙/ㄉㄧˊ	K-eumdok:	jeok
Unihan	U+7684	JP-Onyomi:	teki	K-hundok:	gwanyeok
Kangxi Dictionary	P786	JP-Kunyomi:	mato	Vietnamese:	của

VARIANTS | 旳

COMBINATIONS

的當 - proper, suitable or appropriate	目的地 - destination	有的 - some	
目的 - purpose	唱歌的 (人) - singing (person)		
我的 - mine	的確 - indeed		
冷的 - cold	的士 - taxi		

SAYINGS

一語中的 - make a pointed comment
無的放矢 - shooting aimlessly, words can be pointless
衆矢之的 - common target

衆怨之的 - common resentment
熱鍋上的螞蟻 - in a state of anxiety
搬起石頭砸自己的脚 - reap as one has sows

HISTORICAL

甲骨文 (2000BC)	金文 (1000BC)	篆文 (200BC)	隷 (200AD)

FONTS

楷　行　草　宋

266AD Jing Dynasty Wang Xizhi

1280AD Yuan Dynasty Zhao Mengfu

1280AD Yuan Dynasty Zhao Mengfu

1829AD Ming Dynasty Zhang Bi

THE GENIUS OF CHINESE CHARACTERS

STANDARD	SIMPLIFIED	MEANING
是	是	• to be: 我是 • yes: 是的 • that: 是日 • right: 是非

| 正 | 丨 | 冂 | 日 | 日 | 旦 | 旱 | 早 | 昻 | 是 |
| 简 | 丨 | 冂 | 日 | 日 | 旦 | 旱 | 早 | 昻 | 是 |

ETYMOLOGY
Radical: 日 plus 正
Pictograph: The sun 日 in the correct position 正: right, correct.

DATA

		PRONUNCIATION			
Radical (部首)	72: 日	Pinyin:	shì	J-音読み:	ゼ,シ
Strokes	9 | 9	Wade-Giles:	shih	J-訓読み:	こ・れ/の/こ
HSK	1	Cantonese:	si6	Korean 音读:	시
Frequency	3	Minnan:	sī	Korean 训读:	이것, 여기, 옳다
Big5	AC4F	Bopomofo:	ㄕˋ	K-eumdok:	si
Unihan	U+662F	JP-Onyomi:	ze,shi	K-hundok:	igeot, yeogi, olta
Kangxi Dictionary	P493	JP-Kunyomi:	ko·re/no/ko	Vietnamese:	đúng

VARIANTS | 徥, 昰

COMBINATIONS

這是 - this is
是不是 - is it or is it not
是否 - whether
是日 - that day
是非 - right and wrong

SAYINGS

似是而非 - appear right but actually wrong
實事求是 - based on facts, natural situation of things
莫衷一是 - no consensus

唯利是圖 - do things only to gain profits
口是心非 - say one thing and mean another
物是人非 - things are still the same but the men have changed

HISTORICAL

甲骨文 (2000BC)	金文 (1000BC)	篆文 (200BC)	隸 (200AD)

FONTS

楷　行　草　宋

266AD
Jing Dynasty
Wang Xizhi

778BC
Tang Dynasty
Liu Gongquan

1280AD
Yuan Dynasty
Zhao Mengfu

1829AD
Ming Dynasty
Dong Qichang

THE GENIUS OF CHINESE CHARACTERS

STANDARD	SIMPLIFIED	MEANING
有	有	• to have: 有没有 • some: 有歲數 • own: 擁有 • possess: 私有 • some: 有的

正 一 ナ 𠂇 有 有 有
简 一 ナ 𠂇 有 有 有

ETYMOLOGY Radical: 月
Pictograph: A hand holding meat 肉: to have

DATA

Radical (部首)	74: 月	Pinyin:	yǒu	J-音読み: ユウ, ウ
Strokes	6 | 6	Wade-Giles:	you	J-訓読み: あ･る, も･つ
HSK	1	Cantonese:	yau5	Korean 音读: 유
Frequency	8	Minnan:	iú	Korean 训读: 있다
Big5	A6B3	Bopomofo:	ㄧㄡˇ	K-eumdok: yu
Unihan	U+6709	JP-Onyomi:	yū, u	K-hundok: itda
Kangxi Dictionary	P504	JP-Kunyomi:	a·ru, mo·tsu	Vietnamese: có

VARIANTS 㞢

COMBINATIONS

國有 - state-owned	有趣 - interesting	有名 - famous	有意 - intentional
私有 - privately-owned	有的 - some	有限 - limited	有緣 - fated
富有 - wealthy	有機 - organic	有效 - effective	
有錢 - rich	有理 - reasonable	有事 - occupied	
有情 - affectionate	有禮 - courteous	有時 - sometimes	

SAYINGS

別有洞天 - hidden but beautiful, in another realm
粗中有細 - seems careless, but actually wise
大有可爲 - have a bright future
化爲烏有 - come to nothing, all is lost

豈有此理 - ridiculous or 'how dare you!'
有聲有色 - vivid speech/performance
當之有愧 - ashamed, one not living up to one's own standards, "you flatter me"

HISTORICAL

甲骨文 (2000BC)	金文 (1000BC)	篆文 (200BC)	隸 (200AD)

FONTS

楷 行 草 宋

266AD Jing Dynasty Wang Xizhi
778BC Tang Dynasty Liu Gongquan
1280AD Yuan Dynasty Zhao Mengfu
1829AD Ming Dynasty Dong Qichang

THE GENIUS OF CHINESE CHARACTERS

STANDARD	SIMPLIFIED	MEANING
這	这	• this: 這個 • these: 這些 • here: 這裏 • the

正	丶	亠	扌	丰	产	言	言	訁	這	
简	丶	亠	方	文	汶	这				

ETYMOLOGY | Radical: 辶 辶 = movement + 言 = words. "This" is a borrowed meaning. In Tang Dynasty (618-907), replaced 者 (similar pronunciation) with the meaning of "this" / "here"

DATA

		PRONUNCIATION			
Radical (部首)	156: 辶	Pinyin:	zhè	J-音読み:	シャ
Strokes	10 | 7	Wade-Giles:	chê	J-訓読み:	は・う, これ
HSK	1	Cantonese:	je2	Korean 音读:	저
Frequency	11	Minnan:	che	Korean 训读:	이, 이것
Big5	B36F	Bopomofo:	ㄓㄜˋ	K-eumdok:	jeo
Unihan	U+8FD9	JP-Onyomi:	sha	K-hundok:	i, igeot
Kangxi Dictionary	P1258	JP-Kunyomi:	ha·u, kore	Vietnamese:	điều này

VARIANTS | 這(J)

COMBINATIONS

這個 - this
這人 - this person
這回 - this time
這麼 - so (as, so good!)
這樣 - like this

這年 - this year
這邊 - here
這個這裏 - here
這些 - these

SAYINGS

這山望着那山高 - the grass is greener on the other side

HISTORICAL

甲骨文 (2000BC)	金文 (1000BC)	(200BC)	隸 (200AD)
		這	这

FONTS

楷	行	草	宋
这	这	这	这

266AD
Jing Dynasty
Wang Xizhi

THE GENIUS OF Chinese Characters

STANDARD	SIMPLIFIED	MEANING
個	个	• a measure word: 三個 • general classifier: 這個 • individual: 個性

| 正 | ノ | 亻 | 亻 | 仴 | 佀 | 個 | 個 | 個 | 個 |
| 簡 | ノ | 人 | 个 | | | | | | |

ETYMOLOGY | Radical: 人 + 固 (Phonetic)

DATA

Radical (部首)	9: 人
Strokes	10 | 3
HSK	1
Frequency	12
Big5	ADD3
Unihan	U+4E2A
Kangxi Dictionary	P107

PRONUNCIATION

Pinyin:	gè
Wade-Giles:	kê
Cantonese:	goh3
Minnan:	ê
Bopomofo:	ㄍㄜˋ/ㄍㄜ
JP-Onyomi:	ko, ka
JP-Kunyomi:	N/A

J-音読み:	コ, カ
J-訓読み:	N/A
Korean 音读:	개
Korean 训读:	낱
K-eumdok:	gae
K-hundok:	nat
Vietnamese:	máy tính

VARIANTS | 箇

COMBINATIONS

個別 - individually
個體 - independent entity
個個 - every one
個性 - personality

個人 - individual
個人主義 - individualism
個子 - physique

SAYINGS

個中滋味 - bitterness of an experience
個中妙趣 - interesting/fun
各個擊破 - solve a problem one step at a time
一步一個脚印 - work steadily, step by step

一個巴掌拍不響 - it takes two to tango
一個蘿蔔一個坑 - everything in its place

HISTORICAL

甲骨文 (2000BC)	金文 (1000BC)	篆文 (200BC)	隸 (200AD)
		箇	个

FONTS

楷	行	草	宋
个	个	个	个

266AD
Jing Dynasty
Wang Xizhi

778BC
Tang Dynasty
Tang Yin

1280AD
Yuan Dynasty
Xian Yushu

1829AD
Ming Dynasty
Wu Kuan

THE GENIUS OF CHINESE CHARACTERS

STANDARD	SIMPLIFIED	MEANING
和	和	• and: 他和我; mix together: 混合 • harmony singing: 合唱; to blend: 和味 • kimono: 和服; peace: 和平 • soft: 温和; warm: 暖和 • together with: 我和你

| 正 | 一 | 二 | 千 | 禾 | 禾 | 和 | 和 | 和 | | | |
| 简 | 一 | 二 | 千 | 禾 | 禾 | 和 | 和 | 和 | | | |

ETYMOLOGY — Radical: 口 Pictograph: variant is 龠 playing wind instruments + 禾 signifying wind instruments arranged as rice shoots: harmony.

DATA

Radical (部首)	30: 口
Strokes	8 | 8
HSK	1
Frequency	19
Big5	A94D
Unihan	U+548C
Kangxi Dictionary	P185

PRONUNCIATION

Pinyin:	hé	J-音読み:	ワ, オ, カ
Wade-Giles:	han	J-訓読み:	なご・む
Cantonese:	woh4	Korean 音读:	화
Minnan:	hô	Korean 训读:	화목하다
Bopomofo:	ㄏㄜˊ/ㄏㄜˋ/ㄏㄢˋ/ㄏㄨㄛˊ/ㄏㄨㄛˋ	K-eumdok:	hwa
JP-Onyomi:	wa, o, ka	K-hundok:	hwamokada
JP-Kunyomi:	nago·mu	Vietnamese:	với

VARIANTS: 咊, 盉

COMBINATIONS

我和他 - I and him	和好 - friendly	和聲 - harmony
和約 - peace treaty	和解 - reconciliation	和弦 - chord
和談 - peace talks	和美 - soothing	和諧 - appease
和風 - gentle breeze	和平 - peace	和服 - kimono
暖和 - warm	和尚 - monk	和順 - accommodating

SAYINGS

風和日麗 - the wind is mild and the sun is bright
和睦相處 - live together in peace
和顏悅色 - have a kind face
心平氣和 - even-tempered and good-humoured

一唱一和 - echo each other
隨聲附和 - echoing

HISTORICAL

甲骨文 (2000BC) | 金文 (1000BC) | 篆文 (200BC) | 隸 (200AD)

FONTS

楷 行 草 宋

266AD Jing Dynasty Wang Xizhi
778BC Tang Dynasty Liu Gongquan
1280AD Yuan Dynasty Zhao Mengfu
1829AD Ming Dynasty Dong Qichang

THE GENIUS OF CHINESE CHARACTERS

STANDARD	SIMPLIFIED	MEANING
日	日	• sun: 日出 • Japan: 日本 • day: 日子 • date: 一月一日 • daily: 日日

正 丨 冂 日 日
简 丨 冂 日 日

ETYMOLOGY Radical: 日
Pictograph: the sun

DATA

Radical (部首)	72: 日
Strokes	4 | 4
HSK	1
Frequency	101
Big5	A4E9
Unihan	U+65E5
Kangxi Dictionary	P489

PRONUNCIATION

Pinyin:	rì
Wade-Giles:	jih
Cantonese:	yat6
Minnan:	jit
Bopomofo:	日ˋ
JP-Onyomi:	nichi, jitsu
JP-Kunyomi:	hi, ka

J-音読み:	ニチ, ジツ
J-訓読み:	ひ, か
Korean 音读:	일
Korean 训读:	날
K-eumdok:	il
K-hundok:	nal
Vietnamese:	ngày

VARIANTS 囸

COMBINATIONS

日光 - sunshine	昔日 - formerly	日期 - date	平日 - usually
日出 - sunrise	吉日 - auspicious day	今日 - today	連日 - day after day
日落 - sunset	佳日 - good day	近日 - recently	日文 - Japanese
日間 - daytime	假日 - holiday	日夕, 日夜 - day and night	日本 - Japan
每日, 日日, 日記 - diary	日子 - days		日常 - usual

SAYINGS

重見天日 - regain freedom/to be delivered from oppression

度日如年 - a day passes as if a year - in deep anxiety

不見天日 - never see the sun or sky- suffering oppression

撥雲見日 - clearing doubt to gain understanding

HISTORICAL

甲骨文 (2000BC)	金文 (1000BC)	篆文 (200BC)	隸 (200AD)
日	⊙	日	日

FONTS

楷	行	草	宋
日	日	日	日

266AD Jing Dynasty — Wang Xizhi

778BC Tang Dynasty — Liu Gongquan

1280AD Yuan Dynasty — Zhao Mengfu

1829AD Ming Dynasty — Dong Qichang

THE GENIUS OF CHINESE CHARACTERS

STANDARD	SIMPLIFIED	MEANING
月	月	• month: 月份 • moon: 月亮

| 正 | ノ | 刀 | 月 | 月 |
| 簡 | ノ | 刀 | 月 | 月 |

ETYMOLOGY Radical: 月 Variant of 夕.
Pictograph: crescent moon.

DATA

		PRONUNCIATION			
Radical (部首)	74: 月	Pinyin:	yuè	J-音読み:	ゲツ, ガツ
Strokes	4 | 4	Wade-Giles:	yüeh	J-訓読み:	つき
HSK	1	Cantonese:	yuet6	Korean 音读:	월
Frequency	169	Minnan:	goat	Korean 训读:	달
Big5	A4EB	Bopomofo:	ㄩㄝˋ	K-eumdok:	wol
Unihan	U+6708	JP-Onyomi:	getsu, gatsu	K-hundok:	dal
Kangxi Dictionary	P504	JP-Kunyomi:	tsuki	Vietnamese:	tháng

VARIANTS | 囝, 肼

COMBINATIONS

新月 - new moon	下月 - next month	月刊 - monthly magazine	月亮 - moon
滿月 - full moon	月初 - beginning of the month	月餅 - mooncake	月食 - eclipse of moon
每月 - every month			
月月 - each month	月底 - end of the month	月球 - moon	
上月 - last month	三月 - March	月經 - menstruation	

SAYINGS

春花秋月 - passing of time
成年累月 - year in year out
花好月圓 - conjugal bliss
清風明月 - at leisure

窮年累月 - for years on end

HISTORICAL

甲骨文 (2000BC)	金文 (1000BC)	篆文 (200BC)	隸 (200AD)
(	D	月	月

FONTS

楷	行	草	宋
月	月	月	月

266AD Jing Dynasty Wang Xizhi

778BC Tang Dynasty Liu Gongquan

1280AD Yuan Dynasty Zhao Mengfu

1829AD Ming Dynasty Dong Qichang

THE GENIUS OF Chinese Characters

STANDARD	SIMPLIFIED	MEANING
時	时	• time: 時間 • period: 時段 • era: 古時 • when: 何時 • o'clock: 子時

正 丨 冂 日 日 旷 旷 旷 旷 時 時
简 丨 冂 日 日 旷 时 时

ETYMOLOGY: Radical: 日 The sun 日 + 寺 = phonetic. In Oracle bones, 止 = arrival. The sun arrive at one place = Time.

DATA

		PRONUNCIATION			
Radical (部首)	72: 日	Pinyin:	shí	J-音読み:	ジ
Strokes	10 | 7	Wade-Giles:	shih	J-訓読み:	とき
HSK	1	Cantonese:	si4	Korean 音读:	시
Frequency	25	Minnan:	sî	Korean 训读:	때
Big5	AEC9	Bopomofo:	ㄕˊ	K-eumdok:	si
Unihan	U+65F6	JP-Onyomi:	ji	K-hundok:	ttae
Kangxi Dictionary	P494	JP-Kunyomi:	toki	Vietnamese:	thời gian

VARIANTS

COMBINATIONS

時間 - time　　　　即時 - instantly　　　準時 - on time　　　時光 - time
暫時 - temporarily　及時 - timely　　　　時代 - era　　　　　時候 - time
何時 - when　　　　臨時 - temporary　　時尚 - fashion　　　時間 - time
當時 - then　　　　隨時 - anytime　　　時差 - time difference　時時 - always
同時 - at the same time　時期 - period　　時代 - epoch

SAYINGS

生不逢時 - born in wrong era　　　　名震一時 - temporary fame
時至今日 - even to this day　　　　　及時行樂 - enjoy life while you can
不合時宜 - inopportune
風行一時 - popular for a while

HISTORICAL | FONTS

甲骨文 (2000BC)	金文 (1000BC)	篆文 (200BC)	隸 (200AD)	楷　行　草　宋
		𣅱	时	时　时　时　时

 266AD Jing Dynasty Wang Xizhi

 778BC Tang Dynasty Liu Gongquan

 1280AD Yuan Dynasty Zhao Mengfu

 1829AD Ming Dynasty Dong Qichang

THE GENIUS OF CHINESE CHARACTERS

STANDARD	SIMPLIFIED	MEANING
期	期	• a period of time: 時期 • to hope: 期望; phase: 期間 • courses of study: 學期; time limit: 到期 • issue of a periodical: 第一期

正	一	十	卄	卄	卄	甘	其	其	期	期	期	期
简	一	十	卄	卄	卄	甘	其	其	期	期	期	期

ETYMOLOGY — Radical: 月 The moon 月 + 其 (phonetic). In ancient China, people marked time with the cycles of the moon → cycle/period

DATA

Radical (部首)	74: 月		
Strokes	12 | 12		
HSK	1		
Frequency	253		
Big5	B4C1		
Unihan	U+671F		
Kangxi Dictionary	P506		

PRONUNCIATION

Pinyin:	qī	J-音読み:	キ, ゴ
Wade-Giles:	ch'i	J-訓読み:	とき
Cantonese:	kei4	Korean 音读:	기
Minnan:	kî	Korean 训读:	기약하다
Bopomofo:	ㄑ一/ㄑ一´ㄐ一	K-eumdok:	gi
JP-Onyomi:	ki, go	K-hundok:	giyakada
JP-Kunyomi:	toki	Vietnamese:	giai đoạn = stage

VARIANTS | 其, 朞, 稘

COMBINATIONS

日期 - date	延期 - delay	期間 - period
定期 - regular	過期 - expired	期限 - deadline
學期 - semester	期望 - hope	
假期 - holiday	期待 - look forward to	
到期 - at maturity	期貨 - futures	

SAYINGS

如期而至 - as scheduled	爲期不遠 - in the near future
不期而遇 - chance encounter	計日可期 - in the near future
後會有期 - we'll meet again	
遙遙無期 - not within the foreseeable future	

HISTORICAL

甲骨文 (2000BC)	金文 (1000BC)	篆文 (200BC)	隸 (200AD)
		𦕁	期

FONTS

楷	行	草	宋
期	期	期	期

266AD Jing Dynasty Wang Xizhi

778BC Tang Dynasty Liu Gongquan

1280AD Yuan Dynasty Zhao Mengfu

1829AD Ming Dynasty Chen Daofu

THE GENIUS OF CHINESE CHARACTERS

STANDARD	SIMPLIFIED	MEANING
明	明	• bright: 光明; clear: 明確; open: 明顯 • next: 明年; to understand: 明白 • Ming dynasty: 明朝; brilliant: 明星 • wise: 明王

正 丨 冂 日 日 日 明 明 明
简 丨 冂 日 日 日 明 明 明

ETYMOLOGY: Radical: 日 plus 月 Sun 日 + moon 月 = brightness/light. Another explanation: window 囧 + moon 月 = moonlight streaming through an open window.

DATA

		PRONUNCIATION			
Radical (部首)	72: 日	Pinyin:	míng	J-音読み:	メイ, ミョウ
Strokes	8 | 8	Wade-Giles:	ming	J-訓読み:	あか・るい
HSK	1	Cantonese:	ming4	Korean 音读:	명
Frequency	121	Minnan:	bêng	Korean 训读:	밝다
Big5	A9FA	Bopomofo:	ㄇㄧㄥˊ	K-eumdok:	myeong
Unihan	U+660E	JP-Onyomi:	mei, myō	K-hundok:	bakda
Kangxi Dictionary	P491	JP-Kunyomi:	aka·rui	Vietnamese:	sáng

VARIANTS | 朙, 眀

COMBINATIONS

明代 - Ming Dynasty
明顯 - obviously
明德 - enlightened
聰明 - clever
光明 - bright

明天 - tomorrow
明白 - understand
明日 - tomorrow
明星 - movie star

SAYINGS

愛恨分明 - clear views
不明不白 - obscure
黑白分明 - in sharp contrast
春光明媚 - sunlit scene of spring

冰雪聰明 - extremely intelligent
光明正大 - just and honorable

HISTORICAL

甲骨文 (2000BC)	金文 (1000BC)	篆文 (200BC)	隸 (200AD)
		明	明

FONTS

楷 行 草 宋
明 明 明 明

266AD Jing Dynasty Wang Xizhi
778BC Tang Dynasty Liu Gongquan
1280AD Yuan Dynasty Zhao Mengfu
1829AD Ming Dynasty Dong Qichang

THE GENIUS OF CHINESE CHARACTERS

STANDARD	SIMPLIFIED	MEANING
朋	朋	• friend: 朋友 • sounds of wind: 朋朋

正) 刀 月 月 月 朋 朋 朋
简) 刀 月 月 月 朋 朋 朋

ETYMOLOGY
Radical: 月
String of shells threaded together = wealth → friend.

DATA

		PRONUNCIATION			
Radical (部首)	74: 月	Pinyin:	péng	J-音読み:	ホウ
Strokes	8 | 8	Wade-Giles:	p'êng	J-訓読み:	とも
HSK	1	Cantonese:	pang4	Korean 音读:	붕
Frequency	882	Minnan:	pêng	Korean 训读:	벗,친구
Big5	AA42	Bopomofo:	ㄆㄥˊ	K-eumdok:	bung
Unihan	U+670B	JP-Onyomi:	hō	K-hundok:	beot,chingu
Kangxi Dictionary	P504	JP-Kunyomi:	tomo	Vietnamese:	bạn bè

VARIANTS | 倗

COMBINATIONS
朋友 - friend
朋克 - punk
朋黨 - political clique

SAYINGS
酒肉朋友 - fair weather friends
呼朋喚友 - inviting friends with similar interests
賓朋滿座 - a house full of guests
朋比爲奸 - act in collusion

狐朋狗友 - disreputable friend
碩大無朋 - gigantic

HISTORICAL

甲骨文 (2000BC)	金文 (1000BC)	篆文 (200BC)	隸 (200AD)

FONTS
楷 行 草 宋

266AD Jing Dynasty Wang Xizhi
778BC Tang Dynasty Du Mu
1280AD Yuan Dynasty Zhao Mengfu
1829AD Ming Dynasty Dong Qichang

THE GENIUS OF CHINESE CHARACTERS

STANDARD	SIMPLIFIED	MEANING
會	会	• can (be able): 會做; association: 協會前 • accounting: 會計; to assemble: 會合 • be possible: 會好; meeting: 會議 • meet together: 會見

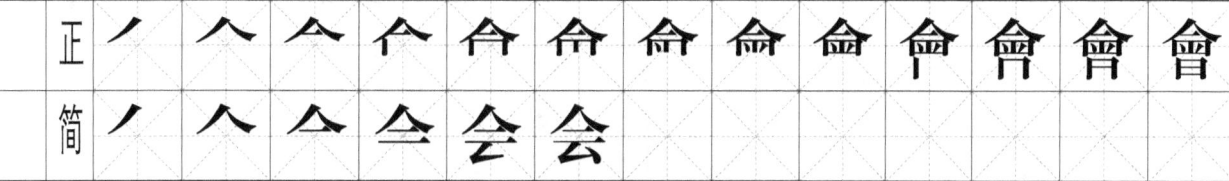

ETYMOLOGY — Radical: 日 To gather 亼 to eat 口 a meal (pictograph of a covered vessel containing rice). Pictograph: Traditional grain barn → together.

DATA

Radical (部首)	73: 日
Strokes	13 | 6
HSK	1
Frequency	29
Big5	B77C
Unihan	U+4F1A
Kangxi Dictionary	P503

PRONUNCIATION

Pinyin:	huì
Wade-Giles:	hui
Cantonese:	wooi4, wooi6
Minnan:	hōe
Bopomofo:	ㄏㄨㄟˋ
JP-Onyomi:	kai, e
JP-Kunyomi:	a·u
J-音読み:	カイ, エ
J-訓読み:	あ・う
Korean 音读:	회
Korean 训读:	모이다
K-eumdok:	hoe
K-hundok:	moida
Vietnamese:	gặp gỡ

VARIANTS: 会(J)

COMBINATIONS

會不會 - is it likely?	會員 - member	會説 - eloquent
會面 - to meet	會所 - clubhouse	
會合 - meet	會議 - conference	
會話 - conversation	會費 - membership fees	
會見 - meeting		

SAYINGS

會逢其適 - coincidentally
能説會道 - to have the gift of the gab
心領神會 - understand tacitly
千載一會 - a very rare opportunity

HISTORICAL

甲骨文 (2000BC)	金文 (1000BC)	篆文 (200BC)	隸 (200AD)

FONTS

楷　行　草　宋

266AD
Jing Dynasty
Wang Xizhi

778BC
Tang Dynasty
Liu Gongquan

1280AD
Yuan Dynasty
Zhao Mengfu

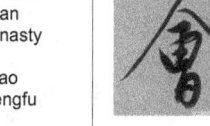
1829AD
Ming Dynasty
Dong Qichang

THE GENIUS OF CHINESE CHARACTERS

STANDARD	SIMPLIFIED	MEANING
		• to come: 來往 • to come to: 來到 • time won't allow: 來不及 • to bring: 來飯 • future: 來年

正	一	ｒ	ｒ	邧	苁	來	來	來
简	一	一	一	卆	半	来	来	

ETYMOLOGY	Radical: 人 Pictograph: Wheat plant. In ancient times, people believed wheat was a gift from god → come

DATA

		PRONUNCIATION			
Radical (部首)	9: 人	Pinyin:	lái	J-音読み:	ライ, タイ
Strokes	8 | 7	Wade-Giles:	lai	J-訓読み:	く･る, きた･す
HSK	1	Cantonese:	loi4	Korean 音读:	래, 내
Frequency	15	Minnan:	lâi	Korean 训读:	오다, 돌아오다
Big5	A8D3	Bopomofo:	ㄌㄞˊ	K-eumdok:	rae, nae
Unihan	U+6765	JP-Onyomi:	rai, tai	K-hundok:	oda, doraoda
Kangxi Dictionary	P513	JP-Kunyomi:	ku·ru, kita·su	Vietnamese:	đến

	VARIANTS	来(J)

COMBINATIONS

來吧 - come on	做不來 - can't do it	後來 - later	來客 - guest
來不及 - too late	上來 - come up	以來 - since	來臨 - arrival
亂來 - mess up	來月 - next month	從來 - never	來年 - next year
慢慢來 - take your time	十來個 - approx.ten	來賓 - guests	來源 - origin/source
來回 - there and back	將來 - in the future	來回 - back and forth	

SAYINGS

紫氣東來 - a propitious omen
本來面目 - true colors
飛來橫禍 - unexpected disaster
古往今來 - throughout the ages

歸去來兮 - homeward bound
跑來跑去 - running around

HISTORICAL

甲骨文 (2000BC)	金文 (1000BC)	篆文 (200BC)	隸 (200AD)
		來	来

FONTS

楷	行	草	宋
来	来	来	来

266AD
Jing Dynasty
Wang Xizhi

778BC
Tang Dynasty
Liu Gongquan

1280AD
Yuan Dynasty
Zhao Mengfu

1829AD
Ming Dynasty
Dong Qichang

THE GENIUS OF CHINESE CHARACTERS

STANDARD	SIMPLIFIED	MEANING
家	家	• home: 家庭 • family: 家族 • expert: 專家 • school of thought: 道家

正 ` 丶 宀 宀 宀 宁 宁 冢 家 家
简 ` 丶 宀 宀 宀 宁 宁 冢 家 家

ETYMOLOGY

Radical: 宀

宀 roof/building + 豕 pig/boar : Pig shed → house/household → home /family.

DATA

Radical (部首)	40: 宀
Strokes	10 | 10
HSK	1
Frequency	56
Big5	AE61
Unihan	U+5BB6
Kangxi Dictionary	P286

PRONUNCIATION

Pinyin:	jiā
Wade-Giles:	chia
Cantonese:	ga1
Minnan:	ke
Bopomofo:	ㄐㄧㄚ
JP-Onyomi:	ka, ke
JP-Kunyomi:	ie, ya, uchi

J-音読み:	カ, ケ
J-訓読み:	いえ, や, うち
Korean 音读:	가
Korean 训读:	집
K-eumdok:	ga
K-hundok:	jip
Vietnamese:	trang chủ

VARIANTS | 傢

COMBINATIONS

家庭 - family
想家 - homesick
回家 - go home
藝術家 - artist
專家 - expert

畫家 - painter
家長 - parent
家具 - furniture
家人 - family
家族 - extended family

SAYINGS

安家立業 - establish a home and business
白手起家 - starting from scratch
大方之家 - generous home
大家風範 - refined manners

百家爭鳴 - hundred schools of thought contend

HISTORICAL

甲骨文 (2000BC)	金文 (1000BC)	篆文 (200BC)	隸 (200AD)
	家	家	家

FONTS

楷 行 草 宋

家 家 家 家

 266AD Jing Dynasty Wang Xizhi

 778BC Tang Dynasty Liu Gongquan

 1280AD Yuan Dynasty Zhao Mengfu

 1829AD Ming Dynasty Dong Qichang

THE GENIUS OF CHINESE CHARACTERS

STANDARD	SIMPLIFIED	MEANING
生	生	• Life: 生命 • to give birth: 生孩子; to be born: 出生 • student: 學生 • lifetime: 一生 • living being: 生靈

正 ノ 一 ㄜ 牛 生
简 ノ 一 ㄜ 牛 生

ETYMOLOGY
Radical: 生
Grass 屮 sprouting and grows out of the ground 土 = birth/start.

DATA
- Radical (部首): 100: 生
- Strokes: 5 | 5
- HSK: 1
- Frequency: 34
- Big5: A5CD
- Unihan: U+751F
- Kangxi Dictionary: P754

PRONUNCIATION
- Pinyin: shēng
- Wade-Giles: shēng
- Cantonese: saang1
- Minnan: se^n
- Bopomofo: ㄕㄥ
- JP-Onyomi: sei, shō
- JP-Kunyomi: nama, i·kiru
- J-音読み: セイ, ショウ
- J-訓読み: なま, い·きる
- Korean 音读: 생
- Korean 训读: 나다
- K-eumdok: saeng
- K-hundok: nada
- Vietnamese: sức khỏe

VARIANTS | 甥

COMBINATIONS
生活 - life	生育 - fertility	生命 - life
養生 - health	陌生 - strangeness	生日 - birthday
永生 - immortality	生病 - to become sick	生死 - life and death
學生 - student	生產 - production	生物學 - biology
發生 - occurrence	生氣 - to be angry	生意 - business

SAYINGS
別開生面 - To break fresh ground
不生不滅 - unborn and imperishable
長生不滅 - immortal
超度眾生 - save mankind from the sea of misery

出生入死 - risk one's life
寸草不生 - infertile land, barren soil

HISTORICAL
- 甲骨文 (2000BC)
- 金文 (1000BC)
- 篆文 (200BC)
- 隸 (200AD)

FONTS
楷 行 草 宋

266AD Jing Dynasty — Wang Xizhi
778BC Tang Dynasty — Liu Gongquan
1280AD Yuan Dynasty — Zhao Mengfu
1829AD Ming Dynasty — Dong Qichang

THE GENIUS OF Chinese CHARACTERS

STANDARD	SIMPLIFIED	MEANING
們	们	• plural marker for personal pronouns: 我們

正 ノ 亻 亻' 亻' 亻' 伊 伊 們 們 們
简 ノ 亻 亻 亻 们

ETYMOLOGY Radical: 人
man 人 + 門 (phonetic). In Tang Dynasty, the plural ending was added.

DATA

		PRONUNCIATION			
Radical (部首)	9: 人	Pinyin:	men	J-音読み:	モン
Strokes	10 | 5	Wade-Giles:	mên	J-訓読み:	ともがら
HSK	1	Cantonese:	moon4	Korean 音读:	문
Frequency	13	Minnan:		Korean 训读:	들
Big5	ADCC	Bopomofo:	ㄇㄣˊ	K-eumdok:	mun
Unihan	U+4EEC	JP-Onyomi:	mon	K-hundok:	deul
Kangxi Dictionary	P107	JP-Kunyomi:	tomogara	Vietnamese:	chúng tôi

VARIANTS

COMBINATIONS

我們 - us
你們 - you
他們 - they (male/male&female)
她們 - they (female)

它們 - they (it)

SAYINGS

n/a

HISTORICAL

甲骨文 (2000BC)	金文 (1000BC)	篆文 (200BC)	隸 (200AD)
		們	们

FONTS

楷 行 草 宋
们 们 们 们

77

THE GENIUS OF CHINESE CHARACTERS

STANDARD	SIMPLIFIED	MEANING
對	对	• Correct (answer): 對 • To answer: 對答; To face, encounter: 反對 • Check (number of something): 對號頭 • Agree: 對胃口 • Deal with: 對待

正: 一 丷 业 业 业 业 业 業 業 業 業 對
對
简: 丆 又 又 对 对

ETYMOLOGY: Radical: 寸 Hold a ceremonial staff 業 in hands寸: hold up → a pair of/ relatively (ceremonial objects usually used in pairs).

DATA

Radical (部首)	41: 寸	Pinyin:	duì
Strokes	14 | 5	Wade-Giles:	tui
HSK	1	Cantonese:	dui3
Frequency	33	Minnan:	tùi
Big5	B9EF	Bopomofo:	ㄉㄨㄟˋ
Unihan	U+5BF9	JP-Onyomi:	tai, tsui
Kangxi Dictionary	P293	JP-Kunyomi:	mu·kau

PRONUNCIATION

J-音読み:	タイ, ツイ
J-訓読み:	む・かう
Korean 音读:	대
Korean 训读:	대하다
K-eumdok:	dae
K-hundok:	daehada
Vietnamese:	chính xác

VARIANTS: 封(J)

COMBINATIONS

一對 - pair
相對 - relatively
反對 - against
絕對 - absolutely
對面 - opposite
核對 - check
對不起 - sorry

對岸 - opposite bank
對換 - swap
對于 - for
對外 - externally
對白 - dialogue
對待 - treat
對方 - opponent

SAYINGS

成雙作對 - in couples
對牛彈琴 - cast pearls before swine
對癥下藥 - the right antidote
門當戶對 - perfect match
文不對題 - irrelevant
針鋒相對 - give tit for tat
對月獨酌 - drinking alone under the moonlight

HISTORICAL

甲骨文 (2000BC)	金文 (1000BC)	篆文 (200BC)	隸 (200AD)
		對	对

FONTS

楷 对　行 对　草 对　宋 对

266AD
Jing Dynasty
Wang Xizhi

778BC
Tang Dynasty
Liu Gongquan

1280AD
Yuan Dynasty
Zhao Mengfu

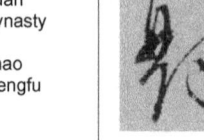
1829AD
Ming Dynasty
Dong Qichang

THE GENIUS OF CHINESE CHARACTERS

STANDARD	SIMPLIFIED	MEANING
能	能	• capability: 能力 • energy: 電能 • able to: 能够 • good at: 能說 • tolerate: 積不相能

正	ㄅ	ㄙ	厃	台	台	台	台ˊ	能	能	能
简	ㄅ	ㄙ	厃	台	台	台	台ˊ	能	能	能

ETYMOLOGY — Radical: 肉 Pictograph: a black bear. Bears are always strong → capable. Related to 熊 = bear with meat 肉 in its mouth and two claws

DATA

		PRONUNCIATION			
Radical (部首)	130: 肉	Pinyin:	néng	J-音読み:	ノウ
Strokes	10 | 10	Wade-Giles:	nêng	J-訓読み:	よ・く
HSK	1	Cantonese:	nang4	Korean 音读:	능,내
Frequency	35	Minnan:	lêng	Korean 训读:	능하다
Big5	AFE0	Bopomofo:	ㄋㄥˊ	K-eumdok:	neung, nae
Unihan	U+80FD	JP-Onyomi:	nō	K-hundok:	neunghada
Kangxi Dictionary	P981	JP-Kunyomi:	yo·ku	Vietnamese:	có thể

		VARIANTS	螚, 骴

COMBINATIONS

能幹 - competency   可能 - possibility
能力 - ability   能够 - ability
技能 - skill   能量 - energy
太陽能 - solar energy
全能 - omnipotence

SAYINGS

百無一能 - no way out of a predicament
愛莫能助 - helpless
不能自拔 - can't help oneself
各盡所能 - each doing his best

過而能改 - willing to change faults, correct one's behavior
力所能及 - do as much as possible

HISTORICAL

甲骨文 (2000BC)	金文 (1000BC)	篆文 (200BC)	隸 (200AD)
			能

FONTS

楷	行	草	宋
能	能	能	能

266AD
Jing Dynasty
Wang Xizhi

778BC
Tang Dynasty
Liu Gongquan

1280AD
Yuan Dynasty
Zhao Mengfu

1829AD
Ming Dynasty
Dong Qichang

THE GENIUS OF CHINESE CHARACTERS

STANDARD	SIMPLIFIED	MEANING
本	本	• plant root: 逐本 • foundation: 本末 • origins: 源本; orginal: 本籍 • capital (investment): 資本 • edition: 原刻本; this: 本日

正	一	十	才	木	本
简	一	十	才	木	本

ETYMOLOGY Radical: 木
Mark the location of the root一on the tree木 = Origin/Basis/Root

DATA

		PRONUNCIATION			
Radical (部首)	75: 木	Pinyin:	běn	J-音読み:	ホン
Strokes	5 | 5	Wade-Giles:	pên	J-訓読み:	もと
HSK	1	Cantonese:	boon2	Korean 音读:	본
Frequency	92	Minnan:	pún	Korean 训读:	근본
Big5	A5BB	Bopomofo:	ㄅㄣˇ	K-eumdok:	bon
Unihan	U+672C	JP-Onyomi:	hon	K-hundok:	geunbon
Kangxi Dictionary	P509	JP-Kunyomi:	moto	Vietnamese:	điều này

VARIANTS | 夲,榃,榃

COMBINATIONS

資本 - capital
本錢 - capital
本日 - today
本月 - this month
本年 - this year

本國 - home country
本人 - I, myself
本土 - the local
本來 - originally
本地 - local

本州 - Honshu
本身 - itself
本性 - nature
本意 - the original
       intention

SAYINGS

本來面目 - true colors
本性難移 - a Chinese version of can a leopard
       change his spots?
變本加厲 - increasingly

一本正經 - playing it straight
照本宣科 - scripted
捨本逐末 - have the order reversed

HISTORICAL

甲骨文 (2000BC)	(1000BC)	篆文 (200BC)	隸 (200AD)
	木	木	本

FONTS

楷	行	草	宋
本	夲	夲	本

266AD Jing Dynasty — Wang Xizhi
778BC Tang Dynasty — Liu Gongquan
1280AD Yuan Dynasty — Zhao Mengfu
1829AD Ming Dynasty — Dong Qichang

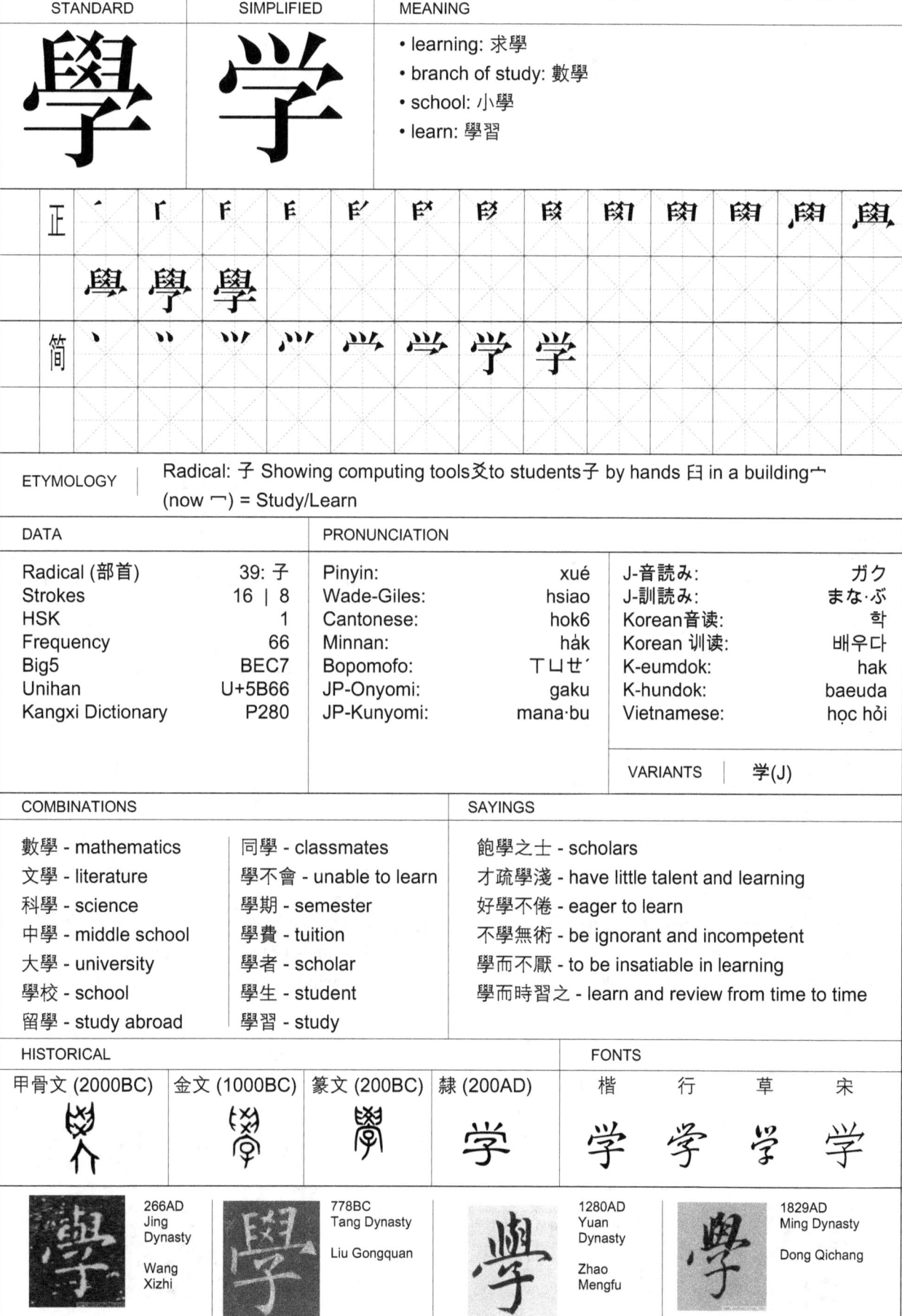

THE GENIUS OF CHINESE CHARACTERS

STANDARD	SIMPLIFIED	MEANING
現	现	• cash: 現金; to appear: 出現 • now: 現在; immediate: 現賣 • current; available: 現貨 • to express: 表現, 現出來

| 正 | 一 | 三 | 干 | 王 | 玗 | 玑 | 玑 | 玥 | 現 | 現 |
| 简 | 一 | 三 | 干 | 王 | 玗 | 玑 | 现 | 现 | | |

ETYMOLOGY

Radical: 玉
見 appear + 玉 jewel: gem appearing from the earth when excavated = appear/emerge

DATA

Radical (部首)	96: 玉		
Strokes	11 | 8		
HSK	1		
Frequency	70		
Big5	B27B		
Unihan	U+73B0		
Kangxi Dictionary	P728		

PRONUNCIATION

Pinyin:	xiàn	J-音読み:	ゲン
Wade-Giles:	hsien	J-訓読み:	あらわ·す
Cantonese:	yin6	Korean 音读:	현
Minnan:	hiān	Korean 训读:	나타나다
Bopomofo:	ㄒㄧㄢˋ	K-eumdok:	hyeon
JP-Onyomi:	gen	K-hundok:	natanada
JP-Kunyomi:	arawa·su	Vietnamese:	hiện nay

VARIANTS

COMBINATIONS

現金 - cash 現場 - live
出現 - emergence 現有 - existing
表現 - performance 先前 - previous
現在 - present 現實 - reality
現代 - modern 現實主義 - realism

SAYINGS

安于現狀 - happy with the status quo
曇花一現 - short-lived
丟人現眼 - make a fool of oneself
活靈活現 - vivid

若隱若現 - looming
現身說法 - advise others using one's own experience

HISTORICAL

甲骨文 (2000BC)	金文 (1000BC)	篆文 (200BC)	隸 (200AD)
		現	現

FONTS

楷	行	草	宋
現	现	现	现

266AD
Jing Dynasty
Wang Xizhi

778BC
Tang Dynasty
Liu Gongquan

1280AD
Yuan Dynasty
Zhao Mengfu

1829AD
Ming Dynasty
Dong Qichang

THE GENIUS OF CHINESE CHARACTERS

STANDARD	SIMPLIFIED	MEANING
說	说	• to say: 說 • to speak: 說話 • scold: 數說 • theory: 學說 • to explain: 解說

正 說 說 說 說 說 說 說 說 說 說 說 說 說

简 丶 讠 讠 讠 讠 说 说 说 说

ETYMOLOGY — Radical: 言
Make people feel happy by talking = Speak/Say → Persuade(politically)/Happy

DATA

Radical (部首)	149: 言
Strokes	14 | 9
HSK	1
Frequency	24
Big5	BBA1
Unihan	U+8BF4
Kangxi Dictionary	P1164

PRONUNCIATION

Pinyin:	shuō
Wade-Giles:	shui
Cantonese:	suet3
Minnan:	soeh
Bopomofo:	ㄕㄨㄛ/ㄕㄨㄟˋ
JP-Onyomi:	setsu, zei
JP-Kunyomi:	to·ku

J-音読み:	セツ, ゼイ
J-訓読み:	と·く
Korean 音读:	말씀
Korean 训读:	말씀
K-eumdok:	seol
K-hundok:	malsseum
Vietnamese:	nói

VARIANTS | 説(J)

COMBINATIONS

說話 - speak
說大話 - exaggerate
說不清 - inexplainable
說不出 - cannot say
胡說 - nonsense
說明 - explain

說白 - to be frank
說不定 - maybe
說法 - saying (s)
說服 - persuade
說服力 - power to persuade

SAYINGS

說來說去 - after all is said and done
說溜了嘴 - inadvertently blurt out
實話實說 - to be honest
欲說還休 - hesitant
談天說地 - talk of everything under the sun
自說自話 - talk to oneself

HISTORICAL

(2000BC)	金文 (1000BC)	(200BC)	(200AD)

FONTS

楷 行 草 宋
说 说 说 说

266AD
Jing Dynasty
Wang Xizhi

778BC
Tang Dynasty
Yan Zhenqing

1280AD
Yuan Dynasty
Zhao Mengfu

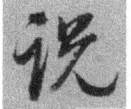
1829AD
Ming Dynasty
Dong Qichang

THE GENIUS OF Chinese CHARACTERS

STANDARD	SIMPLIFIED	MEANING
作	作	• to make: 作衣服 • to do: 作工 • engage in work: 作事 • work: 工作 • writer: 作家

正 ノ 亻 亻 乍 作 作 作
简 ノ 亻 亻 乍 作 作 作

ETYMOLOGY | Radical: 人
create a pile 乍 + 人 (distinguishing form) = make/do → regard as

DATA

Radical (部首)	9: 人	Pinyin:	zuò
Strokes	7 | 7	Wade-Giles:	tso
HSK	1	Cantonese:	jok6
Frequency	49	Minnan:	chok
Big5	A740	Bopomofo:	ㄗㄨㄛˋ
Unihan	U+4F5C	JP-Onyomi:	saku, sa
Kangxi Dictionary	P99	JP-Kunyomi:	tsuku·ru

J-音読み:	サク, サ
J-訓読み:	つく·る
Korean 音读:	작
Korean 训读:	짓다, 만들다
K-eumdok:	jak
K-hundok:	jitda, mandeulda
Vietnamese:	làm

VARIANTS | 佐, 乍, 胙

COMBINATIONS

作事 - do things   作廢 - make invalid   作業 - homework
作衣服 - make clothes   作風 - style   作用 - role
作別 - bid farewell   作家 - writer
作曲 - compose   作夢 - dream
作法 - method   作品 - work

SAYINGS

自作自受 - of their own making   日出而作 - work from sunrise
爲虎作倀 - help a villain do evil   始作俑者 - instigator
狂風大作 - gusty wind
一鼓作氣 - at one fling

HISTORICAL

(2000BC)	(1000BC)	(200BC)	隸 (200AD)
		作	作

FONTS

楷	行	草	宋
作	作	作	作

266AD Jing Dynasty Wang Xizhi

778BC Tang Dynasty Liu Gongquan

1280AD Yuan Dynasty Zhao Mengfu

1829AD Ming Dynasty Dong Qichang

THE GENIUS OF CHINESE CHARACTERS

STANDARD	SIMPLIFIED	MEANING
電	电	• electricity: 電力 • electrical: 電器 • lightning: 雷電 • telegram: 電報

正: 一 厂 宀 冖 襾 雨 雨 雨 雨 雪 雷 雷 電
简: 丨 冂 日 日 电

ETYMOLOGY

Radical: 雨
A bolt of lightning 申 (now 电) in the rain 雨 = lightning/fast → electricity

DATA

		PRONUNCIATION			
Radical (部首)	173: 雨	Pinyin:	diàn	J-音読み:	デン
Strokes	13 | 5	Wade-Giles:	tien	J-訓読み:	いなずま
HSK	1	Cantonese:	din6	Korean 音读:	전
Frequency	230	Minnan:	tiān	Korean 训读:	번개, 전기
Big5	B971	Bopomofo:	ㄉㄧㄢˋ	K-eumdok:	jeon
Unihan	U+7535	JP-Onyomi:	den	K-hundok:	beongae, jeongi
Kangxi Dictionary	P1373	JP-Kunyomi:	inazuma	Vietnamese:	điện lực

VARIANTS

COMBINATIONS

電氣 - electric	電報 - telegraph	電池 - batteries	電臺 - radio station
電力 - electricity	電話 - telephone	電燈 - lights	電壓 - voltage
電器 - appliances	雷電 - lightnings	電腦 - computers	電影 - movies
電瓶 - batteries	電匯 - wire transfer	電綫 - wires	發電 - power generation
静電 - static electricity	電波 - radio waves	電視 - televisions	

SAYINGS

電光火石 - lightning flint
電閃雷鳴 - thunder and lightning
目光如電 - sharp eyes
雷電交加 - thunderstorm

逐電追風 - chasing the wind

HISTORICAL

甲骨文 (2000BC)	金文 (1000BC)	篆文 (200BC)	隸 (200AD)
		電	电

FONTS

楷 行 草 宋
电 电 电 电

266AD
Jing Dynasty
Wang Xizhi

778BC
Tang Dynasty
Liu Gongquan

1280AD
Yuan Dynasty
Zhao Mengfu

1829AD
Ming Dynasty
Dong Qichang

THE GENIUS OF CHINESE CHARACTERS

STANDARD	SIMPLIFIED	MEANING
前	前	• before: 以前; front: 前面 • former: 前任; preceding: 前天 • forward: 前来; beforehand: 前知

正 ` ⸍ 丷 丷 艹 丷 艹

正: ` 丷 丷 艹 艹 艹 艹 艹 前 前
简: ` 丷 丷 艹 艹 艹 艹 艹 前 前

ETYMOLOGY
Radical: 刀
Original meaning = scissors 剪. before/front is a borrowed meaning.

DATA

Radical (部首)	18: 刀		
Strokes	9 | 9		
HSK	1		
Frequency	93		
Big5	AB65		
Unihan	U+524D		
Kangxi Dictionary	P140		

PRONUNCIATION

Pinyin:	qián	J-音読み:	ゼン
Wade-Giles:	ch'ien	J-訓読み:	まえ
Cantonese:	chin4	Korean 音读:	전
Minnan:	chêng	Korean 训读:	앞, 먼저
Bopomofo:	ㄑㄧㄢˊ	K-eumdok:	jeon
JP-Onyomi:	zen	K-hundok:	ap, meonjeo
JP-Kunyomi:	mae	Vietnamese:	trước

VARIANTS | 偂, 歬

COMBINATIONS

前面 - front	目前 - present	前往 - to move towards	前者 - former
前邊 - front	面前 - ahead, in front	前程 - prospect	前例 - precedent
前排 - front row	前天 - previous day	前方 - forward	前年 - year before last
前鋒 - forward	前夫 - ex-husband	前後 - back and forth	前途 - future
向前 - forward	前妻 - ex-wife	前回 - previous time	前言 - preface

SAYINGS

前程似錦 - the future looks bright
前仰後合 - laughing their heads off
門前冷落 - snub in front of the door
空前絕後 - unprecedented

人前背後 - do one thing before a man and another behind his back
停滯不前 - stagnate

HISTORICAL

甲骨文 (2000BC)	金文 (1000BC)	篆文 (200BC)	隸 (200AD)
	肯	𩠐	前

FONTS

楷	行	草	宋
前	前	前	前

266AD Jing Dynasty Wang Xizhi

778BC Tang Dynasty Liu Gongquan

1280AD Yuan Dynasty Zhao Mengfu

1829AD Ming Dynasty Dong Qichang

THE GENIUS OF CHINESE CHARACTERS

STANDARD	SIMPLIFIED	MEANING
開	开	• to open: 開門; start: 開始 • to set: 開單; to drive: 開車 • initiate: 開頭

正	｜	ヨ	ヨ	戶	門	門	門	門	門	閂	開	開
简	一	二	开	开								

ETYMOLOGY

Radical: 門
Removing the bolt 一 from the door 門 with hands 廾 = open / start

DATA

Radical (部首)	169: 門
Strokes	12 | 4
HSK	1
Frequency	94
Big5	B67D
Unihan	U+5F00
Kangxi Dictionary	P1331

PRONUNCIATION

Pinyin:	kāi	J-音読み:	カイ
Wade-Giles:	k'ai	J-訓読み:	ひら･く
Cantonese:	hoi1	Korean 音读:	개
Minnan:	khui	Korean 训读:	열다
Bopomofo:	ㄎㄞ	K-eumdok:	gae
JP-Onyomi:	kai	K-hundok:	yeolda
JP-Kunyomi:	hira·ku	Vietnamese:	mở

VARIANTS

COMBINATIONS

開門 - open the door	開頭 - to begin	開除 - expel	分開 - separate
開燈 - turn on the light	開市 - to open	開出 - to issue	離開 - leave
開眼界 - see new horizons	開工 - to start	開店 - open a shop	滾開 - go away!
	開花 - flower	開車 - drive a vehicle	躲開 - avoid
開始 - start	開拓 - develop	打開 - open	開場 - opening

SAYINGS

開門大吉 - grand opening
异想天開 - asking for the moon
開門見山 - straight to the point
開誠布公 - speak frankly and sincerely

眉開眼笑 - smile from ear to ear
鐵樹開花 - seldom seen

HISTORICAL

(2000BC)	金文 (1000BC)	篆文 (200BC)	隸 (200AD)
		開	开

FONTS

楷	行	草	宋
开	开	开	开

266AD
Jing Dynasty
Wang Xizhi

778BC
Tang Dynasty
Liu Gongquan

1280AD
Yuan Dynasty
Zhao Mengfu

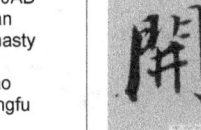
1829AD
Ming Dynasty
Dong Qichang

THE GENIUS OF CHINESE CHARACTERS

STANDARD	SIMPLIFIED	MEANING
京	京	• capital: 京城; Beijing: 北京 • metropolitan city: 京都 • Peking-related: 京劇

正	、	亠	亠	亠	亩	宁	亨	京		
简	、	亠	亠	亠	亩	宁	亨	京		

ETYMOLOGY Radical: 亠 Pictograph: A pavilion built on high ground. Man-made structures → high hill → capital/capital city

DATA
- Radical (部首): 8: 亠
- Strokes: 8 | 8
- HSK: 1
- Frequency: 566
- Big5: A8CA
- Unihan: U+4EAC
- Kangxi Dictionary: P88

PRONUNCIATION
- Pinyin: jīng
- Wade-Giles: ching
- Cantonese: ging1
- Minnan: kia^n
- Bopomofo: ㄐㄧㄥ
- JP-Onyomi: kyō, kei
- JP-Kunyomi: miyako
- J-音読み: キョウ, ケイ
- J-訓読み: みやこ
- Korean 音读: 경
- Korean 训读: 수도
- K-eumdok: gyeong
- K-hundok: sudo
- Vietnamese: bắc kinh

VARIANTS 京

COMBINATIONS
京都 - Kyoto
北京 - Beijing
京城 - Beijing
京劇 - Beijing Opera

SAYINGS
京解之才 - have the talent to pass the Beijing test

HISTORICAL
(2000BC)	金文 (1000BC)	篆文 (200BC)	隸 (200AD)

FONTS
楷　行　草　宋

266AD
Jing Dynasty
Wang Xizhi

778BC
Tang Dynasty
Liu Gongquan

1280AD
Yuan Dynasty
Zhao Mengfu

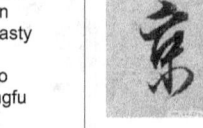
1829AD
Ming Dynasty
Dong Qichang

THE GENIUS OF CHINESE CHARACTERS

STANDARD	SIMPLIFIED	MEANING
分	分	• to divide: 分心; a measure word: 三分 • a unit of length: 公分; separate: 分開 • minute: 分鐘; to divide into: 兩分利 • distinguish: 分別; part: 分內

| 正 | ノ | 八 | 分 | 分 |
| 简 | ノ | 八 | 分 | 分 |

ETYMOLOGY

Radical: 刀
Split right and left 八 with a knife 刀 = split / divide / separate

DATA

Radical (部首)	18: 刀		
Strokes	4 | 4		
HSK	1		
Frequency	79		
Big5	A4C0		
Unihan	U+5206		
Kangxi Dictionary	P136		

PRONUNCIATION

Pinyin:	fēn	J-音読み:	ブン, フン, ブ
Wade-Giles:	fên	J-訓読み:	わ·ける
Cantonese:	fan1	Korean 音读:	분
Minnan:	hūn	Korean 训读:	나누다
Bopomofo:	ㄈㄣ	K-eumdok:	bun
JP-Onyomi:	bun, fun, bu	K-hundok:	nanuda
JP-Kunyomi:	wa·keru	Vietnamese:	phút

VARIANTS | 份, 紛

COMBINATIONS

公分 - centimeters	分散 - disperse	百分之百 - one hundred percent	分居 - separation
分鐘 - minutes	分開 - separate	分工 - division of labor	分局 - branch
十分 - tenths	分別 - separate	分公司 - branch	分發 - distribute
百分比 - percentages	分不清 - indistinguishable	分發 - distribution	分割 - cutup
分手 - break up			分化 - disintegrate

SAYINGS

公私分明 - separating public from private interests
分庭抗禮 - rival
主次不分 - no distinction between primary and secondary
不分勝敗 - regardless of victory or defeat
入木三分 - penetrating

HISTORICAL

甲骨文 (2000BC)	金文 (1000BC)	篆文 (200BC)	隸 (200AD)
		分	分

FONTS

楷 行 草 宋
分 分 分 分

266AD Jing Dynasty — Wang Xizhi
778BC Tang Dynasty — Liu Gongquan
1280AD Yuan Dynasty — Zhao Mengfu
1829AD Ming Dynasty — Dong Qichang

THE GENIUS OF CHINESE CHARACTERS

STANDARD	SIMPLIFIED	MEANING
高	高	• high: 高度; tall: 高低 • noble: 高贵; old: 高年 • elevated: 高架; higher: 高级 • lofty: 高人

正	丶	亠	广	亣	亩	户	亭	高	高	高
简	丶	亠	广	亣	亩	户	亭	高	高	高

ETYMOLOGY
Radical: 高
Pictograph: A double-storey tower with windows and gate 口 = tall/high

DATA

		PRONUNCIATION			
Radical (部首)	189: 高	Pinyin:	gāo	J-音読み:	コウ
Strokes	10 | 10	Wade-Giles:	kao	J-訓読み:	たか·い
HSK	1	Cantonese:	go1	Korean 音读:	고
Frequency	134	Minnan:	ko	Korean 训读:	높다
Big5	B0AA	Bopomofo:	ㄍㄠ	K-eumdok:	go
Unihan	U+9AD8	JP-Onyomi:	kō	K-hundok:	nopda
Kangxi Dictionary	P1451	JP-Kunyomi:	taka·i	Vietnamese:	cao

VARIANTS | 髙

COMBINATIONS

高低 - height	高架 - elevated	高尚 - noble	高傲 - proud
高矮 - height	高舉 - high	高價 - high price	高潮 - orgasm
高度 - height	高山 - alpine	高齡 - senior	高中 - high school
高大 - tall	高樓 - high - rise	高級 - senior	高齡 - senior
高個子 - tall person	高貴 - noble	高手 - expert	高徒 - senior

SAYINGS

高枕无忧 - sit back and relax
高门大户 - a wealthy and puissant family
人高马大 - tall and strong
高耸入云 - touch the sky

自命清高 - acting as if one is morally better than other people
眼高手低 - have grandiose aims but puny abilities
高歌一曲 - sing a song loudly

HISTORICAL

甲骨文 (2000BC)	金文 (1000BC)	篆文 (200BC)	隸 (200AD)
高	高	高	高

FONTS

楷	行	草	宋
高	高	高	高

266AD Jing Dynasty Wang Xizhi

778BC Tang Dynasty Liu Gongquan

1280AD Yuan Dynasty Zhao Mengfu

1829AD Ming Dynasty Dong Qichang

THE GENIUS OF Chinese CHARACTERS

STANDARD	SIMPLIFIED	MEANING
都	都	• all: 都來了; metropolis: 京都 • both (if two things are involved): 他們都 • capital: 省都; city: 都市

正: 一 十 土 耂 耂 者 者 者 者 都 都
简: 一 十 土 耂 耂 者 者 者 者 都 都

ETYMOLOGY

Radical: 邑
village 邑 + 者 (phonetic) = metropolis / capital → all

DATA

Radical (部首)	163: 邑
Strokes	10 | 10
HSK	1
Frequency	68
Big5	B3A3
Unihan	U+90FD
Kangxi Dictionary	P1274

PRONUNCIATION

Pinyin:	dōu	J-音読み:	ト, ツ
Wade-Giles:	tou	J-訓読み:	みやこ
Cantonese:	doh1	Korean 音读:	도, 지
Minnan:	to	Korean 训读:	도읍, 도시
Bopomofo:	ㄉㄨ/ㄉㄨ	K-eumdok:	do, ji
JP-Onyomi:	to, tsu	K-hundok:	doeup, dosi
JP-Kunyomi:	miyako	Vietnamese:	tất cả

VARIANTS

COMBINATIONS

首都 - capital
都城 - metropolis
大都 - mostly
都市 - city
我都要 - I want all

SAYINGS

通都大邑 - metropolis
都頭異姓 - the most noble appellation
一身都是膽 - be full of courage

HISTORICAL

甲骨文 (2000BC)	金文 (1000BC)	篆文 (200BC)	隸 (200AD)
		都	都

FONTS

楷 行 草 宋
都 都 都 都

266AD Jing Dynasty Wang Xizhi
778BC Tang Dynasty Liu Gongquan
1280AD Yuan Dynasty Zhao Mengfu
1829AD Ming Dynasty Dong Qichang

THE GENIUS OF CHINESE CHARACTERS

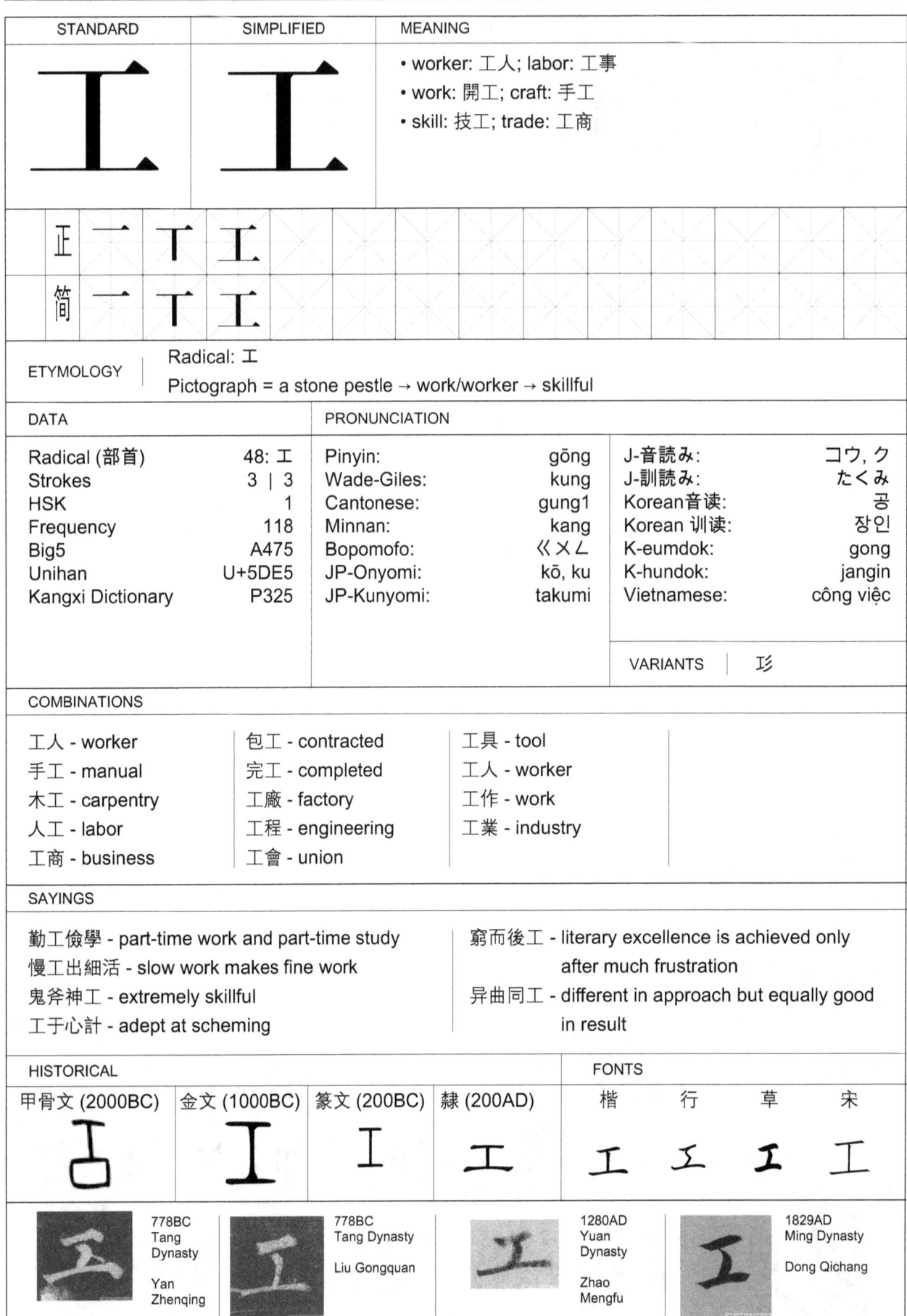

THE GENIUS OF Chinese Characters

STANDARD	SIMPLIFIED	MEANING
面	面	• face: 面部, 面門 • to face: 面對 • surface: 表面 • upside: 上面 • aspect: 方面

| 正 | 一 | 丆 | 㕫 | 靣 | 面 | 面 | 面 | 面 |
| 简 | 一 | 丆 | 㕫 | 靣 | 面 | 面 | 面 | 面 |

ETYMOLOGY — Radical: 面
face with a circle round it = face / surface

DATA

		PRONUNCIATION			
Radical (部首)	176: 面	Pinyin:	miàn	J-音読み:	メン, ベン
Strokes	9 | 9	Wade-Giles:	mien	J-訓読み:	おも, つら
HSK	1	Cantonese:	min6	Korean 音读:	면
Frequency	74	Minnan:	bīn	Korean 训读:	낯, 얼굴
Big5	ADB1	Bopomofo:	ㄇㄧㄢˋ	K-eumdok:	myeon
Unihan	U+9762	JP-Onyomi:	men, ben	K-hundok:	nat, eolgul
Kangxi Dictionary	P1383	JP-Kunyomi:	omo, tsura	Vietnamese:	bề mặt

VARIANTS | 麵, 面

COMBINATIONS

臉面 - face	正面 - front	面面 - every aspect	面談 - face to face discussion
面孔 - face	四面 - four sides	面目 - demeanor	
面對面 - face to face	面壁 - do nothing	面色 - complexion	
前面 - in front	面試 - interview	面子 - self - respect	
對面 - opposite	面具 - mask	面熟 - looks familiar	

SAYINGS

面紅耳赤 - flush with shame or anger
兩面三刀 - two-faced
人面桃花 - romantic memories
泪流滿面 - burst into tears

HISTORICAL | FONTS

| 甲骨文 (2000BC) | 金文 (1000BC) | (200BC) | (200AD) | 楷 | 行 | 草 | 宋 |

266AD Jing Dynasty Wang Xizhi

778BC Tang Dynasty Yan Zhenqing

1280AD Yuan Dynasty Zhao Mengfu

1829AD Ming Dynasty Dong Qichang

THE GENIUS OF CHINESE CHARACTERS

STANDARD	SIMPLIFIED	MEANING
機	机	• machine: 機制; opportunity: 機會 • secret: 機密; airplane: 飛機 • chance: 機遇; helicopter: 直升機

正 一 十 十 木 朩 朾 朹 机 机 机 杉 楼
機 機 機
简 一 十 十 木 机 机

ETYMOLOGY
Radical: 木
Pictograph: A tree with branches and roots = tree, wood, wooden

DATA
Radical (部首)	75: 木
Strokes	16 | 6
HSK	1
Frequency	111
Big5	BEF7
Unihan	U+673A
Kangxi Dictionary	P554

PRONUNCIATION
Pinyin:	jī
Wade-Giles:	chi
Cantonese:	gei1
Minnan:	ki
Bopomofo:	ㄐㄧ
JP-Onyomi:	ki
JP-Kunyomi:	hata

J-音読み:	キ
J-訓読み:	はた
Korean 音读:	기
Korean 训读:	틀, 기계
K-eumdok:	gi
K-hundok:	teul, gigye
Vietnamese:	máy móc

VARIANTS

COMBINATIONS
機械 - mechanical
機器 - machine
照相機 - camera
電視機 - TV set
飛機 - air plane
機制 - machine-made
時機 - opportunity

投機 - speculate
神機 - dark secrets
機場 - airport
機構 - organization
機關 - public organization
機會 - opportunity

SAYINGS
日理萬機 - attend to numerous affairs everyday
機關算盡 - rack one's brains over sth
危機四伏 - be plagued by crises
有機可乘 - an opportunity to take advantage of
天賜良機 - a heaven-sent chance
一綫生機 - a slim chance of survival

HISTORICAL
甲骨文 (2000BC)	金文 (1000BC)	(200BC)	隸 (200AD)

FONTS
楷 行 草 宋

266AD Jing Dynasty Wang Xizhi
778BC Tang Dynasty Yan Zhenqing
1280AD Yuan Dynasty Zhao Mengfu
1829AD Ming Dynasty Dong Qichang

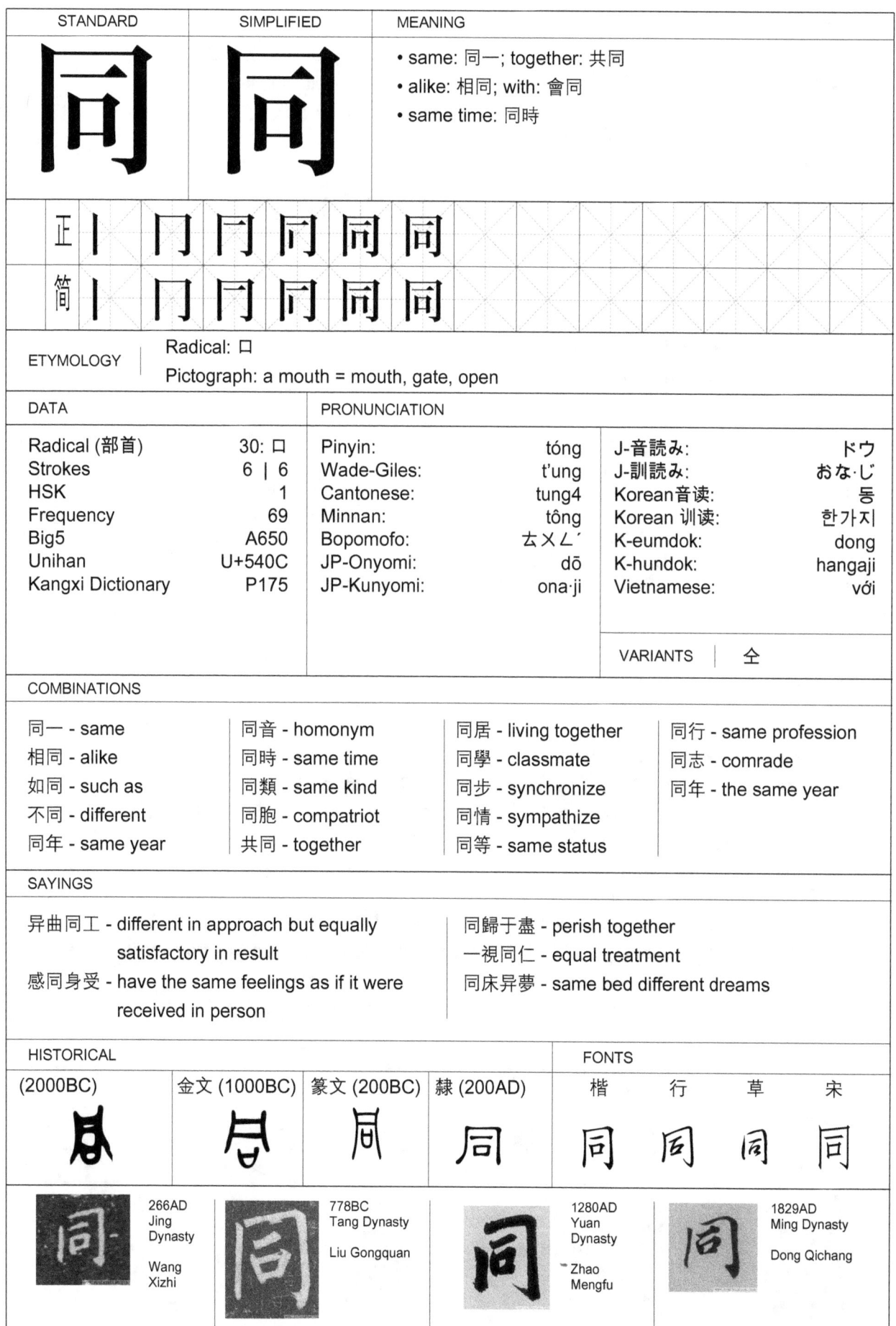

THE GENIUS OF CHINESE CHARACTERS

STANDARD	SIMPLIFIED	MEANING
車	车	• a vehicle (on land): 車子; car: 汽車 • machine; to shape with a lathe • to transport in a cart: 車水

正 一 厂 厅 盲 盲 亘 車
简 一 ナ 左 车

ETYMOLOGY
Radical: 車
Pictograph: a chariot, as in a two-wheeled vehicle drawn by horses = vehicle, car, cart

DATA

		PRONUNCIATION			
Radical (部首)	159: 車	Pinyin:	chē	J-音読み:	シャ
Strokes	7 | 4	Wade-Giles:	ch'ê	J-訓読み:	くるま
HSK	1	Cantonese:	wah4	Korean 音读:	자
Frequency	361	Minnan:	chhia	Korean 训读:	수레
Big5	A8AE	Bopomofo:	ㄔㄜ	K-eumdok:	ja
Unihan	U+8F66	JP-Onyomi:	sha	K-hundok:	sure
Kangxi Dictionary	P1239	JP-Kunyomi:	kuruma	Vietnamese:	xe hơi

VARIANTS

COMBINATIONS

火車 - train	電車 - tram	坐車 - ride in a car	車站 - station
馬車 - chariot, wagon	貨車 - truck	上車 - get in a car	車架 - frame of a car
坦克車 - tank	警車 - police car	車禍 - traffic accident	車輛 - vehicles
自行車 - bicycle	人力車/黃包車 - rickshaw	風車 - windmill	車床 - lathe
摩托車 - motorbike		車道 - traffic lane	

SAYINGS

舟車勞頓 - exhausted from a long travel
學富五車 - be wealthy in knowledge
車到山前必有路 - things will eventually sort themselves out

安步當車 - walk rather than ride
閉門造車 - divorce oneself from reality and act blindly
車水馬龍 - heavy traffic

HISTORICAL

甲骨文 (2000BC)	金文 (1000BC)	篆文 (200BC)	隸 (200AD)
		車	车

FONTS

楷 行 草 宋
车 车 车 车

266AD
Jing Dynasty
Wang Xizhi

778BC
Tang Dynasty
Liu Gongquan

1280AD
Yuan Dynasty
Zhao Mengfu

1829AD
Ming Dynasty
Dong Qichang

THE GENIUS OF CHINESE CHARACTERS

STANDARD	SIMPLIFIED	MEANING
關	关	• frontier pass: 關口; to shut: 關門 • a surname; to concern/related: 關洗 • to turn off: 關機

正: 丨 ⺄ ⺄ 阝 鬥 門 門 門 門 門 門 門 鬧 鬧 鬧 關 關 關 關

简: 丶 丷 丷 关 关 关

ETYMOLOGY — Radical: 門 Pictograph: a two-leaved door = a doorway, gate or opening; a sect, category, class, school of thought

DATA

Radical (部首)	169: 門	
Strokes	19 | 6	
HSK	1	
Frequency	127	
Big5	C3F6	
Unihan	U+5173	
Kangxi Dictionary	P1341	

PRONUNCIATION

Pinyin:	guān
Wade-Giles:	kuan
Cantonese:	gwaan1
Minnan:	koan
Bopomofo:	ㄍㄨㄢ
JP-Onyomi:	kan
JP-Kunyomi:	kaka·waru, seki

J-音読み:	カン
J-訓読み:	かか·わる, せき
Korean 音读:	관
Korean 训读:	관계하다
K-eumdok:	gwan
K-hundok:	gwangyehada
Vietnamese:	tắt

VARIANTS | 関(J)

COMBINATIONS

海關 - customs
關鍵 - crucial
開關 - on/off switch
關聯 - linked
關系 - relationship
關心 - concerned
關節 - joints

關注 - pay attention to
關于 - regarding

SAYINGS

關懷備至 - show the utmost solicitude
過關斬將 - overcome all difficulties
關系重大 - make a difference
無關痛癢 - irrelevant

HISTORICAL

甲骨文 (2000BC)	金文 (1000BC)	篆文 (200BC)	(200AD)
		關	关

FONTS

楷	行	草	宋
关	关	关	关

266AD Jing Dynasty — Wang Xizhi

778BC Tang Dynasty — Yan Zhenqing

1280AD Yuan Dynasty — Zhao Mengfu

1829AD Ming Dynasty — Dong Qichang

THE GENIUS OF Chinese CHARACTERS

STANDARD	SIMPLIFIED	MEANING
裏	里	• inside: 裏面 • interior; within

正: 丶 亠 广 亣 亨 言 审 車 重 東 㐂 裵 裏
简: 丨 冂 日 曰 甲 甼 里

ETYMOLOGY
Radical: 衣
Pictograph: clothes (sleeves and robes) = clothes, clothing, to dress, to cover

DATA

Radical (部首)	145: 衣	Pinyin:	lǐ
Strokes	12 | 7	Wade-Giles:	li
HSK	1	Cantonese:	lui5
Frequency	50	Minnan:	lí
Big5	B8CC	Bopomofo:	ㄌㄧˇ
Unihan	U+91CC	JP-Onyomi:	ri
Kangxi Dictionary	P1291	JP-Kunyomi:	ura, uchi

J-音読み:	リ
J-訓読み:	うら, うち
Korean 音读:	리
Korean 训读:	속, 내부
K-eumdok:	ri
K-hundok:	sok, naebu
Vietnamese:	trong

VARIANTS | 裏, 裡

COMBINATIONS

裏頭 - inside
裏子 - lining of clothing
裏衣 - underwear

SAYINGS

表裏不一 - two-faced
一瀉千裏 - flow down vigorously
下裏巴人 - popular literature or art
霧裏看花 - have blurred vision

裏外受敵 - enemies within and without

HISTORICAL

甲骨文 (2000BC)	金文 (1000BC)	(200BC)	隸 (200AD)
		裏	里

FONTS

楷 行 草 宋
里 里 里 里

266AD Jing Dynasty Wang Xizhi
778BC Tang Dynasty Yan Zhenqing
1280AD Yuan Dynasty Zhao Mengfu
1829AD Ming Dynasty Dong Qichang

THE GENIUS OF CHINESE CHARACTERS

STANDARD	SIMPLIFIED	MEANING
好	好	• good: 好人; be fond of: 嗜好 • well: 做好; fine: 很好; friendly: 友好 • easy to: 好做; very: 好久

正 ㄑ 女 女 好 好 好
简 ㄑ 女 女 好 好 好

ETYMOLOGY	Radical: 女
	Pictograph: A kneeling figure with arms crossed = woman, girl, feminine

DATA

		PRONUNCIATION			
Radical (部首)	38: 女	Pinyin:	hǎo	J-音読み:	コウ
Strokes	6 | 6	Wade-Giles:	hao	J-訓読み:	この·む, す·く
HSK	1	Cantonese:	ho2	Korean 音读:	호
Frequency	82	Minnan:	hó	Korean 训读:	좋다
Big5	A66E	Bopomofo:	ㄏㄠˇ/ㄏㄠˋ	K-eumdok:	ho
Unihan	U+597D	JP-Onyomi:	kō	K-hundok:	jota
Kangxi Dictionary	P255	JP-Kunyomi:	kono·mu, su·ku	Vietnamese:	nó tốt

VARIANTS	竓

COMBINATIONS

好像 - as if
好吃 - tasty
好處 - advantage
好象 - apparently
好多 - a lot

好多了 - much better
好看 - good looking
好些 - so many
好久 - quite a while

SAYINGS

好善樂施 - always glad to give to charities
好高鶩遠 - reach for what is beyond one's grasp
葉公好龍 - professed love of what one actually fears

投其所好 - cater to another's pleasure
花好月圓 - elixir of love

HISTORICAL | FONTS

| 甲骨文 (2000BC) | 金文 (1000BC) | 篆文 (200BC) | 隸 (200AD) | 楷 | 行 | 草 | 宋 |

| 266AD Jing Dynasty Wang Xizhi | 778BC Tang Dynasty Liu Gongquan | 1280AD Yuan Dynasty Zhao Mengfu | 1829AD Ming Dynasty Dong Qichang |

THE GENIUS OF CHINESE CHARACTERS

STANDARD	SIMPLIFIED	MEANING
没	没	• have not: 没有; did not: 没做 • disappear: 泯没 • to drown: 沉没; never: 没齒 • without: 没縫兒

正	丶	冫	氵	氵	沪	没	没
简	丶	冫	氵	氵	沪	没	没

ETYMOLOGY
Radical: 水
Pictograph: Flowing water with side boundaries = water, liquid

DATA

			PRONUNCIATION			
Radical (部首)	85: 水		Pinyin:	méi	J-音読み:	ボツ
Strokes	7 | 7		Wade-Giles:	mei	J-訓読み:	しず・む
HSK	1		Cantonese:	moot6	Korean 音读:	몰
Frequency	72		Minnan:	bu̍t	Korean 训读:	(물에)빠지다
Big5	A853		Bopomofo:	ㄇㄟˊ/ㄇㄛˋ	K-eumdok:	mol
Unihan	U+6CA1		JP-Onyomi:	botsu	K-hundok:	(mure) ppajida
Kangxi Dictionary	P611		JP-Kunyomi:	shizu·mu	Vietnamese:	không

VARIANTS	圽,殁,沒,没(J)

COMBINATIONS

没有 - not have
没吃 - have not eaten
没看 - have not seen

SAYINGS

没心没肺 - heartless
神出鬼没 - appear and disappear mysteriously
没事找事 - asking for trouble or finding faults
没世不忘 - shall not forget

没上没下 - lacking in manners

HISTORICAL

甲骨文 (2000BC)	金文 (1000BC)	篆文 (200BC)	隸 (200AD)
		𣳚	没

FONTS

楷	行	草	宋
没	没	没	没

266AD
Jing Dynasty
Wang Xizhi

778BC
Tang Dynasty
Liu Gongquan

1280AD
Yuan Dynasty
Xian Yushu

1829AD
Ming Dynasty
Dong Qichang

THE GENIUS OF CHINESE CHARACTERS

STANDARD	SIMPLIFIED	MEANING
看	看	• to look at: 看见; to read: 看书 • watch: 看电影; point of view: 看法 • guard: 看门; detain: 看押 • see a doctor: 看病

正 一 二 三 干 手 看 看 看 看
简 一 二 三 干 手 看 看 看 看

ETYMOLOGY | Radical: 目 Pictograph: a sideways human eye (the pupil being the box in the center) = eye, item, section, look, see

DATA

		PRONUNCIATION			
Radical (部首)	109: 目	Pinyin:	kàn	J-音読み:	カン
Strokes	9 | 9	Wade-Giles:	k'an	J-訓読み:	み·る
HSK	1	Cantonese:	hon3	Korean音读:	간
Frequency	76	Minnan:	khòa^n	Korean 训读:	보다
Big5	ACDD	Bopomofo:	ㄎㄢˋ	K-eumdok:	gan
Unihan	U+770B	JP-Onyomi:	kan	K-hundok:	boda
Kangxi Dictionary	P803	JP-Kunyomi:	mi·ru	Vietnamese:	nhìn

VARIANTS

COMBINATIONS

算算看 - let me calculate	好看 - it looks good	看重 - value highly
數數看 - count	不好看 - ugly	看透 - see though a trick
找找看 - looking around	看孩子 - look after a kid	
看一下 - take a look	看病 - see a doctor	
	看法 - point of view	

SAYINGS

刮目相看 - look at somebody with new eyes
看人下菜 - make up to some people and look down on others
狗眼看人低 - snob

另眼相看 - regarded with special respect
中看不中用 - be pleasant to the eye but of no use
看破紅塵 - be disillusioned with the mortal world

HISTORICAL

甲骨文 (2000BC)	(1000BC)	篆文 (200BC)	隸 (200AD)
		眚	看

FONTS

楷 行 草 宋
看 看 看 看

266AD
Jing Dynasty
Wang Xizhi

778BC
Tang Dynasty
Du Mu

1280AD
Yuan Dynasty
Zhao Mengfu

1829AD
Ming Dynasty
Dong Qichang

THE GENIUS OF CHINESE CHARACTERS

STANDARD	SIMPLIFIED	MEANING
點	点	• dot: 雨點; point: 起點 • o'clock: 點鐘; speck: 污點; beckon: 點手 • mark: 點定; point out: 點名; light (fire): 點火

正 丨 冂 冂 囙 甲 甲 里 黒 黑 黑 黑 黒
點 點 點 點
简 丨 卜 广 占 占 占 点 点 点

ETYMOLOGY
Radical: 黑
black, dark, evil + 占 (phonetic) = dot, speck, spot

DATA
Radical (部首)	203: 黑
Strokes	17 | 9
HSK	1
Frequency	128
Big5	C249
Unihan	U+70B9
Kangxi Dictionary	P1519

PRONUNCIATION
Pinyin:	diǎn
Wade-Giles:	tien
Cantonese:	dim2
Minnan:	tiám
Bopomofo:	ㄉㄧㄢˇ
JP-Onyomi:	ten
JP-Kunyomi:	ta·teru

J-音読み:	テン
J-訓読み:	た·てる
Korean 音读:	점
Korean 训读:	점, 얼룩
K-eumdok:	jeom
K-hundok:	jeom, eolluk
Vietnamese:	điểm

VARIANTS | 点(J)

COMBINATIONS
雨點 - rain drops
一點 - a little
一點點 - a little
大一點 - a little bigger
起點 - a starting point
重點 - focus

零點一 - zero point one
點心 - dim sum
點頭 - nodding
點菜 - ordering
兩點鐘 - two o/clock

SAYINGS
畫龍點睛 - to give it the final touch
點頭道是 - to nod
文不加點 - the writing is faultless
蜻蜓點水 - touch on sth. without going into it deeply

HISTORICAL
甲骨文 (2000BC)	(1000BC)	篆文 (200BC)	隸 (200AD)
		點	点

FONTS
楷 行 草 宋
点 点 点 点

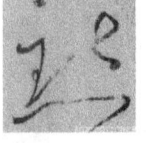
778BC
Tang Dynasty
Huai Su

960BC
Song Dynasty
Su Shi

1280AD
Yuan Dynasty
Zhao Mengfu

1829AD
Ming Dynasty
Dong Qichang

THE GENIUS OF Chinese Characters

STANDARD	SIMPLIFIED	MEANING
起	起	• to rise: 興起; to get up: 起床 • begin: 起頭; stand up: 站起來 • to start: 起始; rise up: 起落; load: 起貨

正	一	十	土	キ	キ	走	走	起	起	起
简	一	十	土	キ	キ	走	走	起	起	起

ETYMOLOGY

Radical: 走
sit + 巳 (phonetic) = to raise, to get up, to start

DATA

		PRONUNCIATION			
Radical (部首)	156: 走	Pinyin:	qǐ	J-音読み:	キ
Strokes	10 | 10	Wade-Giles:	ch'i	J-訓読み:	お·きる/こる
HSK	1	Cantonese:	hei2	Korean 音读:	기
Frequency	75	Minnan:	khí	Korean 训读:	일어나다
Big5	B05F	Bopomofo:	ㄑㄧˇ	K-eumdok:	gi
Unihan	U+8D77	JP-Onyomi:	ki	K-hundok:	ireonada
Kangxi Dictionary	P1215	JP-Kunyomi:	o·kiru/koru	Vietnamese:	lên

VARIANTS | 玘

COMBINATIONS

起來 - arise
一起 - together
起義 - uprise
起飛 - to take off
起初 - in the beginning

起點 - starting point

SAYINGS

起死回生 - bring back to life
風生水起 - to prosper
大起大落 - ups and downs
白手起家 - Start from scratch

此起彼伏 - as one falls another rises
起承轉合 - four steps in the composition of an essay

HISTORICAL

(2000BC)	金文 (1000BC)	篆文 (200BC)	隸 (200AD)
		𧺆	起

FONTS

楷　行　草　宋
起　起　起　起

266AD Jing Dynasty Wang Xizhi
778BC Tang Dynasty Liu Gongquan
1280AD Yuan Dynasty Zhao Mengfu
1829AD Ming Dynasty Dong Qichang

THE GENIUS OF CHINESE CHARACTERS

STANDARD	SIMPLIFIED	MEANING
星	星	• star: 恒星; planet: 行星 • satellite: 衛星; star (person): 明星 • tiny amount: 零星; scattered: 星散

| 正 | 丨 | 冂 | 日 | 旦 | 尸 | 尸 | 戸 | 屌 | 星 |
| 简 | 丨 | 冂 | 日 | 旦 | 尸 | 尸 | 戸 | 屌 | 星 |

ETYMOLOGY

Radical: 日
sun radical + 生 (phonetic) = a star, satellite, planet

DATA

Radical (部首)	72: 日
Strokes	9 | 9
HSK	1
Frequency	537
Big5	AC50
Unihan	U+661F
Kangxi Dictionary	P492

PRONUNCIATION

Pinyin:	xīng
Wade-Giles:	hsing
Cantonese:	sing1
Minnan:	chhi^n
Bopomofo:	ㄒㄧㄥ
JP-Onyomi:	sei, shō
JP-Kunyomi:	hoshi

J-音読み:	セイ, ショウ
J-訓読み:	ほし
Korean 音读:	성
Korean 训读:	별
K-eumdok:	seong
K-hundok:	byeol
Vietnamese:	ngôi sao

VARIANTS | 曐

COMBINATIONS

衛星 - satellite
彗星 - comet
火星 - Mars, sparks
明星 - (movie) star
星球 - planet

球星 - (football) star
星星 - stars
救星 - savior
星座 - constellation

SAYINGS

星移斗轉 - time passing by
物換星移 - things change
星羅棋布 - spread all over the place
月落星沉 - at dawn

福星高照 - come into good luck
月明星稀 - the moon is bright and the stars are sparse
滿天星斗 - a starry sky

HISTORICAL

甲骨文 (2000BC)	金文 (1000BC)	篆文 (200BC)	隸 (200AD)
		曐	星

FONTS

楷	行	草	宋
星	星	星	星

266AD Jing Dynasty Wang Xizhi

778BC Tang Dynasty Liu Gongquan

1280AD Yuan Dynasty Zhao Mengfu

1829AD Ming Dynasty Dong Qichang

THE GENIUS OF CHINESE CHARACTERS

STANDARD	SIMPLIFIED	MEANING
些	些	• some - 有些; few: 一些 • (indicating plural): 這些 • quite a few: 好些人

| 正 | 丨 | 卜 | 止 | 止 | 此 | 此 | 些 |
| 简 | 丨 | 卜 | 止 | 止 | 此 | 此 | 些 |

ETYMOLOGY | Radical: 二
two + 此 = a couple

DATA

Radical (部首)	7: 二
Strokes	8 | 8
HSK	1
Frequency	86
Big5	A8C7
Unihan	U+4E9B
Kangxi Dictionary	P87

PRONUNCIATION

Pinyin:	xiē
Wade-Giles:	hsieh
Cantonese:	se1
Minnan:	
Bopomofo:	ㄒ一ㄝ
JP-Onyomi:	sa
JP-Kunyomi:	isasa·ka

J-音読み:	サ
J-訓読み:	いささ·か
Korean 音读:	사
Korean 训读:	적다
K-eumdok:	sa
K-hundok:	jeokda
Vietnamese:	một số

VARIANTS | 㱔

COMBINATIONS

那些 - those
多些 - more
少些 - less

SAYINGS

n/a

HISTORICAL

甲骨文 (2000BC)	金文 (1000BC)	(200BC)	隸 (200AD)
			些

FONTS

楷	行	草	宋
些	些	些	些

105

THE GENIUS OF CHINESE CHARACTERS

STANDARD	SIMPLIFIED	MEANING
三	三	• the number three : 3 • third: 第三 • three times: 三次

正 一 二 三
简 一 二 三

ETYMOLOGY Pictograph = three

DATA

		PRONUNCIATION			
Radical (部首)	1: 一	Pinyin:	sān	J-音読み:	サン
Strokes	3 | 3	Wade-Giles:	san	J-訓読み:	み
HSK	1	Cantonese:	saam1	Korean 音读:	삼
Frequency	125	Minnan:	sa^n	Korean 训读:	석, 셋
Big5	A454	Bopomofo:	ㄙㄢ	K-eumdok:	sam
Unihan	U+4E09	JP-Onyomi:	san	K-hundok:	seok, set
Kangxi Dictionary	P76	JP-Kunyomi:	mi	Vietnamese:	số ba

VARIANTS | 叁, 弎, 叄

COMBINATIONS

三棱鏡 - a prism
三只手 - a pickpocket
三二 - several
三部曲 - a trilogy
三脚猫 - an odd fellow

三明治 - sandwich
三月 - March

SAYINGS

夜半三更 - late at night
低三下四 - servile
丟三落四 - forgetful
火冒三丈 - fly into a rage

日上三竿 - already late in the morning
舉一反三 - judging the whole from one sample

HISTORICAL

甲骨文 (2000BC)	金文 (1000BC)	篆文 (200BC)	隸 (200AD)
三	三	三	三

FONTS

楷 行 草 宋

三 三 三 三

266AD Jing Dynasty Wang Xizhi

778BC Tang Dynasty Liu Gongquan

1280AD Yuan Dynasty Zhao Mengfu

1829AD Ming Dynasty Dong Qichang

THE GENIUS OF CHINESE CHARACTERS

STANDARD	SIMPLIFIED	MEANING
很	很	• very: 很好 • much: 很多

正: 丿 ㇒ 彳 彳 彳 彳 很 很 很
简: 丿 ㇒ 彳 彳 彳 彳 很 很 很

ETYMOLOGY

Radical: 彳
left step + 艮 (phonetic) = very much, extremely

DATA

- Radical (部首): 60: 彳
- Strokes: 9 | 9
- HSK: 1
- Frequency: 138
- Big5: ABDC
- Unihan: U+5F88
- Kangxi Dictionary: P366

PRONUNCIATION

- Pinyin: hěn
- Wade-Giles: hên
- Cantonese: han5
- Minnan:
- Bopomofo: ㄏㄣˇ
- JP-Onyomi: kon
- JP-Kunyomi: moto·ru
- J-音読み: コン
- J-訓読み: もと·る
- Korean 音读: 흔
- Korean 训读: 매우, 몹시
- K-eumdok: heun
- K-hundok: maeu, mopsi
- Vietnamese: rất

VARIANTS: 佷, 狠, 詪

COMBINATIONS

- 很對不起 - very sorry
- 很受打擊 - received a heavy blow
- 快得很 - very fast
- 很不好 - not very good

SAYINGS

n/a

HISTORICAL

(2000BC)	金文 (1000BC)	篆文 (200BC)	(200AD)
		很	很

FONTS

楷 行 草 宋
很 很 很 很

THE GENIUS OF CHINESE CHARACTERS

STANDARD	SIMPLIFIED	MEANING
商	商	• commerce: 商人; consult: 相商 • business: 行商; to discuss: 協商 • merchant: 商賈; trade: 商務

正: 丶 亠 六 产 产 产 产 商 商 商
简: 丶 亠 六 产 产 产 产 商 商 商

ETYMOLOGY
Radical: 口
originally composed of fireplace 丙 with bitter 辛 at the top = business, trade

DATA
		PRONUNCIATION			
Radical (部首)	30: 口	Pinyin:	shāng	J-音読み:	ショウ
Strokes	11 | 11	Wade-Giles:	shang	J-訓読み:	あきな·う
HSK	1	Cantonese:	seung1	Korean 音读:	상
Frequency	402	Minnan:	siong	Korean 训读:	장사
Big5	B0D3	Bopomofo:	ㄕㄤ	K-eumdok:	sang
Unihan	U+5546	JP-Onyomi:	shō	K-hundok:	jangsa
Kangxi Dictionary	P194	JP-Kunyomi:	akina·u	Vietnamese:	đơn vị

VARIANTS | 謫

COMBINATIONS
商標 - trademark
商船 - freighter
商港 - seaport
商戰 - trade war
商家 - businessman

商事 - commercial affairs
商賈 - merchants

SAYINGS
從長商議 - give the matter further thought and discuss later
富商大賈 - wealthy man
共商國事 - discuss state affairs

士農工商 - scholar, farmer, artisan and merchant

HISTORICAL
甲骨文 (2000BC)	金文 (1000BC)	篆文 (200BC)	(200AD)
丙	丙	商	商

FONTS
楷 行 草 宋
商 商 商 商

778BC Tang Dynasty — Ouyang Xun
960BC Song Dynasty — Su Shi
1280AD Yuan Dynasty — Zhao Mengfu
1829AD Ming Dynasty — Dong Qichang

THE GENIUS OF CHINESE CHARACTERS

STANDARD	SIMPLIFIED	MEANING
麼	么	• what: 什麼; what for: 幹麼 • (question final particle): 你來麼 • (exclamation particle): 也麼

正 ノ 幺 么
简 ノ 幺 么

ETYMOLOGY
Radical: 麻
to bother + 幺(phonetic) = small, insignificant

DATA

		PRONUNCIATION			
Radical (部首)	200: 麻	Pinyin:	me	J-音読み:	バ, マ, モ
Strokes	14 | 3	Wade-Giles:	ma	J-訓読み:	N/A
HSK	1	Cantonese:	ma3	Korean 音读:	마
Frequency	63	Minnan:	mah	Korean 训读:	작다
Big5	BBF2	Bopomofo:	ㄇㄛ/ㄇㄜ˙	K-eumdok:	ma
Unihan	U+4E48	JP-Onyomi:	ba, ma, mo	K-hundok:	jakda
Kangxi Dictionary	P1515	JP-Kunyomi:	N/A	Vietnamese:	gì

VARIANTS

COMBINATIONS

什麼 - what?
幹麼 - what are you doing?

SAYINGS

n/a

HISTORICAL

(2000BC) | 金文 (1000BC) | 篆文 (200BC) | 隸 (200AD)

FONTS

楷 行 草 宋

266AD Jing Dynasty Wang Xizhi

960BC Song Dynasty Su Shi

960BC Song Dynasty Mi Fu

1829AD Ming Dynasty Dong Qichang

THE GENIUS OF Chinese CHARACTERS

STANDARD	SIMPLIFIED	MEANING
樣	样	• appearance: 樣子; pattern: 圖樣 • way: 同樣; form: 式樣; style: 樣式 • sample: 樣品; varieties: 三樣食物

正	一	十	才	木	术	杧	栏	栏	样	样	样	样
样	樣											
简	一	十	才	木	术	杧	栏	栏	样			

ETYMOLOGY

Radical: 木
wood + 羕 (phonetic - flowing water) = shape, appearance

DATA		PRONUNCIATION			
Radical (部首)	75: 木	Pinyin:	yàng	J-音読み:	ヨウ
Strokes	15 | 10	Wade-Giles:	yang	J-訓読み:	さま
HSK	1	Cantonese:	yeung6	Korean 音读:	양
Frequency	88	Minnan:	iūⁿ	Korean 训读:	모양
Big5	BCCB	Bopomofo:	ㄧㄤˋ	K-eumdok:	yang
Unihan	U+6837	JP-Onyomi:	yō	K-hundok:	eojosa
Kangxi Dictionary	P551	JP-Kunyomi:	sama	Vietnamese:	tốt bụng
				VARIANTS	様(J)

COMBINATIONS

樣本 - a sample copy
樣品 - sample goods
樣樣 - everything
樣式 - form
圖樣 - blueprint
走樣 - out of shape

SAYINGS

裝模作樣 - put on airs
一模一樣 - be exactly alike
人模狗樣 - pretending to be what one is not
大模大樣 - arrogant
各式各樣 - assorted, a mixture

HISTORICAL

(2000BC)	金文 (1000BC)	篆文 (200BC)	隸 (200AD)
		羕	样

FONTS

楷	行	草	宋
样	样	样	样

266AD Jing Dynasty Wang Xizhi

960BC Song Dynasty Su Shi

1280AD Yuan Dynasty Zhao Mengfu

1829AD Ming Dynasty Tang Yin

THE GENIUS OF CHINESE CHARACTERS

STANDARD	SIMPLIFIED	MEANING
那	那	• that: 那個; those: 那些 • there: 那兒; in such a manner: 那樣 • even if: 那怕 • so: 那麼

正　丁　丮　㝕　刋　邪　那

简

ETYMOLOGY | Radical: 邑 Original meaning was 'to be rich' then later 'so what?' A city 邑 whose inhabitants wore rough garments 冉 (phonetic - weak) = that, those, which

DATA

Radical (部首)	163: 邑	Pinyin:	nà	J-音読み:	ナ, ダ
Strokes	6 | 6	Wade-Giles:	na	J-訓読み:	なに, いかん·ぞ
HSK	1	Cantonese:	na5	Korean 音读:	나
Frequency	38	Minnan:	ná	Korean 训读:	어찌, 어찌하여
Big5	A8BA	Bopomofo:	ㄋㄚˋ	K-eumdok:	na
Unihan	U+90A3	JP-Onyomi:	na, da	K-hundok:	moyang
Kangxi Dictionary	P1268	JP-Kunyomi:	nani, ikan·zo	Vietnamese:	cái đó

VARIANTS	哪

COMBINATIONS

那位 - that person
那時 - at that time
那陣兒 - that moment
那得 - how can?
那裏 - where

那其間 - during the interval

SAYINGS

這山望着那山高 - never happy with one's lot, or the grass is always greener on the other side

HISTORICAL | FONTS

甲骨文 (2000BC)	金文 (1000BC)	(200BC)	(200AD)	楷	行	草	宋
		𨛜	那	那	那	那	那

266AD Jing Dynasty Wang Xizhi

960BC Song Dynasty Su Shi

960BC Song Dynasty Mi Fu

1829AD Ming Dynasty Dong Qichang

THE GENIUS OF CHINESE CHARACTERS

STANDARD	SIMPLIFIED	MEANING
東	东	• east: 東邊; eastern: 東方 • owner: 房東; East Asia: 東亞

正: 一 厂 厃 亘 亘 車 束 東
简: 一 土 左 东 东

ETYMOLOGY
Radical: 木
the sun (日) rising behind a tree (木) = east

DATA

		PRONUNCIATION			
Radical (部首)	75: 木	Pinyin:	dōng	J-音読み:	トウ
Strokes	8 | 5	Wade-Giles:	tung	J-訓読み:	ひがし
HSK	1	Cantonese:	dung1	Korean 音读:	동
Frequency	194	Minnan:	tong	Korean 训读:	동녘
Big5	AA46	Bopomofo:	ㄉㄨㄥ	K-eumdok:	dong
Unihan	U+4E1C	JP-Onyomi:	tō	K-hundok:	dongjjok
Kangxi Dictionary	P513	JP-Kunyomi:	higashi	Vietnamese:	phía đông

VARIANTS

COMBINATIONS

股東 - shareholder
東道 - host for party
東亞 - East Asia
東京 - Tokyo
東家 - master, boss

房東 - landlord
東廁 - latrine

SAYINGS

東奔西走 - run about busily
東倒西歪 - reel right and left
東窗事發 - criminal conspiracy unmasked
東山再起 - return to power

東張西望 - look around
付之東流 - efforts wasted

HISTORICAL

甲骨文 (2000BC)	(1000BC)	(200BC)	(200AD)
		東	东

FONTS

楷	行	草	宋
东	东	东	东

266AD Jing Dynasty Wang Xizhi
778BC Tang Dynasty Liu Gongquan
1280AD Yuan Dynasty Zhao Mengfu
1829AD Ming Dynasty Dong Qichang

THE GENIUS OF Chinese Characters

STANDARD	SIMPLIFIED	MEANING
西	西	• west: 西邊; western: 西方 • western (type): 西服 • Spain: 西班牙

正: 一 丆 冂 两 西 西
简: 一 丆 冂 两 西 西

ETYMOLOGY: Radical: 西 Pictograph: said to be a bird's nest; seal character shows bird above; archaic form may have been a package of something from the West

DATA

Radical (部首)	146: 西	
Strokes	6 | 6	
HSK	1	
Frequency	167	
Big5	A6E8	
Unihan	U+897F	
Kangxi Dictionary	P1128	

PRONUNCIATION

Pinyin:	xī
Wade-Giles:	hsi
Cantonese:	sai1
Minnan:	se
Bopomofo:	ㄒ一
JP-Onyomi:	sei, sai
JP-Kunyomi:	nishi

J-音読み:	セイ, サイ
J-訓読み:	にし
Korean 音读:	서
Korean 训读:	서쪽
K-eumdok:	seo
K-hundok:	seojjok
Vietnamese:	oo

VARIANTS: 卥, 卤

COMBINATIONS

西瓜 - watermelon
西紅柿 - tomato
西伯利亞 - Siberia
西岸 - west coast

西醫 - Western medicine

SAYINGS

東張西望 - look around
日薄西山 - the sun sinking in the west
中西合璧 - Chinese and Western (styles) combined

東尋西覓 - to look everywhere
東躲西藏 - hiding here and there

HISTORICAL

甲骨文 (2000BC) | 金文 (1000BC) | 篆文 (200BC) | 隸 (200AD)

FONTS

楷 行 草 宋

266AD Jing Dynasty Wang Xizhi
778BC Tang Dynasty Liu Gongquan
1280AD Yuan Dynasty Zhao Mengfu
1829AD Ming Dynasty Dong Qichang

THE GENIUS OF CHINESE CHARACTERS

STANDARD	SIMPLIFIED	MEANING
想	想	• to think: 別想; to miss: 想家 • to suppose: 想有; to want: 想要 • plan for: 構想; speculate: 構想 • ideal: 理想; ideas: 思想; imagination: 幻想

| 正 | 一 | 十 | 才 | 木 | 村 | 利 | 相 | 相 | 相 | 相 | 想 | 想 | 想 |
| 简 | 一 | 十 | 才 | 木 | 村 | 利 | 相 | 相 | 相 | 相 | 想 | 想 | 想 |

ETYMOLOGY

Radical: 心
To inspect 相 the heart 心 = to want, to miss

DATA

Radical (部首)   61: 心
Strokes   13 | 13
HSK   1
Frequency   99
Big5   B751
Unihan   U+60F3
Kangxi Dictionary   P392

PRONUNCIATION

Pinyin: xiǎng
Wade-Giles: hsiang
Cantonese: seung2
Minnan: siūⁿ
Bopomofo: ㄒㄧㄤˇ
JP-Onyomi: sō, so
JP-Kunyomi: omo·u

J-音読み: ソウ, ソ
J-訓読み: おも・う
Korean 音读: 상
Korean 训读: 생각, 생각하다
K-eumdok: sang
K-hundok: saenggak, saenggakada
Vietnamese: nhớ bạn

VARIANTS

COMBINATIONS

想法 - viewpoints
妄想 - absurd idea
想念 - miss (somebody)
想家 - be homesick
構想 - speculation

幻想 - fantasy

SAYINGS

前思後想 - consider again and again
痴心妄想 - daydreaming
胡思亂想 - entertain foolish ideas
意想不到 - beyond one's expectation

可想而知 - as one can imagine
想方設法 - try by every means

HISTORICAL

甲骨文 (2000BC)	金文 (1000BC)	篆文 (200BC)	隸 (200AD)
		想	想

FONTS

楷	行	草	宋
想	想	想	想

 266AD Jing Dynasty Wang Xizhi

 778BC Tang Dynasty Yan Zhenqing

 1280AD Yuan Dynasty Zhao Mengfu

 1829AD Ming Dynasty Dong Qichang

THE GENIUS OF Chinese CHARACTERS

STANDARD	SIMPLIFIED	MEANING
水	水	• water: 清水 • river: 水流 • clear: 水音 • wild duck: 水鴨

| 正 | 丨 | 才 | 水 | 水 |
| 简 | 丨 | 才 | 水 | 水 |

ETYMOLOGY — Radical: 水
Water flowing within boundaries = water

DATA

Radical (部首)	85: 水		
Strokes	4 | 4		
HSK	1		
Frequency	202		
Big5	A4F4		
Unihan	U+6C34		
Kangxi Dictionary	P603		

PRONUNCIATION

Pinyin:	shuǐ	J-音読み:	スイ
Wade-Giles:	shui	J-訓読み:	みず
Cantonese:	sui2	Korean 音读:	수
Minnan:	chúi	Korean 训读:	물
Bopomofo:	ㄕㄨㄟˇ	K-eumdok:	su
JP-Onyomi:	sui	K-hundok:	mul
JP-Kunyomi:	mizu	Vietnamese:	nước

VARIANTS | 氵

COMBINATIONS

山水 - landscape
蒸溜水 - distilled water
水汪汪 - watery (eyes)
水汊 - tributaries
水芹 - celery

水池 - pond
水患 - floods
水雷 - torpedo
花露水 - eau de cologne

水母 - jellyfish

SAYINGS

水落石出 - situation will be clear when facts are known
車水馬龍 - heavy traffic
水泄不通 - tightly packed

細水長流 - plan on a long-term basis
逆水行舟 - sail against the current
水底撈月 - efforts in vain

HISTORICAL

(2000BC) (1000BC) (200BC) (200AD)

FONTS

楷 行 草 宋

266AD Jing Dynasty Wang Xizhi
778BC Tang Dynasty Yan Zhenqing
1280AD Yuan Dynasty Zhao Mengfu
1829AD Ming Dynasty Dong Qichang

THE GENIUS OF CHINESE CHARACTERS

STANDARD	SIMPLIFIED	MEANING
影	影	• image: 電影; shadow: 影子 • reflection: 小影; photograph: 攝影 • trace: 没影兒

正 丨 冂 日 日 日 旦 旱 昇 昌 景 景 景 景 影
影 影
简 丨 冂 日 日 日 旦 旱 昇 昌 景 景 景 景 影
影 影

ETYMOLOGY
Radical: 彡
Lines 彡 cast by the sun across the landscape 景 = shadow, picture

DATA
- Radical (部首): 59: 彡
- Strokes: 15 | 15
- HSK: 1
- Frequency: 390
- Big5: BC76
- Unihan: U+5F71
- Kangxi Dictionary: P364

PRONUNCIATION
- Pinyin: yǐng
- Wade-Giles: ying
- Cantonese: ying2
- Minnan: iáⁿ
- Bopomofo: ㄧㄥˇ
- JP-Onyomi: ei
- JP-Kunyomi: kage
- J-音読み: エイ
- J-訓読み: かげ
- Korean 音读: 영
- Korean 训读: 그림자
- K-eumdok: yeong
- K-hundok: geurimja
- Vietnamese: bóng

VARIANTS | 景

COMBINATIONS
- 投影 - cast shadow
- 水影 - reflection
- 電影 - movie
- 影院 - movie theater
- 影戤 - forgery
- 影像 - photograph

SAYINGS
- 形影不離 - always together
- 捕風捉影 - make groundless accusations
- 含沙射影 - attack by insinuation
- 立竿見影 - produce an immediate effect
- 形單影衹 - extremely lonely
- 刀光劍影 - engaged in hot battle
- 顧影自憐 - narcissistic

HISTORICAL

(2000BC)	金文 (1000BC)	(200BC)	(200AD)
		景	影

FONTS
楷 行 草 宋
影 影 影 影

- 266AD Jing Dynasty Wang Xizhi
- 778BC Tang Dynasty Yan Zhenqing
- 1280AD Yuan Dynasty Zhao Mengfu
- 1829AD Ming Dynasty Dong Qichang

THE GENIUS OF CHINESE CHARACTERS

STANDARD	SIMPLIFIED	MEANING
話	话	• talk: 談話; conversation: 會話; language: 官話 • spoken words; speech: 俗話; what someone said • words: 話中; to discuss 話下; vernacular: 白話 • language: 普通話

正	丶	亠	亠	言	言	言	訁	訐	訐	話	話
简	丶	讠	讠	讠	评	评	话	话			

ETYMOLOGY Radical: 言
to speak + 舌 (phonetic - tongue) = language, conversation

DATA

Radical (部首)　　　149: 言
Strokes　　　　　　13 | 8
HSK　　　　　　　　1
Xinhua Dictionary　P198
Frequency　　　　　170
Big5　　　　　　　B8DC
Unihan　　　　　　U+8BDD
Kangxi　　　　　　P1158

PRONUNCIATION

Pinyin:　　　huà
Wade-Giles:　hua
Cantonese:　wa6
Minnan:　　ōe
Bopomofo:　ㄏㄨㄚˋ
JP-Onyomi:　wa
JP-Kunyomi:　hanashi

J-音読み:　　わ
J-訓読み:　　はなし
Korean 音读:　화
Korean 训读:　말씀
K-eumdok:　hwa
K-hundok:　malsseum
Vietnamese:　từ ngữ

VARIANTS

COMBINATIONS

話音兒 - tone of one's voice
話料兒 - material for gossip
閑話 - gossip

謊話 - a lie
話鐺 - chatterbox
話筒 - microphone

SAYINGS

说來話長 - It's a long story
二話不说 - without saying anything more
話不投機 - nothing in common to talk about
廢話連篇 - pages of nonsense

話裏有話 - implicit meaning
傳爲佳話 - become a favourite tale

HISTORICAL

甲骨文 (2000BC)	金文 (1000BC)	篆文 (200BC)	隸 (200AD)
			话

FONTS

楷　　行　　草　　宋
话　话　话　话

266AD
Jing Dynasty
Wang Xizhi

778BC
Tang Dynasty
Li Yong

1280AD
Yuan Dynasty
Zhao Mengfu

1829AD
Ming Dynasty
Dong Qichang

THE GENIUS OF CHINESE CHARACTERS

STANDARD	SIMPLIFIED	MEANING
視	视	• to look at: 注視; to inspect: 巡視 • to regard: 視爲; observe: 視野 • see: 偷視; to take charge: 視事

正: 丶 ﹀ 亍 礻 衤 衤 礽 祁 袒 袒 視
简: 丶 ﹀ 亍 礻 衤 礽 视 视

ETYMOLOGY

Radical: 示
見 (phonetic - to see) + to show, reveal = to look at, observe

DATA

Radical (部首)	113: 示	Pinyin:	shì	J-音読み:	シ
Strokes	11 | 8	Wade-Giles:	shih	J-訓読み:	み・る
HSK	1	Cantonese:	si6	Korean 音读:	시
Frequency	438	Minnan:	sī	Korean 训读:	보다
Big5	B5F8	Bopomofo:	ㄕˋ	K-eumdok:	si
Unihan	U+89C6	JP-Onyomi:	shi	K-hundok:	boda
Kangxi Dictionary	P1134	JP-Kunyomi:	mi·ru	Vietnamese:	như

VARIANTS

COMBINATIONS

偷視 - peep at
輕視 - despise
巡視 - patrol
視事 - to take charge
視綫 - line of vision

視野 - field of vision
善視 - treat kindly

SAYINGS

目不斜視 - be entirely absorbed
熟視無睹 - turn a blind eye to
視死如歸 - face death without fear
一視同仁 - treat all alike

相視而笑 - smile into each other's eyes
虎視眈眈 - look at fiercely as a tiger does
視如敝屣 - regard as worn-out shoes

HISTORICAL

甲骨文 (2000BC)	金文 (1000BC)	篆文 (200BC)	隸 (200AD)
		視	视

FONTS

楷 行 草 宋
視 視 視 視

266AD Jing Dynasty Wang Xizhi
778BC Tang Dynasty Li Yong
1280AD Yuan Dynasty Zhao Mengfu
1829AD Ming Dynasty Dong Qichang

THE GENIUS OF Chinese CHARACTERS

STANDARD	SIMPLIFIED	MEANING
果	果	• fruit: 果實; result: 因果 • fill: 果腹; resolute: 果决

| 正 | 丨 | 冂 | 日 | 旦 | 旦 | 甲 | 果 | 果 |
| 简 | 丨 | 冂 | 日 | 旦 | 旦 | 甲 | 果 | 果 |

ETYMOLOGY

Radical: 木
Pictograph: fruit on a tree 木 = fruit, result

DATA

Radical (部首)	75: 木
Strokes	8 | 8
HSK	1
Frequency	165
Big5	AA47
Unihan	U+679C
Kangxi Dictionary	P519

PRONUNCIATION

Pinyin:	guǒ
Wade-Giles:	kuo
Cantonese:	gwoh2
Minnan:	kó
Bopomofo:	ㄍㄨㄛˇ
JP-Onyomi:	ka
JP-Kunyomi:	ha·te/tasu
J-音読み:	カ
J-訓読み:	は・て/たす
Korean 音读:	과
Korean 训读:	열매
K-eumdok:	gwa
K-hundok:	yeolmae
Vietnamese:	trái cây

VARIANTS	菓, 輠

COMBINATIONS

- 果脯 - dried fruits
- 效果 - effect of
- 結果 - consequence
- 果醬 - jam
- 果汁 - fruit juice
- 果毅 - resolute and daring
- 果報 - retribution

SAYINGS

- 食不果腹 - have little food to eat
- 碩果累累 - countless rich fruits or achievements
- 前因後果 - cause and effect
- 自食其果 - suffer the consequences of one's doing
- 果不其然 - just as expected

HISTORICAL

甲骨文 (2000BC) | (1000BC) | (200BC) | 隸 (200AD)

FONTS

楷 行 草 宋

266AD Jing Dynasty Wang Xizhi
778BC Tang Dynasty Li Yong
1280AD Yuan Dynasty Zhao Mengfu
1829AD Ming Dynasty Dong Qichang

THE GENIUS OF CHINESE CHARACTERS

STANDARD	SIMPLIFIED	MEANING
老	老	• old (in age): 老人; tough: 老笋 • experienced: 老绷; middleaged: 老妈 • term of respect: 老王

| 正 | 一 | 十 | 土 | 耂 | 耂 | 老 |
| 简 | 一 | 十 | 土 | 耂 | 耂 | 老 |

ETYMOLOGY: Radical: 老 Pictograph: a man 人 leaning on a cane, hair 毛 and change 匕 indicating age = old, experienced

DATA
Radical (部首)	125: 老			
Strokes	6 | 6			
HSK	1			
Frequency	179			
Big5	A6D1			
Unihan	U+8001			
Kangxi Dictionary	P960			

PRONUNCIATION
Pinyin:	lǎo	J-音読み:	ロウ
Wade-Giles:	lao	J-訓読み:	お·いる/ふ·ける
Cantonese:	lo5	Korean 音读:	로
Minnan:	ló	Korean 训读:	늙다
Bopomofo:	ㄌㄠˇ	K-eumdok:	ro
JP-Onyomi:	rō	K-hundok:	neukda
JP-Kunyomi:	o·iru, fu·keru	Vietnamese:	cũ

VARIANTS

COMBINATIONS
老頭 - old man
老相好 - old sweetheart
老毛病 - a chronic ailment
老貨兒 - old stuff

老虎 - tiger
老鼠 - mouse
老頑固 - a bigot

SAYINGS
舟車勞頓 - exhausted from a long travel
學富五車 - be wealthy in knowledge
車到山前必有路 - where there's a will, there's a way

安步當車 - walk rather than ride
閉門造車 - divorce oneself from reality and act blindly
車水馬龍 - heavy traffic

HISTORICAL
(2000BC) (1000BC) (200BC) 隸 (200AD)

FONTS
楷 行 草 宋

266AD
Jing Dynasty
Wang Xizhi

778BC
Tang Dynasty
Yan Zhenqing

1280AD
Yuan Dynasty
Zhao Mengfu

1829AD
Ming Dynasty
Dong Qichang

THE GENIUS OF CHINESE CHARACTERS

STANDARD	SIMPLIFIED	MEANING
院	院	• courtyard: 庭院; institute: 學院 • court: 法院; hospital: 醫院; yard: 院子

正: 了 阝 阝' 阝' 阝 阝 阝 阡 院
简: 了 阝 阝' 阝' 阝 阝 阝 阡 院

ETYMOLOGY

Radical: 阜
walls + 完 (phonetic - complete) = courtyard, hospital, school

DATA

Radical (部首)	170: 阜
Strokes	9 | 9
HSK	1
Frequency	338
Big5	B07C
Unihan	U+9662
Kangxi Dictionary	P1352

PRONUNCIATION

Pinyin:	yuàn
Wade-Giles:	yüen
Cantonese:	yuen2
Minnan:	ĩⁿ
Bopomofo:	ㄩㄢˋ
JP-Onyomi:	in
JP-Kunyomi:	kaki

J-音読み:	イン
J-訓読み:	かき
Korean 音读:	원
Korean 训读:	집
K-eumdok:	won
K-hundok:	jip
Vietnamese:	bệnh viện

VARIANTS | 完, 寏

COMBINATIONS

院長 - president
院士 - academician
院墙 - courtyard walls
院綫 - cinema chain
劇院 - theater
寺院 - temple
院校 - colleges and universities

SAYINGS

深宅大院 - imposing dwellings and spacious courtyards
三宫六院 - Harem, where the emperor keeps his concubines
後院起火 - internal conflicts

HISTORICAL

甲骨文 (2000BC)	(1000BC)	(200BC)	隸 (200AD)
		阮	院

FONTS

楷 行 草 宋
院 院 院 院

266AD Jing Dynasty Wang Xizhi
778BC Tang Dynasty Liu Gongquan
1280AD Yuan Dynasty Zhao Mengfu
1829AD Ming Dynasty Dong Qichang

THE GENIUS OF CHINESE CHARACTERS

STANDARD	SIMPLIFIED	MEANING
認	认	• to recognize: 認清 • to admit: 認罪 • to know: 認得 • consent: 認可

正: ` ´ ゠ 亠 言 言 言 訂 訒 訒 認 認 認

簡 認
简 ` 讠 讥 认

ETYMOLOGY

Radical: 言

words + 忍 (phonetic - to endure) = to admit, understand

DATA

Radical (部首)	149: 言
Strokes	14 | 4
HSK	1
Frequency	213
Big5	BB7B
Unihan	U+8BA4
Kangxi Dictionary	P1161

PRONUNCIATION

Pinyin:	rèn
Wade-Giles:	jên
Cantonese:	ying4
Minnan:	jīn
Bopomofo:	ㄖㄣˋ
JP-Onyomi:	nin
JP-Kunyomi:	mito·meru

J-音読み:	ニン
J-訓読み:	みと·める
Korean 音读:	인
Korean 训读:	알다, 인식하다
K-eumdok:	in
K-hundok:	alda, insikada
Vietnamese:	nhìn nhận

VARIANTS | 認(J)

COMBINATIONS

認真 - earnest
認可 - endorse
認生 - be shy
認許 - acknowledge
認錯 - admit one's mistake

承認 - admit
自認 - concede

SAYINGS

矢口否認 - flatly deny
六親不認 - not to recognize one's closest relatives
認賊作父 - take the foe for one's father
供認不諱 - confess everything
認祖歸宗 - find one's origin
翻臉不認人 - deny a friend

HISTORICAL

甲骨文 (2000BC)	(1000BC)	篆文 (200BC)	隸 (200AD)

FONTS

楷	行	草	宋	
认	认	认	认	认

THE GENIUS OF CHINESE CHARACTERS

STANDARD	SIMPLIFIED	MEANING
打	打	• to strike: 打鈴; to fight: 打仗; to hunt: 打獵 • to build (make): 打毛衣; to pack: 打包 • to make (decision): 打主意; to dial: 打電話 • to play: 打牌; to carry: 打旗子

正 一 丁 扌 扩 打

简

ETYMOLOGY — Radical: 手
手 = action indicator, 丁 = nail. To strike a nail

DATA

Radical (部首)	64: 手	Pinyin:	dǎ	J-音読み:	ダ
Strokes	5 | 5	Wade-Giles:	ta	J-訓読み:	う・つ
HSK	1	Cantonese:	da2	Korean 音读:	타
Frequency	223	Minnan:	táⁿ	Korean 训读:	치다
Big5	A5B4	Bopomofo:	ㄉㄚˇ	K-eumdok:	ta
Unihan	U+6253	JP-Onyomi:	da	K-hundok:	chida
Kangxi Dictionary	P417	JP-Kunyomi:	u·tsu	Vietnamese:	đánh

PRONUNCIATION

VARIANTS

COMBINATIONS

打包 - to pack
打賭 - to wager
打嗝 - to hiccup
打針 - to have an injection

打開 - to open up
打旗子 - carry a flag
打官司 - file a lawsuit
打火機 - lighter

SAYINGS

無精打采 - in low spirits
歪打正著 - hit the mark by a fluke
精打細算 - careful calculation and strict budgeting
屈打成招 - confess to false charges under torture

打草驚蛇 - act rashly and alert the enemy
趁火打劫 - to loot a burning house

HISTORICAL

甲骨文 (2000BC)	金文 (1000BC)	篆文 (200BC)	隸 (200AD)
		朳	打

FONTS

楷 行 草 宋

打 打 打 打

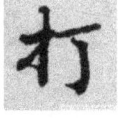 778BC Tang Dynasty Guo Quan

 960BC Song Dynasty Huang Tingjian

 960AD Song Dynasty Mi Fu

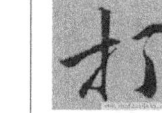 1829AD Ming Dynasty Tang Yin

THE GENIUS OF CHINESE CHARACTERS

STANDARD	SIMPLIFIED	MEANING
做	做	• to make: 做菜; to do: 做工 • to celebrate: 做生日; to pretend: 做派 • to plot: 做計; to show off: 做闊

正 ノ 亻 亻 什 仕 估 估 估 伿 做 做
简 ノ 亻 亻 什 仕 估 估 估 伿 做 做

ETYMOLOGY

Radical: 人

A person + 故 (phonetic - causes something) = work, make

DATA

		PRONUNCIATION			
Radical (部首)	9: 人	Pinyin:	zuò	J-音読み:	サ,サク
Strokes	11 | 11	Wade-Giles:	tso	J-訓読み:	な·す
HSK	1	Cantonese:	jo6	Korean 音读:	주
Frequency	246	Minnan:	chò	Korean 训读:	만들다
Big5	B0B5	Bopomofo:	ㄗㄨㄛˋ	K-eumdok:	ju
Unihan	U+505A	JP-Onyomi:	sa,saku	K-hundok:	mandeulda
Kangxi Dictionary	P110	JP-Kunyomi:	na·su	Vietnamese:	làm

VARIANTS

COMBINATIONS

做計 - to scheme
做壽 - hold birthday celebrations
做手脚 - make secret arrangements

做飯 - prepare a meal
做鬼兒 - irregularities
做聲 - break silence

SAYINGS

小題大做 - make a great fuss over a trifle, much ado about nothing
白日做夢 - indulge in wishful thinking
做小伏低 - stoop to compromise

説到做到 - live up to one's word
好吃懶做 - a good-for-nothing
做賊心虛 - to have a guilty conscience

HISTORICAL

甲骨文 (2000BC)	(1000BC)	(200BC)	隸 (200AD)

FONTS

楷	行	草	宋
做	做	做	做

1829AD
Ming Dynasty

Tang Yin

THE GENIUS OF Chinese CHARACTERS

STANDARD	SIMPLIFIED	MEANING
先	先	• first: 以先; beginnings: 先河; foresight: 先見 • prophet: 先知; ancestors: 先人; previously: 先前 • road ahead: 先路; the deceased: 先大夫 • forefathers: 先輩

正　ノ　┌　亠　生　牛　先
简　ノ　┌　亠　生　牛　先

ETYMOLOGY

Radical: 儿
A 儿 man who 之 moves forward = first, early

DATA

Radical (部首)	10: 儿
Strokes	6 | 6
HSK	1
Frequency	188
Big5	A5FD
Unihan	U+5148
Kangxi Dictionary	P124

PRONUNCIATION

Pinyin:	xiān
Wade-Giles:	hsien
Cantonese:	sin1
Minnan:	seng
Bopomofo:	ㄒ一ㄢ
JP-Onyomi:	sen
JP-Kunyomi:	saki, mazu

J-音読み:	セン
J-訓読み:	さき, まず
Korean 音读:	선
Korean 训读:	먼저, 미리
K-eumdok:	seon
K-hundok:	meonjeo, miri
Vietnamese:	đầu tiên

VARIANTS

COMBINATIONS

先輩 - elder generation
先兆 - omen
先覺 - prophet
先人 - ancestors
先生 - mister

先識 - foresight
先後 - successively
先驅 - vanguard
先期 - beforehand

SAYINGS

身先士卒 - lead one's men in a charge
先苦後甜 - no sweet without sweat
先睹爲快 - take delight in being the first to read or see something

爭先恐後 - to strive to be the first and fear to lag behind
欲揚先抑 - compliment goes after a criticism
一馬當先 - take the lead

HISTORICAL

甲骨文 (2000BC) | (1000BC) | (200BC) | (200AD)

FONTS

楷　行　草　宋

266AD Jing Dynasty Wang Xizhi
778BC Tang Dynasty Liu Gongquan
1280AD Yuan Dynasty Zhao Mengfu
1829AD Ming Dynasty Dong Qichang

THE GENIUS OF CHINESE CHARACTERS

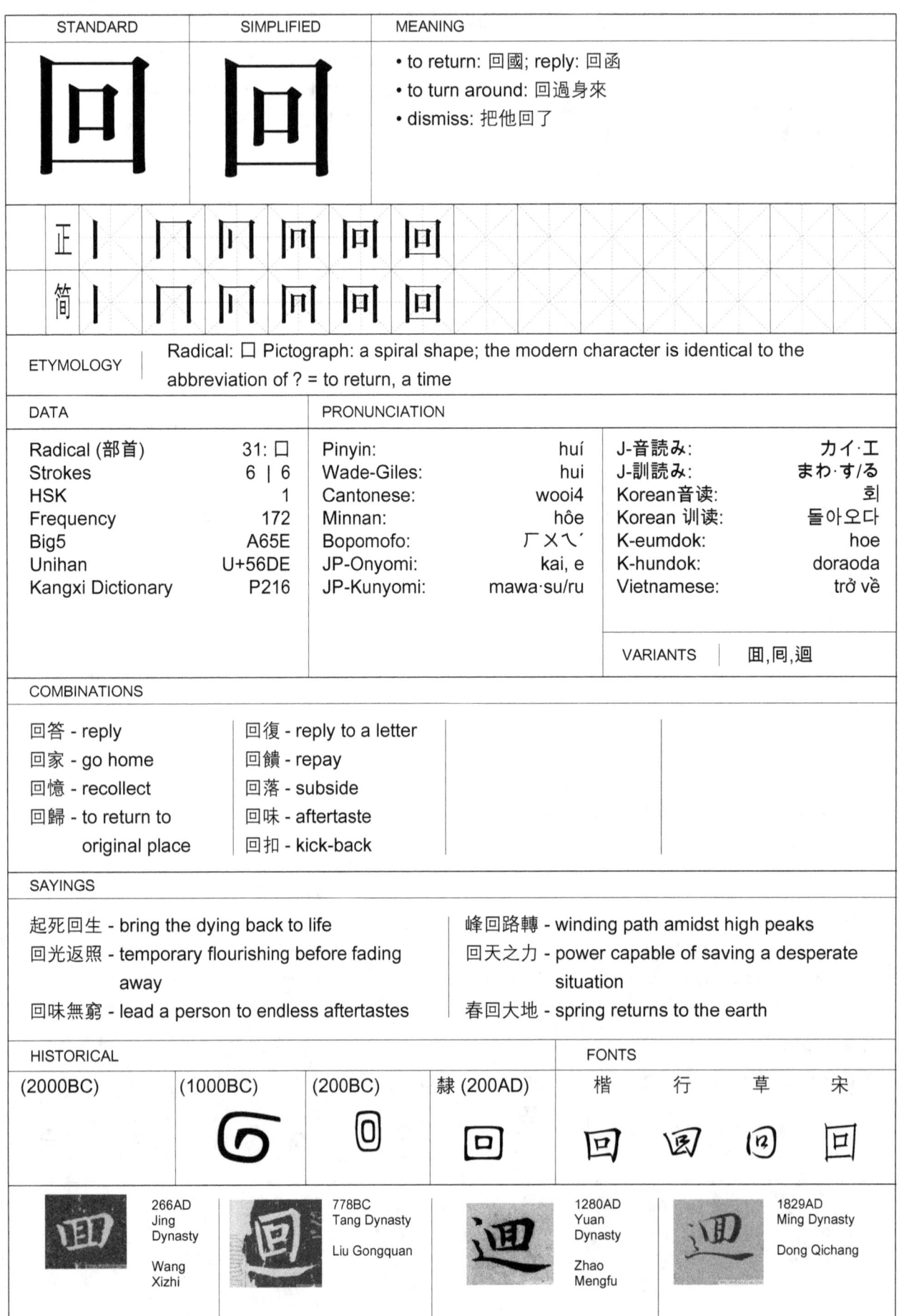

STANDARD	SIMPLIFIED	MEANING
回	回	• to return: 回國; reply: 回函 • to turn around: 回過身來 • dismiss: 把他回了

正 丨 冂 冂 冋 回 回
简 丨 冂 冂 冋 回 回

ETYMOLOGY — Radical: 囗 Pictograph: a spiral shape; the modern character is identical to the abbreviation of ? = to return, a time

DATA

Radical (部首) 31: 囗
Strokes 6 | 6
HSK 1
Frequency 172
Big5 A65E
Unihan U+56DE
Kangxi Dictionary P216

PRONUNCIATION

Pinyin: huí
Wade-Giles: hui
Cantonese: wooi4
Minnan: hôe
Bopomofo: ㄏㄨㄟˊ
JP-Onyomi: kai, e
JP-Kunyomi: mawa·su/ru

J-音読み: カイ・エ
J-訓読み: まわ・す/る
Korean 音读: 회
Korean 训读: 돌아오다
K-eumdok: hoe
K-hundok: doraoda
Vietnamese: trở về

VARIANTS | 囬, 回, 迴

COMBINATIONS

回答 - reply
回家 - go home
回憶 - recollect
回歸 - to return to original place
回復 - reply to a letter
回饋 - repay
回落 - subside
回味 - aftertaste
回扣 - kick-back

SAYINGS

起死回生 - bring the dying back to life
回光返照 - temporary flourishing before fading away
回味無窮 - lead a person to endless aftertastes
峰回路轉 - winding path amidst high peaks
回天之力 - power capable of saving a desperate situation
春回大地 - spring returns to the earth

HISTORICAL

(2000BC) (1000BC) (200BC) 隸 (200AD)

FONTS

楷 行 草 宋

266AD Jing Dynasty Wang Xizhi
778BC Tang Dynasty Liu Gongquan
1280AD Yuan Dynasty Zhao Mengfu
1829AD Ming Dynasty Dong Qichang

THE GENIUS OF Chinese CHARACTERS

STANDARD	SIMPLIFIED	MEANING
系	系	• system: 系統; lineage: 世系; faction: 直系 • department: 文學系; to involve: 系絆 • a series (of events): 系列; distantly related: 系孫

正	一	丆	亠	幺	糸	系	系
简	一	丆	亠	幺	糸	系	系

ETYMOLOGY | Radical: 糸
make connections + 爪 (phonetic - to pull) = department, relation, connect

DATA

		PRONUNCIATION			
Radical (部首)	120: 糸	Pinyin:	xì	J-音読み:	ケイ
Strokes	7 | 7	Wade-Giles:	hsi	J-訓読み:	すじ
HSK	1	Cantonese:	hai6	Korean 音读:	계
Frequency	216	Minnan:	hē	Korean 训读:	매다
Big5	A874	Bopomofo:	ㄒㄧˋ	K-eumdok:	gye
Unihan	U+7CFB	JP-Onyomi:	kei	K-hundok:	maeda
Kangxi Dictionary	P915	JP-Kunyomi:	suji	Vietnamese:	hệ thống

VARIANTS	係

COMBINATIONS

系絆 - to entangle 系統 - a system
系列 - a series (of events) 系族 - the clan
系念 - to be concerned
系孫 - distantly related

SAYINGS

赤繩系足 - be united in wedlock   長繩系景 - try to stop the passage of time
感慨系之 - sigh with deep feeling   比肩系踵 - crowded, shoulder to shoulder
解鈴還需系鈴人 - the one who creates a problem
should be the one to solve it

HISTORICAL

甲骨文 (2000BC)	(1000BC)	篆文 (200BC)	隸 (200AD)

FONTS

楷 行 草 宋
系 系 系 系

266AD
Jing Dynasty
Wang Xizhi

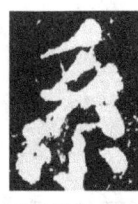
778BC
Tang Dynasty
Liu Gongquan

1280AD
Yuan Dynasty
Den Wenyuan

1829AD
Ming Dynasty
Dong Qichang

THE GENIUS OF CHINESE CHARACTERS

STANDARD	SIMPLIFIED	MEANING
氣	气	• breath: 屏氣; energy: 元氣; physical strength: 力氣 • ambition: 志氣; courage: 勇氣; brilliance: 英氣 • habit: 習氣; morale: 士氣; fragrance: 香氣 • type: 氣派; get angry: 生氣; personal character: 氣格 • weather: 天气

正: 丿 ⺈ 气 气 气 氕 氖 氚 氣 氣
简: 丿 ⺈ 气 气

ETYMOLOGY
Radical: 气
vapors + 米 (phonetic - rice) = gas, weather, mood

DATA

		PRONUNCIATION			
Radical (部首)	84: 气	Pinyin:	qì	J-音読み:	キ, ケ
Strokes	10 | 4	Wade-Giles:	ch'i	J-訓読み:	いき
HSK	1	Cantonese:	hei3	Korean 音读:	기
Frequency	217	Minnan:	khùi	Korean 训读:	기운
Big5	AEF0	Bopomofo:	ㄑㄧˋ	K-eumdok:	gi
Unihan	U+6C14	JP-Onyomi:	ki, ke	K-hundok:	giun
Kangxi Dictionary	P599	JP-Kunyomi:	iki	Vietnamese:	khí ga

VARIANTS: 気(J)

COMBINATIONS

氣球 - balloon
氣忿 - anger
氣恨 - to hate
氣化 - to vaporize
氣節 - moral integrity

氣悶 - suffocating
氣性 - person's temperament
氣數 - fate
氣温 - air temperature

運氣 - luck

SAYINGS

氣宇軒昂 - inspiring looks
蕩氣回腸 - soul-stirring
垂頭喪氣 - lose one's spirits
正氣凜然 - awe-inspiring righteousness

心平氣和 - be in a calm mood
一氣呵成 - to complete a job at one go

HISTORICAL

(2000BC) | 金文 (1000BC) | 篆文 (200BC) | 隸 (200AD)

FONTS

楷 行 草 宋

266AD Jing Dynasty Wang Xizhi
778BC Tang Dynasty Liu Gongquan
1280AD Yuan Dynasty Zhao Mengfu
1829AD Ming Dynasty Dong Qichang

THE GENIUS OF CHINESE CHARACTERS

STANDARD	SIMPLIFIED	MEANING
服	服	• clothes: 便服; to dress: 服裝 • dose (of medicine): 一服藥; swallow (medicine): 服毒 • mourning: 有服; to serve: 服務; respect: 佩服 • admire: 服膺

| 正 | 丿 | 刀 | 月 | 月 | 月￢ | 朋 | 服 | 服 |
| 简 | 丿 | 刀 | 月 | 月 | 月￢ | 朋 | 服 | 服 |

ETYMOLOGY
Radical: 月
boat + Fu (phonetic - govern) = clothes, wear

DATA

		PRONUNCIATION			
Radical (部首)	74: 月	Pinyin:	fú	J-音読み:	フク
Strokes	8 | 8	Wade-Giles:	fu	J-訓読み:	したが・う
HSK	1	Cantonese:	fuk6	Korean 音读:	복
Frequency	365	Minnan:	hȯk	Korean 训读:	웃, 의복
Big5	AA41	Bopomofo:	ㄈㄨˊ	K-eumdok:	bok
Unihan	U+670D	JP-Onyomi:	fuku	K-hundok:	ot, uibok
Kangxi Dictionary	P505	JP-Kunyomi:	shitaga·u	Vietnamese:	quần áo

VARIANTS 箙

COMBINATIONS

- 服喪 - mourning
- 服輸 - admit defeat
- 服罪 - to be sentenced
- 服從 - obey
- 服膺 - admire
- 降服 - surrender
- 服色 - color of dress
- 服飾 - attire

SAYINGS

- 心服口服 - sincere admiration
- 奇裝异服 - fanciful costumes
- 水土不服 - not acclimatized
- 以德服人 - win people by virtue
- 華冠麗服 - be gaudily or grandly attired
- 安生服業 - live and work

HISTORICAL

甲骨文 (2000BC)	金文 (1000BC)	篆文 (200BC)	隸 (200AD)

FONTS

楷　行　草　宋

| 266AD Jing Dynasty Wang Xizhi | 778BC Tang Dynasty Liu Gongquan | 1280AD Yuan Dynasty Zhao Mengfu | 1829AD Ming Dynasty Dong Qichang |

THE GENIUS OF CHINESE CHARACTERS

STANDARD	SIMPLIFIED	MEANING
再	再	• again: 再次; repeatedly: 一再 • good-bye: 再見; furthermore: 再者 • re-marry: 再婚

正 一 丆 冂 币 再 再
简 一 丆 冂 币 再 再

ETYMOLOGY

Radical: 冂
To weigh 冓 + twice 二 = again

DATA

		PRONUNCIATION			
Radical (部首)	13: 冂	Pinyin:	zài	J-音読み:	サイ, サ
Strokes	6 | 6	Wade-Giles:	tsai	J-訓読み:	ふたた·び
HSK	1	Cantonese:	joi3	Korean 音读:	재
Frequency	242	Minnan:	chài	Korean 训读:	두, 두번, 재차
Big5	A641	Bopomofo:	ㄗㄞˋ	K-eumdok:	jae
Unihan	U+518D	JP-Onyomi:	sai, sa	K-hundok: du, du beon, jaecha
Kangxi Dictionary	P129	JP-Kunyomi:	futata·bi	Vietnamese:	lần nữa

VARIANTS

COMBINATIONS

再次 - again
再度 - once again
再來 - come again
再見 - goodbye
再説 - moreover

再審 - review
再發 - to reissue
再三 - over and over again
不再 – no more

SAYINGS

一呼再諾 - pass down the orders from above used to describe obedience
一而再, 再而三 - again and again
一錯再錯 - to repeat errors

東山再起 - to make a comeback
再生父母 - like a second parent, to be one's great benefactor

HISTORICAL

甲骨文 (2000BC)	金文 (1000BC)	篆文 (200BC)	隸 (200AD)
		再	再

266AD Jing Dynasty Wang Xizhi

778BC Tang Dynasty Yan Zhenqing

FONTS

楷 行 草 宋
再 再 再 再

1280AD Yuan Dynasty Zhao Mengfu

1829AD Ming Dynasty Dong Qichang

THE GENIUS OF CHINESE CHARACTERS

STANDARD	SIMPLIFIED	MEANING
兒	儿	• child: 兒子; male: 兒馬; a son: 兒郎 • husband: 兒夫; a stallion: 兒馬 • familiar fellow: 老兒

正: 丨 丆 丆 臼 臼 臼 兒 兒
简: 丿 儿

ETYMOLOGY
Radical: 儿
A person 儿 with its head 囟 not closed yet (臼) = child, oneself

DATA

		PRONUNCIATION			
Radical (部首)	10: 儿	Pinyin:	ér	J-音読み:	ジ, ニ
Strokes	8 | 2	Wade-Giles:	êrh	J-訓読み:	こ
HSK	1	Cantonese:	yi4	Korean 音读:	아
Frequency	192	Minnan:	jî	Korean 训读:	아이
Big5	A8E0	Bopomofo:	ㄦˊ	K-eumdok:	a
Unihan	U+513F	JP-Onyomi:	ji, ni	K-hundok:	ai
Kangxi Dictionary	P125	JP-Kunyomi:	ko	Vietnamese:	đứa trẻ

VARIANTS | 児(J)

COMBINATIONS

兒子 - son
女兒 - daughter
這兒 - here
兒童 - child
那兒 - there

頭兒 - leader

SAYINGS

兒女情長 - the lasting affection of boys and girls
吊兒郎當 - sloppy and careless
視同兒戲 - treat something as child's play

妻兒老小 - a married man's wife and the entire family
非同兒戲 - it isn't child's play not to be taken lightly

HISTORICAL

甲骨文 (2000BC)	金文 (1000BC)	篆文 (200BC)	隸 (200AD)

FONTS

楷　行　草　宋

266AD Jing Dynasty Wang Xizhi

778BC Tang Dynasty Ouyang Xun

1280AD Yuan Dynasty Zhao Mengfu

1829AD Ming Dynasty Dong Qichang

THE GENIUS OF CHINESE CHARACTERS

STANDARD	SIMPLIFIED	MEANING
住	住	• to reside: 住所; stop for rest: 住歇 • to stop: 住手; residence: 住宅 • accommodation: 住所; inhabitant: 住户

正 ノ 亻 亻 亻 佇 住 住
简 ノ 亻 亻 亻 佇 住 住

ETYMOLOGY
Radical: 人
people + 主 (phonetic - master) = dwell, live

DATA

		PRONUNCIATION			
Radical (部首)	9: 人	Pinyin:	zhù	J-音読み:	ジュウ
Strokes	7 | 7	Wade-Giles:	chu	J-訓読み:	す·む
HSK	1	Cantonese:	jue6	Korean 音读:	주
Frequency	309	Minnan:	chū	Korean 训读:	살다
Big5	A6ED	Bopomofo:	ㄓㄨˋ	K-eumdok:	ju
Unihan	U+4F4F	JP-Onyomi:	jū	K-hundok:	salda
Kangxi Dictionary	P98	JP-Kunyomi:	su·mu	Vietnamese:	trực tiếp

VARIANTS

COMBINATIONS

居住 - to reside   停住 - to stop
站住 - to stand   住宅 - residence
不住 - constantly
記住 - to remember
住房 - housing

SAYINGS

久停久住 - to linger/ stay for a long time
久别重逢 - reunion after long separation

HISTORICAL

甲骨文 (2000BC)	金文 (1000BC)	篆文 (200BC)	隸 (200AD)

FONTS

楷 行 草 宋
住 住 住 住

266AD Jing Dynasty Wang Xizhi
778BC Tang Dynasty Yan Zhenqing
1280AD Yuan Dynasty Zhao Mengfu
1829AD Ming Dynasty Dong Qichang

THE GENIUS OF CHINESE CHARACTERS

STANDARD	SIMPLIFIED	MEANING
什	什	• miscellaneous (utensils): 什器; odds and ends: 什碎 • tenfold (or hundredfold): 什百; one tenth: 什一 • huh?: 什麼

正 ノ 亻 仁 什
简 ノ 亻 仁 什

ETYMOLOGY
Radical: 人
person radical + 十(phonetic - ten) = a tenth, mixed, ruse

DATA
Radical (部首) 9: 人
Strokes 4 | 4
HSK 1
Frequency 156
Big5 A4B0
Unihan U+4EC0
Kangxi Dictionary P91

PRONUNCIATION
Pinyin: shí
Wade-Giles: shê
Cantonese: sam6
Minnan:
Bopomofo: ㄕˊ/ㄕㄣˊ
JP-Onyomi: jū
JP-Kunyomi: tō

J-音読み: ジュウ
J-訓読み: とお
Korean 音读: 십, 집
Korean 训读: 열 사람
K-eumdok: sip, jip
K-hundok: yeol saram
Vietnamese: gì

VARIANTS | 十, 卄

COMBINATIONS
什麼 - what
什菜 - mixed vegetables
家什 - furniture

SAYINGS
什一之利 - ten percent profit

HISTORICAL
甲骨文 (2000BC) | 金文 (1000BC) | (200BC) | (200AD)

FONTS
楷 行 草 宋

960BC Song Dynasty Zhu Xi
1280AD Yuan Dynasty Deng Wenyuan

133

THE GENIUS OF CHINESE CHARACTERS

STANDARD	SIMPLIFIED	MEANING
書	书	• books: 圖書; letter (of correspondence): 書渣 • certificate: 證書; script: 楷書; storytelling: 說書 • to write: 書寫; calligraphist: 書家

正 ㄱ ㄲ 㠯 肀 肀 聿 書 書 書 書

简 ㄱ ㄋ 书 书

ETYMOLOGY
Radical: 曰
Uses a pen (聿) to 者 (phonetic - express/write) = Book, letter, document

DATA

		PRONUNCIATION			
Radical (部首)	73: 曰	Pinyin:	shū	J-音読み:	ショ
Strokes	10 | 4	Wade-Giles:	shu	J-訓読み:	かく, ふみ
HSK	1	Cantonese:	sue1	Korean 音读:	서
Frequency	282	Minnan:	su	Korean 训读:	글, 글씨
Big5	AED1	Bopomofo:	ㄕㄨ	K-eumdok:	seo
Unihan	U+4E66	JP-Onyomi:	sho	K-hundok:	geul, geulssi
Kangxi Dictionary	P502	JP-Kunyomi:	ka·ku, fumi	Vietnamese:	sách

VARIANTS

COMBINATIONS

秘書 - secretary
圖書 - books
證書 - certificate
書店 - bookstore
看書 - to read

SAYINGS

書不釋手 - not to part from one's book
牛角書生 - a diligent learner
廢書而嘆 - stop reading and sigh over what the book says

讀書百遍, 其義自見 - read a book many (hundreds of) times and its meaning becomes clear
刺股讀書 - study hard in defiance of hardships

HISTORICAL

甲骨文 (2000BC)	金文 (1000BC)	(200BC)	隸 (200AD)
		書	书

FONTS

楷 行 草 宋
书 书 书 书

- 266AD Jing Dynasty — Wang Xizhi
- 778BC Tang Dynasty — Liu Gongquan
- 1280AD Yuan Dynasty — Zhao Mengfu
- 1829AD Ming Dynasty — Dong Qichang

THE GENIUS OF Chinese CHARACTERS

STANDARD	SIMPLIFIED	MEANING
		• rice: 白米 • meter: 米突 • grain of rice: 米粒 • small sun-dried object: 蝦米

| 正 | 丶 | 丷 | 半 | 米 | 米 |
| 简 | 丶 | 丷 | 半 | 米 | 米 |

ETYMOLOGY

Radical: 米

Pictograph: 6 grains of rice split horozontally (3 top – 3 bottom) split by threshing = rice

DATA

Radical (部首)	119: 米
Strokes	6 | 6
HSK	1
Frequency	575
Big5	A6CC
Unihan	U+7C73
Kangxi Dictionary	P906

PRONUNCIATION

Pinyin:	mǐ	J-音読み:	ベイ, マイ
Wade-Giles:	mi	J-訓読み:	こめ
Cantonese:	mai5	Korean 音读:	미
Minnan:	bí	Korean 训读:	쌀
Bopomofo:	ㄇㄧˇ	K-eumdok:	mi
JP-Onyomi:	bei, mai	K-hundok:	ssal
JP-Kunyomi:	kome	Vietnamese:	mét

VARIANTS

COMBINATIONS

玉米 - corn
大米 - rice
厘米 - centimeter
米飯 - cooked rice

SAYINGS

不爲五鬥米折腰 - to describe someone as virtuous and noble, of moral integrity

偷雞不著蝕把米 - go for wool and come back shorn

生米煮成熟飯 - fait accompli, what is done cannot be undone

無米之炊 - cook a meal without rice to make bricks without straw

HISTORICAL

甲骨文 (2000BC)	金文 (1000BC)	(200BC)	隸 (200AD)
𣥠	米	米	米

FONTS

楷	行	草	宋
米	米	米	米

266AD
Jing Dynasty
Wang Xizhi

778BC
Tang Dynasty
Li Yong

1280AD
Yuan Dynasty
Xian Yushu

1829AD
Ming Dynasty
Dong Qichang

THE GENIUS OF CHINESE CHARACTERS

STANDARD	SIMPLIFIED	MEANING
師	师	• teacher: 老師; a division (milit.): 師長 • master: 師父; (professional person): 律師 • troops: 雄師; imitate: 師古

正 ′ 丨 丫 卢 自 自 白 卣 師 師
简 丨 丿 丿 广 戶 师

ETYMOLOGY Radical: 巾 Able to make a full circlet 帀 (phonetic) around the mound: numerous, army = official post, teacher, study/learn

DATA

Radical (部首)	50: 巾	Pinyin:	shī	J-音読み:	シ
Strokes	10 | 6	Wade-Giles:	shih	J-訓読み:	いくさ
HSK	1	Cantonese:	si1	Korean 音读:	사
Frequency	333	Minnan:	su	Korean 训读:	스승
Big5	AE76	Bopomofo:	ㄕ	K-eumdok:	sa
Unihan	U+5E08	JP-Onyomi:	shi	K-hundok:	seuseung
Kangxi Dictionary	P331	JP-Kunyomi:	ikusa	Vietnamese:	bộ phận

VARIANTS

COMBINATIONS

老師 - teacher　　技師 - technician
律師 - lawyer
師傅 - master
導師 - tutor
厨師 - cook

SAYINGS

名師出高徒 - a great teacher trains a fine student
三人行必有我師 - one can learn from anyone in any place
出師不利 - get off on the wrong foot

一日爲師, 終身爲父 - teacher for a day, father for life
師出有名 - there must be a reason for doing something

HISTORICAL

(2000BC) | 金文 (1000BC) | 篆文 (200BC) | 隸 (200AD)

FONTS: 楷　行　草　宋

266AD Jing Dynasty Wang Xizhi
778BC Tang Dynasty Liu Gongquan
1280AD Yuan Dynasty Zhao Mengfu
1829AD Ming Dynasty Dong Qichang

THE GENIUS OF Chinese CHARACTERS

STANDARD	SIMPLIFIED	MEANING
五	五	• the number five: 5; may: 五月 • five generations: 五世 • pentagon: 五角大厦

正 一 丁 五 五
简 一 丁 五 五

ETYMOLOGY — Radical: 二
Yin and Yang interlace between heaven and earth: a figure in the middle = five

DATA
- Radical (部首): 7: 二
- Strokes: 4 | 4
- HSK: 1
- Frequency: 279
- Big5: A4AD
- Unihan: U+4E94
- Kangxi Dictionary: P86

PRONUNCIATION
- Pinyin: wǔ
- Wade-Giles: wu
- Cantonese: ng5
- Minnan: gō
- Bopomofo: ㄨˇ
- JP-Onyomi: go
- JP-Kunyomi: itsu·tsu
- J-音読み: ゴ
- J-訓読み: いつ・つ
- Korean 音读: 오
- Korean 训读: 다섯
- K-eumdok: o
- K-hundok: daseot
- Vietnamese: vợ

VARIANTS | 伍

COMBINATIONS
- 第五 - fifth
- 五月 - May
- 五級 - grade 5
- 五洲 - five continents

SAYINGS
- 三年五載 - several years
- 一五一十 - detailed narration
- 三五成群 - in groups of three or four
- 三令五申 - to order again and again
- 五十步笑百步 - the pot calling the kettle black
- 五光十色 - a riot of colors
- 五湖四海 - everywhere

HISTORICAL

甲骨文 (2000BC)	金文 (1000BC)	篆文 (200BC)	隸 (200AD)
X	8	X	五

FONTS

楷 行 草 宋
五 五 五 五

- 266AD Jing Dynasty Wang Xizhi
- 778BC Tang Dynasty Liu Gongquan
- 1280AD Yuan Dynasty Zhao Mengfu
- 1829AD Ming Dynasty Dong Qichang

THE GENIUS OF Chinese CHARACTERS

STANDARD	SIMPLIFIED	MEANING
見	见	• to see: 見到; call on: 拜見 • extend welcome to: 接見; views: 意見 • farsighted: 遠見; get thinner: 見瘦 • square: 見方

| 正 | 丨 | 冂 | 冃 | 月 | 目 | 目 | 見 |
| 简 | 丨 | 冂 | 见 | 见 |

ETYMOLOGY

Radical: 見
Someone 儿 with eyes 目 opening: see/observe = interview/behold

DATA

		PRONUNCIATION			
Radical (部首)	147: 見	Pinyin:	jiàn	J-音読み:	ケン
Strokes	7 | 4	Wade-Giles:	chien	J-訓読み:	み·る/える
HSK	1	Cantonese:	gin3	Korean 音读:	견
Frequency	153	Minnan:	kiàn	Korean 训读:	보다
Big5	A8A3	Bopomofo:	ㄐㄧㄢˋ	K-eumdok:	gyeon
Unihan	U+89C1	JP-Onyomi:	ken	K-hundok:	boda
Kangxi Dictionary	P1133	JP-Kunyomi:	mi·ru/eru	Vietnamese:	xem

VARIANTS

COMBINATIONS

看見 - to see
意見 - idea
聽見 - to hear
見過 - have seen
見面 - to meet

再見 - goodbye
夢見 - to dream

SAYINGS

一見如故 - familiarity at first sight; become friends at first sight
一針見血 - to hit the nail on the head
一見鐘情 - love at first sight

不見棺材不掉泪 - To refuse to repent until complete failure occurs

HISTORICAL

(2000BC)	(1000BC)	(200BC)	隸 (200AD)
		見	见

FONTS

楷	行	草	宋
见	见	见	见

266AD Jing Dynasty Wang Xizhi

778BC Tang Dynasty Liu Gongquan

1280AD Yuan Dynasty Zhao Mengfu

1829AD Ming Dynasty Dong Qichang

THE GENIUS OF Chinese CHARACTERS

STANDARD	SIMPLIFIED	MEANING
熱	热	• hot: 冷熱; hot weather: 熱天 • warmth (of feeling): 熱腸; restless: 熱中 • popular (high demand): 熱門; enthusiastic: 熱心 • heat stroke: 受熱; fervent: 熱烈

正	一	十	士	圥	夫	去	奉	奎	剉	埶	埶	熱
	熱	熱										
简	一	才	才	扌	执	执	执	执	热	热		

ETYMOLOGY
Radical: 火

火 fire + 埶 (phonetic): hot (of weather) = heat/warm

DATA		PRONUNCIATION			
Radical (部首)	86: 火	Pinyin:	rè	J-音読み:	ネツ
Strokes	15 | 10	Wade-Giles:	jê	J-訓読み:	あつ・い
HSK	1	Cantonese:	yit6	Korean 音读:	열
Frequency	606	Minnan:	joah	Korean 训读:	덥다,따듯하다
Big5	BCF6	Bopomofo:	ㄖㄜˋ	K-eumdok:	yeol
Unihan	U+70ED	JP-Onyomi:	netsu	K-hundok:	deopda, ttadeutada
Kangxi Dictionary	P681	JP-Kunyomi:	atsu·i	Vietnamese:	nhiệt

VARIANTS

COMBINATIONS

熱烈 - enthusiastic
熱情 - passion
親熱 - affectionate
熱水 - hot water
熱心 - enthusiasm
熱氣 - steam
熱門 - popular

SAYINGS

冷嘲熱諷 - to mock and ridicule
趁熱打鐵 - strike while the iron is hot
滿腔熱血 - full of zeal
熱氣騰騰 - steaming hot
熱泪盈眶 - eyes brimming with tears of excitement extremely moved
熱鬧哄哄 - clamorous, filled with noise and excitement

HISTORICAL

(2000BC)	(1000BC)	篆文 (200BC)	隸 (200AD)
		𤍨	熱

FONTS

楷	行	草	宋
热	热	热	热

266AD
Jing Dynasty
Wang Xizhi

778BC
Tang Dynasty
Yan Zhenqin

1280AD
Yuan Dynasty
Zhao Mengfu

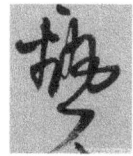
1829AD
Ming Dynasty
Wang Duo

THE GENIUS OF CHINESE CHARACTERS

STANDARD	SIMPLIFIED	MEANING
買	买	• to buy: 買地; bribe: 買官; hire: 買舟 • customer: 買主; pay bribe to: 買通 • purchase: 購買

正: 丨 冂 冂 罒 罒 罘 罘 罘 買 買 買
简: 乛 乛 乛 亝 买 买

ETYMOLOGY
Radical: 貝 with money
shells - used as ancient currency. 罒 catch or gain + 貝. 殼 shell: seek/buy

DATA
- Radical (部首): 154: 貝
- Strokes: 12 | 6
- HSK: 1
- Frequency: 758
- Big5: B652
- Unihan: U+4E70
- Kangxi Dictionary: P1206

PRONUNCIATION
- Pinyin: mǎi
- Wade-Giles: mai
- Cantonese: maai5
- Minnan: bé
- Bopomofo: ㄇㄞˇ
- JP-Onyomi: bai
- JP-Kunyomi: ka·u
- J-音読み: バイ
- J-訓読み: か·う
- Korean 音读: 매
- Korean 训读: 사다
- K-eumdok: mae
- K-hundok: sada
- Vietnamese: mua

VARIANTS

COMBINATIONS
- 購買 - to purchase
- 買到 - bought
- 買主 - customer
- 買回 - repurchase

SAYINGS
- 招兵買馬 - to recruit soliders and buy horses; to expand business; to recruit new staff
- 現買現賣 - hand-to-mouth buying; Zero Stock Buying
- 買櫝還珠 - buy the casket without the jewels; poor judgement
- 買空賣空 - to play the market; to sell hot air

HISTORICAL
- (2000BC)
- 金文 (1000BC)
- 篆文 (200BC)
- 隸 (200AD)

FONTS
楷 行 草 宋

- 960BC Song Dynasty, Mi Fu
- 1280AD Yuan Dynasty, Zhao Mengfu
- 1829AD Ming Dynasty, Dong Qichang
- 1829AD Ming Dynasty, Tang Yin

THE GENIUS OF CHINESE CHARACTERS

STANDARD	SIMPLIFIED	MEANING
醫	医	• medicine: 醫藥; to cure: 醫治 • doctor: 醫生; hospital: 醫院 • physician: 醫家

正: 一 厂 匚 三 歹 矢 医 医 医㇇ 殹⺁ 殹 殹 殹
醫 殹 殹 醫 醫
简: 一 厂 匚 三 歹 歺 医

ETYMOLOGY — Radical: 酉 殹 sick state + 酉 alcohol: in ancient times alcohol was used to cure illness = treat/cure, doctor

DATA

Radical (部首)	164: 酉
Strokes	18 | 7
HSK	1
Frequency	482
Big5	C2E5
Unihan	U+533B
Kangxi Dictionary	P1278

PRONUNCIATION

Pinyin:	yī
Wade-Giles:	i
Cantonese:	yi1
Minnan:	i
Bopomofo:	ㄧ
JP-Onyomi:	i
JP-Kunyomi:	i·yasu

J-音読み:	イ
J-訓読み:	い・やす
Korean 音读:	의
Korean 训读:	의원, 의사
K-eumdok:	ui
K-hundok:	uiwon, uisa
Vietnamese:	y khoa

VARIANTS | 醫, 毉

COMBINATIONS

醫院 - hospital
醫生 - doctor
醫學 - medicine
醫藥 - pharmaceutical
醫療 - medical treatment

SAYINGS

死馬當活馬醫 - to flog a dead horse
諱疾忌醫 - hide a sickness for fear of treatment; conceal a fault to avoid criticism
久病成醫 - a long illness makes the patient a doctor
俗不可醫 - unbearably vulgar

HISTORICAL

甲骨文 (2000BC)	金文 (1000BC)	篆文 (200BC)	隸 (200AD)
		醫	医

FONTS

楷 行 草 宋
医 医 医 医

778BC Tang Dynasty — Guo Quan
1280AD Yuan Dynasty — Xian Yushu
1829AD Ming Dynasty — Wu Kuan
1829AD Ming Dynasty — Dong Qichang

THE GENIUS OF CHINESE CHARACTERS

STANDARD	SIMPLIFIED	MEANING
		• to love: 戀愛; to like: 喜愛; love (romantic): 愛情 • hobby: 愛好; cute: 可愛; to cherish: 愛護 • be prone to: 愛哭; admire: 愛服 • to adore (somebody): 愛慕; lover: 愛人

正	一	二	二	罒	罒	罒	罒	爫	爫	爫	爫	愛	愛
简	一	二	二	罒	罒	罒	爫	爫	爱	爱			

ETYMOLOGY

Radical: 心

夂 feet + ? (phonetic): walking. 愛 replaced ? (similiar phonetic) with the meaning "love"

DATA

		PRONUNCIATION			
Radical (部首)	61: 心	Pinyin:	ài	J-音読み:	アイ
Strokes	13 | 10	Wade-Giles:	ai	J-訓読み:	いと・しい
HSK	1	Cantonese:	oi3	Korean 音读:	애
Frequency	394	Minnan:	ài	Korean 训读:	사랑
Big5	B752	Bopomofo:	ㄞˋ	K-eumdok:	ae
Unihan	U+7231	JP-Onyomi:	ai	K-hundok:	sarang
Kangxi Dictionary	P395	JP-Kunyomi:	ito·shī	Vietnamese:	yêu và quý

VARIANTS

COMBINATIONS

愛情 - romance
可愛 - adorable
愛心 - compassion
喜愛 - to love
愛護 - to treasure

SAYINGS

博愛濟群 - compassion and generosity for all
愛人如己 - love a person as oneself
愛屋及烏 - love me love my dog
愛恨交織 - a mixture of love a hate

愛惜羽毛 - cherish oneself
愛憎分明 - well-defined likes and dislikes
愛才好士 - cherish talented and virtuous persons

HISTORICAL

甲骨文 (2000BC)	金文 (1000BC)	篆文 (200BC)	隸 (200AD)
		壽	爱

FONTS

楷	行	草	宋
爱	爱	愛	爱

778BC
Tang Dynasty
Guo Quan

778BC
Tang Dynasty
Yan Zhenqing

1829AD
Ming Dynasty
Wu Kuan

1829AD
Ming Dynasty
Tang Yin

THE GENIUS OF Chinese CHARACTERS

STANDARD	SIMPLIFIED	MEANING
校	校	• proofread: 校稿; school: 校長; to collate: 校勘 • military rank: 上校; to contest: 校場 • to revise: 校閱

正	一	十	才	木	朩	柠	栌	柊	杦	校
简	一	十	才	木	朩	柠	栌	柊	杦	校

ETYMOLOGY | Radical: 木
Put the wood 木 together 交: a kind of punishment tool = check/proofread, school

DATA
- Radical (部首): 75: 木
- Strokes: 10 | 10
- HSK: 1
- Frequency: 633
- Big5: AED5
- Unihan: U+6821
- Kangxi Dictionary: P522

PRONUNCIATION
- Pinyin: xiào
- Wade-Giles: chiao
- Cantonese: haau6
- Minnan: hāu
- Bopomofo: ㄒㄧㄠˊ/ㄐㄧㄠˋ
- JP-Onyomi: kō, kyō
- JP-Kunyomi: aze, kase

- J-音読み: コウ, キョウ
- J-訓読み: あぜ, かせ
- Korean 音读: 교
- Korean 训读: 학교
- K-eumdok: gyo
- K-hundok: hakgyo
- Vietnamese: trường học

VARIANTS | 挍

COMBINATIONS

學校 - school	校服 - school uniform
校長 - president	
校園 - campus	
校捨 - school building	
校正 - to correct	

SAYINGS

同年而校 - to discuss or treat different people and matters altogether	犯而不校 - not to be offended by insults
校短推長 - to measure someone's merits and shortcomings	

HISTORICAL

甲骨文 (2000BC)	金文 (1000BC)	篆文 (200BC)	隸 (200AD)
		校	校

FONTS

楷	行	草	宋
校	挍	校	校

- 266AD Jing Dynasty, Wang Xizhi
- 778BC Tang Dynasty, Yan Zhenqing
- 1280AD Yuan Dynasty, Zhao Mengfu
- 1829AD Ming Dynasty, Wu Kuan

THE GENIUS OF CHINESE CHARACTERS

STANDARD	SIMPLIFIED	MEANING
昨	昨	• yesterday: 昨天; last night: 昨夜 • the recent past: 日昨

| 正 | 丨 | 冂 | 月 | 日 | 旷 | 旷 | 昨 | 昨 | 昨 |
| 简 | 丨 | 冂 | 月 | 日 | 旷 | 旷 | 昨 | 昨 | 昨 |

ETYMOLOGY
Radical: 日
日 one day + 乍 (phonetic): yesterday/in former times

DATA

Radical (部首)	72: 日	Pinyin:	zuó	J-音読み:	サク
Strokes	9 | 9	Wade-Giles:	tso	J-訓読み:	きのう
HSK	1	Cantonese:	jok6	Korean 音读:	작
Frequency	1475	Minnan:	cháh	Korean 训读:	어제
Big5	AC51	Bopomofo:	ㄗㄨㄛˊ	K-eumdok:	jak
Unihan	U+6628	JP-Onyomi:	saku	K-hundok:	eoje
Kangxi Dictionary	P493	JP-Kunyomi:	kinou	Vietnamese:	hôm qua

VARIANTS

COMBINATIONS

昨天 - yesterday
昨夜 - last night

SAYINGS

今是昨非 - now is right and before was wrong; to repent

HISTORICAL

甲骨文 (2000BC)	金文 (1000BC)	篆文 (200BC)	隸 (200AD)
		昨	昨

FONTS

楷	行	草	宋
昨	昨	昨	昨

266AD Jing Dynasty Wang Xizhi

778BC Tang Dynasty Liu Gongquan

1280AD Yuan Dynasty Zhao Mengfu

1829AD Ming Dynasty Dong Qichang

THE GENIUS OF CHINESE CHARACTERS

STANDARD	SIMPLIFIED	MEANING
站	站	• station: 車站; to stand: 站起來 • to stop: 站住; to stand in line: 站排 • railway platform: 站臺

正: 丶 亠 六 立 立 站 站 站 站 站
简: 丶 亠 六 立 立 站 站 站 站 站

ETYMOLOGY

Radical: 立
占 fixed in place + 立 stand: stand (rigid) = station/lodging

DATA

Radical (部首)	117: 立
Strokes	10 | 10
HSK	1
Frequency	544
Big5	AFB8
Unihan	U+7AD9
Kangxi Dictionary	P870

PRONUNCIATION

Pinyin:	zhàn
Wade-Giles:	chan
Cantonese:	jaam6
Minnan:	chām
Bopomofo:	ㄓㄢˋ
JP-Onyomi:	tan
JP-Kunyomi:	eki, ta·tsu
J-音読み:	タン
J-訓読み:	えき, た・つ
Korean 音读:	참
Korean 训读:	역마을
K-eumdok:	cham
K-hundok:	yeongmaeul
Vietnamese:	ga tàu

VARIANTS	佔

COMBINATIONS

車站 - rail station
站住 - to stand
站臺 - platform
網站 - website

SAYINGS

站不住腳 - ill-founded
站穩腳跟 - to establish oneself

HISTORICAL

甲骨文 (2000BC)	金文 (1000BC)	篆文 (200BC)	隸 (200AD)
		站	站

FONTS

楷	行	草	宋
站	站	站	站

THE GENIUS OF CHINESE CHARACTERS

STANDARD	SIMPLIFIED	MEANING
覺	觉	• go to sleep: 睡覺; feel: 覺疼; find out: 覺出 • discover: 覺察; aware of self: 自覺 • senses (hear, touch, etc.): 聽覺 • to wake up from dream: 夢覺; sensation: 知覺 • hallucination: 幻覺

正: ` ﹁ F F F⁻ F⁼ 臼 臼 臼 臼 臼 臼
學 臼 臼 臼 臼 覺 覺
简: ` ﹀ ﹀﹀ ﹀﹀ 丷 ⺌ ⺍ 觉 觉

ETYMOLOGY
Radical: 見
見 (see) replaced 子 of 學 (acquire knowledge): study/breakthrough/awake/wake up

DATA

Radical (部首)	147: 見	
Strokes	20 | 9	
HSK	1	
Frequency	327	
Big5	C4B1	
Unihan	U+89C9	
Kangxi Dictionary	P1137	

PRONUNCIATION

Pinyin:	jiào	J-音読み:	カク, コウ
Wade-Giles:	chiao	J-訓読み:	おぼ·える, さ·ます
Cantonese:	gok3	Korean 音读:	각
Minnan:	kak	Korean 训读:	깨닫다
Bopomofo:	ㄐㄧㄠˋ	K-eumdok:	gak
JP-Onyomi:	kaku, kou	K-hundok:	kkaedatda
JP-Kunyomi:	obo·eru, sa·masu	Vietnamese:	cảm thấy

VARIANTS | 覚(J)

COMBINATIONS
覺得 - to think
感覺 - to feel
不覺 - unconsciously
睡覺 - to sleep
自覺 - conscious
察覺 - to detect
直覺 - intuition

SAYINGS
不知不覺 - unconsciously
後知後覺 - only realize until an event has ended
神不知, 鬼不覺 - stealth, stealthily
十年一覺揚州夢 - suddenly come to the realization of years wasted
如夢初覺 - to suddenly realize as if waking up from a dream

HISTORICAL

甲骨文 (2000BC)	金文 (1000BC)	篆文 (200BC)	隸 (200AD)
		覺	觉

FONTS
楷 行 草 宋
觉 觉 觉 觉

266AD
Jing Dynasty
Wang Xizhi

778BC
Tang Dynasty
Liu Gongquan

1280AD
Yuan Dynasty
Zhao Mengfu

1829AD
Ming Dynasty
Dong Qichang

THE GENIUS OF CHINESE CHARACTERS

STANDARD	SIMPLIFIED	MEANING
候	候	• to wait: 等候 ; to await: 候示 • when?: 什麼時候 ; duration and degree: 火候 • climate: 氣候

正 ノ 亻 什 伫 伫 伊 倅 俟 候
简 ノ 亻 什 伫 伫 伊 倅 俟 候

ETYMOLOGY

Radical: 人

人 person + target 矣 (phonetic): look on = wait/expect

DATA

Radical (部首)	9: 人	Pinyin:	hòu	J-音読み:	コウ
Strokes	10 | 10	Wade-Giles:	hou	J-訓読み:	そうろう
HSK	1	Cantonese:	hau6	Korean 音读:	후
Frequency	341	Minnan:	hāu	Korean 训读:	기후, 때
Big5	ADD4	Bopomofo:	ㄏㄡˋ	K-eumdok:	hu
Unihan	U+5019	JP-Onyomi:	kō	K-hundok:	gihu, ttae
Kangxi Dictionary	P108	JP-Kunyomi:	sourou	Vietnamese:	chờ đợi

VARIANTS

COMBINATIONS

時候 - time
候選 - candidate
氣候 - climate
等候 - to wait
伺候 - to serve

癥候 - illness, symptoms

SAYINGS

承顏候色 - to flatter
雞鳴候旦 - wake up before dawn to avoid missing important tasks; overly anxious
積薪候燎 - make nooses for one's own neck

HISTORICAL

甲骨文 (2000BC)	金文 (1000BC)	篆文 (200BC)	(200AD)
		候	候

FONTS

楷 行 草 宋
候 候 候 候

266AD Jing Dynasty Wang Xizhi

778BC Tang Dynasty Tang Ren

1280AD Yuan Dynasty Zhao Mengfu

1829AD Ming Dynasty Dong Qichang

147

THE GENIUS OF CHINESE CHARACTERS

STANDARD	SIMPLIFIED	MEANING
飛	飞	• to fly: 飛行; flying: 飛吻; airplane: 飛機 • go quickly: 飛跑; to go up (high): 飛騰 • float in the sky: 飛揚

正 乁 飞 飞 飞 飞 飞 飞 飛 飛
簡 乁 飞 飞

ETYMOLOGY
Radical: 飛
Pictograph: the wings and tail of a flying bird: fly, quickly

DATA

Radical (部首)	183: 飛	Pinyin:	fēi	J-音読み:	ヒ
Strokes	9 | 3	Wade-Giles:	fei	J-訓読み:	と・ぶ/ばす
HSK	1	Cantonese:	fei1	Korean 音读:	비
Frequency	347	Minnan:	hui	Korean 训读:	날다
Big5	ADB8	Bopomofo:	ㄈㄟ	K-eumdok:	bi
Unihan	U+98DE	JP-Onyomi:	hi	K-hundok:	nalda
Kangxi Dictionary	P1415	JP-Kunyomi:	to·bu/basu	Vietnamese:	bay

VARIANTS

COMBINATIONS

飛機 - airplane
飛行 - to fly
飛船 - airship
飛快 - very fast
飛揚 - to rise

飛速 - flying speed
飛躍 - to leap

SAYINGS

一飛衝天 - an overnight success
不翼而飛 - vanish without trace
兔走鳥飛 - time flies
健步如飛 - running as fast as flying

兩鬢飛霜 - white hair from old age
口沫橫飛 - splutter
意氣飛揚 - vigorous spirit
插翅難飛 - hard to escape even if given wings

HISTORICAL

甲骨文 (2000BC)	金文 (1000BC)	篆文 (200BC)	(200AD)

FONTS
楷 行 草 宋

266AD Jing Dynasty Wang Xizhi
778BC Tang Dynasty Guo Quan
1280AD Yuan Dynasty Zhao Mengfu
1829AD Ming Dynasty Dong Qichang

THE GENIUS OF CHINESE CHARACTERS

STANDARD	SIMPLIFIED	MEANING
錢	钱	• money: 金錢; cash: 現錢 • pay cash: 付錢; rich: 有錢 • wallet: 錢包

正: ノ 𠆢 𠆢 𠂉 ᐯ 产 金 金 釒 鈊 鈛 銭 錢
錢 錢 錢

简: ノ 𠂉 𠂉 𠂉 钅 钅 钅 钅 钱 钱

ETYMOLOGY
Radical: 金
metal. 戔 (phonetic) of reduced size: money, coin

DATA
- Radical (部首): 167: 金
- Strokes: 16 | 10
- HSK: 1
- Frequency: 603
- Big5: BFFA
- Unihan: U+94B1
- Kangxi Dictionary: P1311

PRONUNCIATION
- Pinyin: qián
- Wade-Giles: ch'ien
- Cantonese: chin4
- Minnan: chîⁿ
- Bopomofo: ㄑㄧㄢˊ
- JP-Onyomi: sen
- JP-Kunyomi: zeni
- J-音読み: セン
- J-訓読み: ぜに
- Korean 音读: 전
- Korean 训读: 돈
- K-eumdok: jeon
- K-hundok: don
- Vietnamese: tiền bạc

VARIANTS | 銭(J)

COMBINATIONS
- 金錢 - money
- 花錢 - to spend money
- 價錢 - price
- 要錢 - to charge
- 工錢 - salary
- 出錢 - to pay

SAYINGS
- 一分錢, 一分貨 - you get what you paid for
- 一錢不值 - not worth a penny
- 有錢能使鬼推磨 - money makes the world go round
- 多錢善賈 - good trading conditions
- 用錢如水 - to spend money like water
- 要錢不要命 - get rich or die trying

HISTORICAL
甲骨文 (2000BC)	金文 (1000BC)	篆文 (200BC)	隸 (200AD)
		錢	钱

FONTS
楷 行 草 宋
钱 錢 钱 钱

- 778BC Tang Dynasty, Guo Quan
- 778BC Tang Dynasty, Yan Zhenqing
- 1280AD Yuan Dynasty, Zhao Mengfu
- 1829AD Ming Dynasty, Dong Qichang

THE GENIUS OF CHINESE CHARACTERS

STANDARD	SIMPLIFIED	MEANING
歲	岁	• year: 歲歲; age: 年歲; how old?: 幾歲? • annual: 歲出; new year's eve: 歲除 • year's end: 歲杪

正	丨	𠂉	丨丨	步	岁	芦	芦	芦	芦	歩	歳	歳	歲
简	丨	止	山	岁	岁	岁							

ETYMOLOGY
Radical: 止
戌 (phonetic) + 止 arrive: Jupiter. Jupiter moved once every twelve years = year

DATA

		PRONUNCIATION			
Radical (部首)	77: 止	Pinyin:	suì	J-音読み:	さい, せい
Strokes	13 | 6	Wade-Giles:	sui	J-訓読み:	とし
HSK	1	Cantonese:	sui3	Korean 音读:	세
Frequency	772	Minnan:	hòe	Korean 训读:	해, 나이
Big5	B7B3	Bopomofo:	ㄙㄨㄟˋ	K-eumdok:	se
Unihan	U+5C81	JP-Onyomi:	sai, sei	K-hundok:	hae, nai
Kangxi Dictionary	P577	JP-Kunyomi:	toshi	Vietnamese:	tuổi

VARIANTS	歲(J)

COMBINATIONS
歲月 - years
歲時 - season
萬歲 - long live
年歲 - years of age
周歲 - one full year

SAYINGS
崢嶸歲月 - eventful years
千歲一時 - rare opportunity
以日爲歲 - yearn for something fervently
凶年饑歲 - years of famine

歲寒知鬆柏 - adversity reveals virtue
歲寒三友 - pine, bamboo, and plum
日久歲深 - to last for an eternity
歲不我與 - time and tide wait for no one

HISTORICAL

甲骨文 (2000BC)	金文 (1000BC)	篆文 (200BC)	隸 (200AD)
			岁

FONTS

楷	行	草	宋
岁	岁	岁	岁

266AD
Jing Dynasty
Wang Xizhi

778BC
Tang Dynasty
Liu Gongquan

1280AD
Yuan Dynasty
Zhao Mengfu

1829AD
Ming Dynasty
Dong Qichang

THE GENIUS OF CHINESE CHARACTERS

STANDARD	SIMPLIFIED	MEANING
請	请	• please (do sth): 请坐; to invite: 邀請 • to request: 請求; to ask: 請問 • to pray for: 請雨 • invitation card: 請帖

正: 丶 亠 亠 言 言 言 訁 訁 詩 請 請 請 請
請 請
简: 丶 讠 讠 讠 许 许 请 请 请 请

ETYMOLOGY

Radical: 言

言 word + 青 (phonetic): visit = ask/please (do something)

DATA

Radical (部首)	149: 言
Strokes	15 | 10
HSK	1
Frequency	421
Big5	BDD0
Unihan	U+8BF7
Kangxi Dictionary	P1167

PRONUNCIATION

Pinyin:	qǐng
Wade-Giles:	ch'ing
Cantonese:	ching2
Minnan:	chhéng
Bopomofo:	ㄑㄧㄥˇ
JP-Onyomi:	sei, shin
JP-Kunyomi:	kō, u·keru

J-音読み:	セイ, シン
J-訓読み:	こう, う·ける
Korean 音读:	청
Korean 训读:	청하다
K-eumdok:	cheong
K-hundok:	cheonghada
Vietnamese:	xin vui lòng

VARIANTS

COMBINATIONS

申請 - to apply
邀請 - to invite
請求 - request
請問 - excuse me
請客 - to invite to dinner
請示 - to ask for instructions
提請 - to propose

SAYINGS

不請自來 - uninvited
另請高明 - find someone more qualified
三催四請 - coax and plead
負荊請罪 - to offer someone a humble apology

HISTORICAL

甲骨文 (2000BC)	金文 (1000BC)	篆文 (200BC)	隸 (200AD)
		請	请

FONTS

楷　行　草　宋
请　请　请　请

266AD — Jing Dynasty — Wang Xizhi
778BC — Tang Dynasty — Liu Gongquan
1280AD — Yuan Dynasty — Zhao Mengfu
1829AD — Ming Dynasty — Dong Qichang

THE GENIUS OF CHINESE CHARACTERS

STANDARD	SIMPLIFIED	MEANING
識	识	• knowledge: 知識; to know (someone): 相識 • to distinguish: 識別; to recognise: 識拔 • common sense: 常識; literacy: 識字 • to record: 款識

正: 丶 亠 三 言 言 言 訁 訁 訁 訁 訁 訁 訁 訁 訁 訁 訁 識 識 識
简: 丶 讠 讠 识 识 识

ETYMOLOGY

Radical: 言
言 word + make/record 哉 (phonetic): recognize = knowledge

DATA

Radical (部首)	149: 言
Strokes	19 | 7
HSK	1
Frequency	340
Big5	C3D1
Unihan	U+8BC6
Kangxi Dictionary	P1181

PRONUNCIATION

Pinyin:	shí	J-音読み:	シキ
Wade-Giles:	shih	J-訓読み:	しる・す
Cantonese:	sik1	Korean 音读:	식, 지
Minnan:	sek	Korean 训读:	알다, 적다
Bopomofo:	ㄕˊ/ㄕˋ	K-eumdok:	sik, ji
JP-Onyomi:	shiki	K-hundok:	alda, jeokda
JP-Kunyomi:	shiru·su	Vietnamese:	hiểu biết

VARIANTS

COMBINATIONS

認識 - to recognize
知識 - knowledge
意識 - consciousness
相識 - acquaintance
識別 - to distinguish
常識 - common sense

SAYINGS

一般見識 - lower oneself to somebody's level
不打不相識 - no discord, no concord
不識大體 - to fail to grasp the big picture
不識好歹 - unable to tell good from bad
不識泰山 - not recognize a famous/talented/prestigious person

HISTORICAL

甲骨文 (2000BC)	金文 (1000BC)	篆文 (200BC)	隸 (200AD)
		識	識

FONTS

楷	行	草	宋
识	识	识	识

266AD Jing Dynasty Wang Xizhi

778BC Tang Dynasty Liu Gongquan

1280AD Yuan Dynasty Zhao Mengfu

1829AD Ming Dynasty Wang Duo

THE GENIUS OF CHINESE CHARACTERS

STANDARD	SIMPLIFIED	MEANING
火	火	• fire: 生火; anger: 火氣; fiery: 火性 • train: 火車; torch: 火把; flames: 火焰 • firepower: 火力; ham: 火腿

| 正 | 丶 | 丷 | 少 | 火 |
| 简 | 丶 | 丷 | 少 | 火 |

ETYMOLOGY Radical: 火
Pictograph: flames

DATA

Radical (部首)	86: 火
Strokes	4 | 4
HSK	1
Frequency	433
Big5	A4F5
Unihan	U+706B
Kangxi Dictionary	P665

PRONUNCIATION

Pinyin:	huǒ
Wade-Giles:	huo
Cantonese:	foh2
Minnan:	hóe
Bopomofo:	ㄏㄨㄛˇ
JP-Onyomi:	ka
JP-Kunyomi:	hi, ho

J-音読み:	力
J-訓読み:	ひ, ほ
Korean 音读:	화
Korean 训读:	불
K-eumdok:	hwa
K-hundok:	bul
Vietnamese:	ngọn lửa

VARIANTS | 灬

COMBINATIONS

火車 - train	紅火 - prosperous
火箭 - rocket	著火 - to ignite
火灾 - fire	
火星 - Mars	
燈火 - lights	

SAYINGS

人間烟火 - wordly affairs and thoughts
趁火打劫 - to loot a burning house
幹柴烈火 - consuming passion between lovers
刀山火海 - extreme danger

勢同水火 - two sharply opposing parties
如火如荼 - unstoppable like wildfire
如火燎原 - to spread like wildfire
赴湯蹈火 - not afraid of any difficulty

HISTORICAL

甲骨文 (2000BC)	金文 (1000BC)	篆文 (200BC)	隸 (200AD)
ᗰ	✧	火	火

FONTS

楷	行	草	宋
火	火	火	火

266AD
Jing Dynasty
Wang Xizhi

778BC
Tang Dynasty
Liu Gongquan

1280AD
Yuan Dynasty
Zhao Mengfu

1829AD
Ming Dynasty
Dong Qichang

THE GENIUS OF CHINESE CHARACTERS

STANDARD	SIMPLIFIED	MEANING
聽	听	• to hear: 聽見; to listen to: 聽從 • to supervise: 聽政; to obey: 聽話 • earphone: 聽筒; dictation: 聽寫

正: 一 厂 丌 丌 耳 耳 耳 耳 耳 耳 耳 耳
耵 耵 耵 耵 耵 耵 聽 聽 聽

简: 丨 冂 口 叱 听 听 听

ETYMOLOGY | Radical: 耳
Archaic form was ear 耳 listening to mouth 口: hear/listen = listen to/comply with/obey

DATA

		PRONUNCIATION			
Radical (部首)	128: 耳	Pinyin:	tīng	J-音読み:	チョウ
Strokes	22 | 7	Wade-Giles:	t'ing	J-訓読み:	き・く
HSK	1	Cantonese:	ting1	Korean 音读:	청
Frequency	285	Minnan:	thiaⁿ	Korean 训读:	듣다
Big5	C5A5	Bopomofo:	ㄊㄧㄥ	K-eumdok:	cheong
Unihan	U+542C	JP-Onyomi:	chō	K-hundok:	deutda
Kangxi Dictionary	P970	JP-Kunyomi:	ki·ku	Vietnamese:	nghe

VARIANTS | 聴(J)

COMBINATIONS

聽到 - to hear, heard
聽說 - hearsay
好聽 - pleasant to hear
聽懂 - to understand
監聽 - to monitor
聽者 - listener

SAYINGS

俯首聽命 - obey submissively
危言聳聽 - alarmist talk
唯命是聽 - absolute obedience
姑妄聽之 - to hear is not to believe
揣骨聽聲 - incapable of appreciating art
洗耳恭聽 - to listen with respectful attention
耳聽八方 - extremely vigilant

HISTORICAL

甲骨文 (2000BC)	金文 (1000BC)	篆文 (200BC)	隸 (200AD)

FONTS

楷 行 草 宋
听 听 听 听

| 266AD Jing Dynasty Wang Xizhi | 778BC Tang Dynasty Liu Gongquan | 1280AD Yuan Dynasty Zhao Mengfu | 1829AD Ming Dynasty Dong Qichang |

THE GENIUS OF CHINESE CHARACTERS

STANDARD	SIMPLIFIED	MEANING
興	兴	• interest: 興趣; impulse: 詩興; daily life: 興居 • prosper: 興盛; to prevail: 興得開; rejuvenate: 興國 • fashionable: 時興

正: 丶 ㄧ ㄏ F 臼 臼 臼 臼 臼 臼 臼 臼 臼 興 興 興

简: 丶 ㄧㄧ ㅛ 丷 兴 兴

ETYMOLOGY

Radical: 臼 Originally hands 舁 lifting up an object 凡, later 口 was added underneath making it 同: raise/build = interest

DATA

			PRONUNCIATION			
Radical (部首)	134: 臼	Pinyin:	xìng	J-音読み:	コウ, キョウ
Strokes	16 | 6	Wade-Giles:	hsing	J-訓読み:	おこ·す
HSK	1	Cantonese:	hing1	Korean 音读:	흥
Frequency	531	Minnan:	hèng	Korean 训读:	일다, 일으키다
Big5	BFB3	Bopomofo:	ㄒㄧㄥ/ㄒㄧㄥˋ	K-eumdok:	heung
Unihan	U+5174	JP-Onyomi:	kō, kyō	K-hundok:	ilda, ireukida
Kangxi Dictionary	P1005	JP-Kunyomi:	oko·su	Vietnamese:	xing

VARIANTS

COMBINATIONS

高興 - happy
興奮 - excited
興致 - mood
興建 - to build
興盛 - to thrive

SAYINGS

偃武興文 - invest in education, not military
乘興而來 - come in with high spirits
意興索然 - have no interest in something
意興闌珊 - with flagging interest
方興日盛 - continuingly flourishing
天下興亡, 匹夫有責 - everyone bears responsibility for the prosperity of society

HISTORICAL

甲骨文 (2000BC)	金文 (1000BC)	篆文 (200BC)	隸 (200AD)
		興	兴

FONTS

楷 行 草 宋
兴 兴 兴 兴

266AD Jing Dynasty — Wang Xizhi
778BC Tang Dynasty — Liu Gongquan
1280AD Yuan Dynasty — Zhao Mengfu
1829AD Ming Dynasty — Dong Qichang

THE GENIUS OF CHINESE CHARACTERS

STANDARD	SIMPLIFIED	MEANING
習	习	• to practice: 練習; habit: 惡習 • to study: 學習; review: 温習 • customs: 習慣

正: 一 コ ヨ ヨ ヨヨ ヨヨ ヨヨ ヨヨ 習 習 習
简: 丁 ヨ 习

ETYMOLOGY
Radical: 羽
Birds are learning to fly in fine weather: practice/study = be good at

DATA
Radical (部首)	124: 羽
Strokes	11 | 3
HSK	1
Frequency	676
Big5	B2DF
Unihan	U+4E60
Kangxi Dictionary	P956

PRONUNCIATION
Pinyin:	xí	J-音読み:	シュウ
Wade-Giles:	hsi	J-訓読み:	なら·う
Cantonese:	jaap6	Korean 音读:	습
Minnan:	chiap̍	Korean 训读:	익히다
Bopomofo:	ㄒㄧˊ	K-eumdok:	seup
JP-Onyomi:	shū	K-hundok:	ikida
JP-Kunyomi:	nara·u	Vietnamese:	học hỏi

VARIANTS

COMBINATIONS
學習 - to study	自習 - individual study
練習 - practice	預習 - to preview
習慣 - habit	
演習 - exercise	
研習 - research	

SAYINGS
染風習俗 - to get into bad habits through long custom
循常習故 - follow convention and keep old customs

積習難改 - old habits are hard to change
習以爲常 - accustomed to
習以成俗 - to become accustomed to something through long practice

HISTORICAL

甲骨文 (2000BC)	金文 (1000BC)	篆文 (200BC)	隸 (200AD)
		習	習

FONTS
楷 行 草 宋
習 习 习 习

266AD
Jing Dynasty
Wang Xizhi

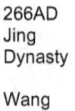
778BC
Tang Dynasty
Yan Zhenqing

1280AD
Yuan Dynasty
Zhao Mengfu

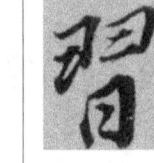
1829AD
Ming Dynasty
Dong Qichang

THE GENIUS OF CHINESE CHARACTERS

STANDARD	SIMPLIFIED	MEANING
語	语	• language: 言語; dialect: 土語; speech: 口語 • pronunciation: 語音; grammar: 語法 • means of communication: 手語; riddle: 謎語 • proverb: 俗語; words: 語辭

正: 丶 亠 圡 言 言 言 訁 訂 語 語 語 語 語
简: 丶 讠 讠 讠 访 语 语 语 语

ETYMOLOGY
Radical: 言
Speak 言 + 吾 (phonetic): talk, saying, language

DATA

Radical (部首)	149: 言	Pinyin:	yǔ	J-音読み:	ゴ
Strokes	14 | 9	Wade-Giles:	yü	J-訓読み:	かた·る
HSK	1	Cantonese:	yu5	Korean 音读:	어
Frequency	493	Minnan:	gí	Korean 训读:	말씀, 말
Big5	BB79	Bopomofo:	ㄩˇ	K-eumdok:	eo
Unihan	U+8BED	JP-Onyomi:	go	K-hundok:	malsseum, mal
Kangxi Dictionary	P1163	JP-Kunyomi:	kata·ru	Vietnamese:	ngôn ngữ

VARIANTS

COMBINATIONS

語言 - language
英語 - English
言語 - words
語氣 - tone
話語 - words
漢語 - Chinese language

語調 - intonation
用語 - term
外語 - foreign language

SAYINGS

一言兩語 - only a few words
一語不發 - not saying a word
一語道破 - point out the truth with one remark
七言八語 - gossip
冷言冷語 - sarcastic comment
竊竊私語 - to whisper
呢喃細語 - murmuring

HISTORICAL

甲骨文 (2000BC)	金文 (1000BC)	篆文 (200BC)	隸 (200AD)
		語	语

FONTS

楷 行 草 宋
语 语 语 语

266AD Jing Dynasty Wang Xizhi
778BC Tang Dynasty Guo Quan
1280AD Yuan Dynasty Zhao Mengfu
1829AD Ming Dynasty Dong Qichang

THE GENIUS OF CHINESE CHARACTERS

STANDARD	SIMPLIFIED	MEANING
腦	脑	• brain: 大腦; skull: 腦殼 • computer: 電腦 • head (leader): 首腦

| 正 | 丿 | 刀 | 月 | 月 | 肊 | 肊 | 肊 | 肊 | 朎 | 腦 | 腦 | 腦 |
| 簡 | 丿 | 刀 | 月 | 月 | 肊 | 肛 | 肛 | 胠 | 脑 | 脑 | | |

ETYMOLOGY
Radical: 月
In the Seal Character : person 人 + head 囟 with hair 巛 = brain/head

DATA

Radical (部首)	130: 肉		
Strokes	13 | 10		
HSK	1		
Frequency	646		
Big5	B8A3		
Unihan	U+8111		
Kangxi Dictionary	P988		

PRONUNCIATION

Pinyin:	nǎo	J-音読み:	ノウ, ドウ
Wade-Giles:	nao	J-訓読み:	N/A
Cantonese:	no5	Korean 音读:	뇌
Minnan:	náu	Korean 训读:	골, 뇌
Bopomofo:	ㄋㄠˇ	K-eumdok:	noe
JP-Onyomi:	nō, dō	K-hundok:	gol, noe
JP-Kunyomi:	N/A	Vietnamese:	óc

VARIANTS | 脳(J)

COMBINATIONS

電腦 - computer
頭腦 - mind
腦門 - forehead
洗腦 - to brainwash
首腦 - leader

SAYINGS

伸頭探腦 - crane one's neck to peep
虎頭虎腦 - looking honest and strong
愣頭愣腦 - rash and impetuous
鬼頭鬼腦 - sneaky and furtive

頭昏腦脹 - dizzy, giddy

HISTORICAL

甲骨文 (2000BC)	金文 (1000BC)	篆文 (200BC)	隸 (200AD)
		𦜝	腦

FONTS

楷	行	草	宋
脑	脑	脑	脑

THE GENIUS OF CHINESE CHARACTERS

STANDARD	SIMPLIFIED	MEANING
店	店	• inn: 客店; shop: 書店; store: 店鋪 • hotel: 酒店; salesperson: 店員

正: 丶 亠 广 广 庐 庐 店 店
简: 丶 亠 广 广 庐 庐 店 店

ETYMOLOGY: Radical: 广 In the Seal Character: 土 earthy + occupy 占 (phonetic): counter made of clay = shop/store

DATA

- Radical (部首): 53: 广
- Strokes: 8 | 8
- HSK: 1
- Frequency: 1041
- Big5: A9B1
- Unihan: U+5E97
- Kangxi Dictionary: P344

PRONUNCIATION

- Pinyin: diàn
- Wade-Giles: tien
- Cantonese: dim3
- Minnan: tiàm
- Bopomofo: ㄉㄧㄢˋ
- JP-Onyomi: ten
- JP-Kunyomi: mise
- J-音読み: テン
- J-訓読み: みせ
- Korean 音读: 점
- Korean 训读: 가게, 상점
- K-eumdok: jeom
- K-hundok: gage, sangjeom
- Vietnamese: cửa tiệm

VARIANTS

COMBINATIONS

- 飯店 - restaurant
- 商店 - store
- 花店 - flower shop
- 書店 - bookstore
- 店鋪 - shop
- 店主 - shop owner
- 店堂 - showroom

SAYINGS

n/a

HISTORICAL

- 甲骨文 (2000BC)
- 金文 (1000BC)
- 篆文 (200BC)
- 隸 (200AD) 店

FONTS

楷 店　行 店　草 店　宋 店

- 1051BC Song Dynasty, Su Shi
- 1280AD Yuan Dynasty, Zhao Mengfu
- 1829AD Ming Dynasty, Tang Yin
- 1829AD Ming Dynasty, Wen Zhengming

THE GENIUS OF CHINESE CHARACTERS

STANDARD	SIMPLIFIED	MEANING
寫	写	• to write: 寫字; compose: 寫稿 • draw: 寫照; treasurer: 寫賬

正 ` ｀ ⺌ 宀 宀 宀 宀 宀 宀 宀 冟 宁 寫 寫 寫
寫 寫

简 ` 宀 冖 写 写

ETYMOLOGY Radical: 宀 Structure/building 宀 + 舃 (phonetic): moved articles into the house, transform, transcribe/copy = draw/write

DATA

Radical (部首)	40: 宀
Strokes	15 | 5
HSK	1
Frequency	448
Big5	BC67
Unihan	U+5199
Kangxi Dictionary	P292

PRONUNCIATION

Pinyin:	xiě
Wade-Giles:	hsieh
Cantonese:	se2
Minnan:	siá
Bopomofo:	ㄒㄧㄝˇ
JP-Onyomi:	sha
JP-Kunyomi:	utsu·su

J-音読み:	シャ
J-訓読み:	うつ·す
Korean 音读:	사
Korean 训读:	베끼다
K-eumdok:	sa
K-hundok:	bekkida
Vietnamese:	viết

VARIANTS 写(J)

COMBINATIONS

寫信 - to write a letter
描寫 - to describe
寫給 - write to somebody
書寫 - to write
寫完 - to finish writing

寫照 - portrayal
寫字 - to write characters

SAYINGS

輕描淡寫 - to play down

HISTORICAL

甲骨文 (2000BC)	金文 (1000BC)	篆文 (200BC)	隸 (200AD)
		寫	寫

FONTS

楷	行	草	宋
寫	寫	写	寫

266AD Jing Dynasty Wang Xizhi

778BC Tang Dynasty Liu Gongquan

1280AD Yuan Dynasty Zhao Mengfu

1829AD Ming Dynasty Dong Qichang

THE GENIUS OF Chinese CHARACTERS

STANDARD	SIMPLIFIED	MEANING
喜	喜	• to congratulate: 賀喜; to like: 喜歡 • expecting (a child): 有喜; announce good news: 報喜 • gratifying: 可喜; happy: 喜色; to love: 喜愛 • celebrate: 喜慶; comedy: 喜劇; joy: 喜悅

正 一 十 士 吉 吉 吉 吉 吉 壴 壴 喜 喜
简 一 十 士 吉 吉 吉 吉 吉 壴 壴 喜 喜

ETYMOLOGY | Radical: 口 People play music when they are happy 壴, laughter came from the mouth 口 = happy/enjoy

DATA
- Radical (部首): 30: 口
- Strokes: 12 | 12
- HSK: 1
- Frequency: 668
- Big5: B3DF
- Unihan: U+559C
- Kangxi Dictionary: P199

PRONUNCIATION
- Pinyin: xǐ
- Wade-Giles: hsi
- Cantonese: hei3
- Minnan: hí
- Bopomofo: ㄒㄧˇ
- JP-Onyomi: ki
- JP-Kunyomi: yoroko·bu
- J-音読み: キ
- J-訓読み: よろこ·ぶ
- Korean 音读: 희
- Korean 训读: 기쁘다
- K-eumdok: hi
- K-hundok: gippeuda
- Vietnamese: giống

VARIANTS | 憙

COMBINATIONS
- 喜歡 - to be fond of
- 歡喜 - to like
- 喜愛 - to love
- 喜悅 - joyous
- 驚喜 - nice surprise
- 喜劇 - comedy
- 喜好 - to like
- 喜車 - wedding car
- 嬉笑 - to laugh

SAYINGS
- 喜上眉梢 - look very happy
- 喜不自勝 - unable to contain one's joy
- 喜新厭舊 - fickle in one's affection
- 歡天喜地 - delighted
- 喜出望外 - overjoyed at the turn of event
- 喜怒無常 - moody
- 喜極而泣 - crying tears of joy
- 喜聞樂見 - love to hear and see to one's liking

HISTORICAL

甲骨文 (2000BC)	金文 (1000BC)	篆文 (200BC)	隸 (200AD)
		喜	喜

FONTS
楷 行 草 宋
喜 喜 喜 喜

- 266AD Jing Dynasty Wang Xizhi
- 778BC Tang Dynasty Liu Gongquan
- 1280AD Yuan Dynasty Zhao Mengfu
- 1829AD Ming Dynasty Dong Qichang

THE GENIUS OF CHINESE CHARACTERS

STANDARD	SIMPLIFIED	MEANING
讀	读	• to study: 讀書; to read: 默讀 • to pronounce: 讀法; attend school: 寄讀 • reader: 讀者

正: 丶 丶 亠 言 言 言 訁 訪 讀 讀 讀 讀
讀 讀 讀 讀 讀 讀 讀 讀 讀

简: 丶 讠 订 讣 讠 讠 读 读 读

ETYMOLOGY

Radical: 言

Speak 言 + 賣 (phonetic): read/pronounce = analysis/understand

DATA

Radical (部首)	149: 言
Strokes	22 | 10
HSK	1
Frequency	752
Big5	C5AA
Unihan	U+8BFB
Kangxi Dictionary	P1185

PRONUNCIATION

Pinyin:	dú	J-音読み:	トク, トウ
Wade-Giles:	tou	J-訓読み:	よ·む
Cantonese:	duk6	Korean 音读:	독
Minnan:	hí	Korean 训读:	읽다
Bopomofo:	ㄉㄨˊ	K-eumdok:	dok
JP-Onyomi:	toku, tō	K-hundok:	ikda
JP-Kunyomi:	yo·mu	Vietnamese:	đọc

VARIANTS | 読(J)

COMBINATIONS

讀書 - to read a book
讀者 - reader
解讀 - to decode
就讀 - to go to school
攻讀 - to major
朗讀 - to read aloud

讀懂 - to read and understand
導讀 - guide

SAYINGS

百讀不厭 - worth reading a hundred times
飽讀詩書 - having read plenty of books; well-read

HISTORICAL

甲骨文 (2000BC)	金文 (1000BC)	篆文 (200BC)	隸 (200AD)
		讀	读

FONTS

楷 行 草 宋

读 读 读 读 读

266AD Jing Dynasty — Wang Xizhi
778BC Tang Dynasty — Liu Gongquan
1280AD Yuan Dynasty — Zhao Mengfu
1829AD Ming Dynasty — Dong Qichang

THE GENIUS OF CHINESE CHARACTERS

STANDARD	SIMPLIFIED	MEANING
館	馆	• teahouse: 茶館; restaurant: 飯館 • accommodation: 旅館; embassy: 使館 • museum: 博物館

正: 丿 亽 今 今 今 食 食 食 食 飠 飠 飠 館 館 館

简: 丿 亽 饣 饣 饣 饣 饣 饣 馆 馆

ETYMOLOGY: Radical: 食 Provide food 食 + an official building 官 (phonetic): a place to meet guests = hotel/government office

DATA

		PRONUNCIATION			
Radical (部首)	184: 食	Pinyin:	guǎn	J-音読み:	カン
Strokes	16 | 11	Wade-Giles:	kuan	J-訓読み:	やかた
HSK	1	Cantonese:	goon2	Korean 音读:	관
Frequency	1011	Minnan:	kóan	Korean 训读:	집, 가게
Big5	C05D	Bopomofo:	ㄍㄨㄢˇ	K-eumdok:	gwan
Unihan	U+9986	JP-Onyomi:	kan	K-hundok:	jip, gage
Kangxi Dictionary	P1422	JP-Kunyomi:	yakata	Vietnamese:	gian hàng

VARIANTS

COMBINATIONS

使館 - embassy
賓館 - guesthouse
旅館 - hotel
餐館 - restaurant
飯館 - restaurant
茶館 - teahouse

酒館 - wine shop
領館 - consulate

SAYINGS: n/a

HISTORICAL

甲骨文 (2000BC)	金文 (1000BC)	篆文 (200BC)	隸 (200AD)
		館	館

FONTS: 楷 行 草 宋 — 馆 馆 馆 馆

266AD Jing Dynasty Wang Xizhi
778BC Tang Dynasty Yan Zhenqing
1280AD Yuan Dynasty Zhao Mengfu
1829AD Ming Dynasty Dong Qichang

THE GENIUS OF CHINESE CHARACTERS

STANDARD	SIMPLIFIED	MEANING
歡	欢	• happy: 歡忭; joyous: 歡樂; cheer: 歡呼 • to enjoy: 歡喜; sweatheart: 所歡 • rejoicing: 歡欣

正: 一 ナ 艹 艹 艹 艹 苗 苗 苗 苜 萑 萑 萑 萑 萑 萑 雚 雚 歡 歡 歡

简: フ 又 又 欢 欢 欢

ETYMOLOGY

Radical: 欠

Open mouth 欠 + 雚 (phonetic): open mouth and laugh = happy

DATA

Radical (部首)	76: 欠
Strokes	21 | 6
HSK	1
Frequency	685
Big5	C577
Unihan	U+6B22
Kangxi Dictionary	P573

PRONUNCIATION

Pinyin:	huān
Wade-Giles:	huan
Cantonese:	foon1
Minnan:	hoan
Bopomofo:	ㄏㄨㄢ
JP-Onyomi:	kan
JP-Kunyomi:	yoroko·bu

J-音読み:	カン
J-訓読み:	よろこ·ぶ
Korean 音读:	환
Korean 训读:	기쁘다
K-eumdok:	hwan
K-hundok:	gippeuda
Vietnamese:	huân

VARIANTS | 懽(J)

COMBINATIONS

喜歡 - to like
歡迎 - to welcome
歡喜 - to like
歡樂 - gladness
歡呼 - to cheer for
聯歡 - celebration

歡快 - lively
歡笑 - to laugh happily
歡心 - favor
歡送 - to send off
狂歡 - carnival

SAYINGS

千歡萬喜 - extremely happy
另結新歡 - to find a new love
尋歡作樂 - pleasure seeking
歡天喜地 - 強顏歡笑 - very happy
悒悒不歡 - depressed and worrisome
悲歡離合 - sorrows and joys, departures and reunions the vicissitudes of life

HISTORICAL

甲骨文 (2000BC)	金文 (1000BC)	篆文 (200BC)	隸 (200AD)
		雚	欢

FONTS

楷	行	草	宋
欢	欢	欢	欢

 266AD Jing Dynasty Wang Xizhi

 778BC Tang Dynasty Yan Zhenqing

 1280AD Yuan Dynasty Zhao Mengfu

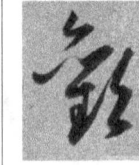 1829AD Ming Dynasty Dong Qichang

THE GENIUS OF Chinese Characters

STANDARD	SIMPLIFIED	MEANING
怎	怎	• how: 怎麼 • why: 怎樣 • how good: 怎好 • how could: 怎得

正: 丿 一 午 乍 乍 乍 怎 怎 怎
简: 丿 一 午 乍 乍 乍 怎 怎 怎

ETYMOLOGY

Radical: 心

Heart 心 + 乍 (phonetic): an interrogative pronoun = how/what/why

DATA

Radical (部首)	61: 心		
Strokes	9 | 9		
HSK	1		
Frequency	382		
Big5	ABE7		
Unihan	U+600E		
Kangxi Dictionary	P379		

PRONUNCIATION

Pinyin:	zěn	J-音読み:	シン, ソ
Wade-Giles:	tsê	J-訓読み:	いか・で
Cantonese:	jam5	Korean 音读:	吾
Minnan:	cháiⁿ	Korean 训读:	어찌
Bopomofo:	ㄗㄣˇ	K-eumdok:	jeum
JP-Onyomi:	shin, so	K-hundok:	eojji
JP-Kunyomi:	ika·de	Vietnamese:	làm sao

VARIANTS

COMBINATIONS

怎麼 - how/what/why
怎樣 - how/why
怎能 - how can
怎生 - how/why
怎麼着 - whatever

怎麼樣 - how are things?

SAYINGS

n/a

HISTORICAL

甲骨文 (2000BC)	金文 (1000BC)	篆文 (200BC)	隸 (200AD)

FONTS

楷	行	草	宋
怎	怎	怎	怎

1829AD Ming Dynasty Tang Yin

THE GENIUS OF Chinese CHARACTERS

STANDARD	SIMPLIFIED	MEANING
杯	杯	• cup: 杯子 • (measure word for cups/drinks): 一杯茶

| 正 | 一 | 十 | 才 | 木 | 札 | 杁 | 杯 | 杯 |
| 简 | 一 | 十 | 才 | 木 | 札 | 杁 | 杯 | 杯 |

ETYMOLOGY

Radical: 木
Wood 木 + 不 (phonetic): cup/glass = a cup of

DATA

Radical (部首)   75: 木
Strokes   8 | 8
HSK   1
Frequency   1396
Big5   AA4D
Unihan   U+676F
Kangxi Dictionary P513

PRONUNCIATION

Pinyin: bēi
Wade-Giles: pei
Cantonese: booi1
Minnan: poe
Bopomofo: ㄅㄟ
JP-Onyomi: hai
JP-Kunyomi: sakazuki

J-音読み: ハイ
J-訓読み: さかずき
Korean 音读: 배
Korean 训读: 잔
K-eumdok: bae
K-hundok: jan
Vietnamese: cốc

VARIANTS | 盃, 桮

COMBINATIONS

幹杯 - cheers
酒杯 - wine glass
杯賽 - prize cup
茶杯 - teacup
獎杯 - trophy

SAYINGS

杯弓蛇影 - a false alarm
杯盤狼籍 - cups and dishes strewn everywhere
杯水車薪 - a drop in the bucket
殘杯冷炙 - dinner leftovers

好酒貪杯 - be fond of the bottle

HISTORICAL

甲骨文 (2000BC) | 金文 (1000BC) | 篆文 (200BC) | 隸 (200AD)

FONTS

楷　行　草　宋

266AD Jing Dynasty Wang Xizhi
778BC Tang Dynasty Yan Zhenqing
1280AD Yuan Dynasty Zhao Mengfu
1829AD Ming Dynasty Tang Yin

THE GENIUS OF CHINESE CHARACTERS

STANDARD	SIMPLIFIED	MEANING
鐘	钟	• bell: 打鐘 • clock: 時鐘 • time of the day: 鐘點

正: 丿 亻 仒 亼 仐 仐 仐 仐 金 鈩 鈩 鈩 鈩
鈩 鈩 鈩 鈩 鐘 鐘 鐘

简: 丿 亻 仒 仒 钅 钅 钅 钅 钟

ETYMOLOGY

Radical: 金
Metal 金 + 童 (phonetic): bell made of copper

DATA

Radical (部首)	167: 金
Strokes	20 | 9
HSK	1
Frequency	905
Big5	C4C1
Unihan	U+949F
Kangxi Dictionary	P1323

PRONUNCIATION

Pinyin:	zhōng
Wade-Giles:	chung
Cantonese:	jung1
Minnan:	cheng
Bopomofo:	ㄓㄨㄥ
JP-Onyomi:	shō
JP-Kunyomi:	kane

J-音読み:	ショウ
J-訓読み:	かね
Korean 音读:	종
Korean 训读:	쇠북
K-eumdok:	jong
K-hundok:	soebuk
Vietnamese:	chuông

VARIANTS

COMBINATIONS

分鐘 - minute
鐘頭 - hour
點鐘 - o'clock
鐘表 - clock

SAYINGS

老態龍鐘 - doddering, old and clumsy
暮鼓晨鐘 - daily call to religious life
一見鐘情 - fall in love at first sight
鐘鼓之色 - one's expression when enjoying music

HISTORICAL

甲骨文 (2000BC)	金文 (1000BC)	篆文 (200BC)	隸 (200AD)
		鐘	钟

FONTS

楷	行	草	宋
钟	钟	钟	钟

266AD Jing Dynasty Wang Xizhi
778BC Tang Dynasty Liu Gongquan
1280AD Yuan Dynasty Zhao Mengfu
1829AD Ming Dynasty Dong Qichang

THE GENIUS OF CHINESE CHARACTERS

STANDARD	SIMPLIFIED	MEANING
呢	呢	• woolen material: 呢子 • murmur: 呢喃 • (emphasis in question): 行呢

Stroke order (正): 丨 口 口 口⁷ 口⁷ 吖 呢 呢
Stroke order (简): 丨 口 口 口⁷ 口⁷ 吖 呢 呢

ETYMOLOGY: Radical: 口 Mouth 口 + 尼 (phonetic): whisper. 呢 is borrowed as a mood word at the end of interrogative sentences

DATA

Radical (部首)	30: 口
Strokes	8 | 8
HSK	1
Frequency	383
Big5	A94F
Unihan	U+5462
Kangxi Dictionary	P181

PRONUNCIATION

Pinyin:	ne
Wade-Giles:	nê
Cantonese:	ni1
Minnan:	ni
Bopomofo:	ㄋㄧˊ/ㄋㄜ˙
JP-Onyomi:	ji, ni
JP-Kunyomi:	N/A
J-音読み:	ジ, ニ
J-訓読み:	N/A
Korean 音读:	니, 이
Korean 训读:	소곤거리다
K-eumdok:	ni, i
K-hundok:	sogongeorida
Vietnamese:	làm thế nào về

VARIANTS: 詑

COMBINATIONS

呢喃 - twittering
人字呢 - Chevron
军服呢 - uniform material
华达呢 - gabardine

SAYINGS

n/a

HISTORICAL

甲骨文 (2000BC)	金文 (1000BC)	篆文 (200BC)	隸 (200AD)
			呢

FONTS

楷	行	草	宋
呢	呢	呢	呢

THE GENIUS OF CHINESE CHARACTERS

STANDARD	SIMPLIFIED	MEANING
租	租	• to rent: 房租 • taxes: 租稅 • sublease: 轉租

Stroke order (正): 一 二 千 千 禾 利 租 租 租 租
Stroke order (简): 一 二 千 千 禾 利 租 租 租 租

ETYMOLOGY

Radical: 禾

Grain 禾 + 且 (phonetic): in ancient China, grain is a part of revenue = tax/rent

DATA

- Radical (部首): 115: 禾
- Strokes: 10 | 10
- HSK: 1
- Frequency: 1397
- Big5: AFB2
- Unihan: U+79DF
- Kangxi Dictionary: P851

PRONUNCIATION

- Pinyin: zū
- Wade-Giles: tsu
- Cantonese: jo1
- Minnan: cho
- Bopomofo: ㄗㄨ
- JP-Onyomi: so
- JP-Kunyomi: mitsu·gi
- J-音読み: ソ
- J-訓読み: みつ·ぎ
- Korean 音读: 조
- Korean 训读: 조세, 빌리다
- K-eumdok: jo
- K-hundok: jose, billida
- Vietnamese: thuê

VARIANTS

COMBINATIONS

- 房租 - house rent
- 租界 - concession
- 月租 - monthly rent
- 租戶 - tenant
- 交付租金 - pay rent

SAYINGS

n/a

HISTORICAL

甲骨文 (2000BC)	金文 (1000BC)	篆文 (200BC)	隸 (200AD)
		租	租

FONTS

楷	行	草	宋
租	租	租	租

THE GENIUS OF CHINESE CHARACTERS

STANDARD	SIMPLIFIED	MEANING
塊	块	• piece: 一塊布 • a bit: 大塊 • standing alone: 塊然

正: 一 十 土 土' 扩 圹 坮 坰 坢 塊 塊 塊
简: 一 十 土 圠 垆 坎 块

ETYMOLOGY

Radical: 土
Soil 土 + 鬼 (phonetic): lumps of soil = piece/chunk

DATA

		PRONUNCIATION			
Radical (部首)	32: 土	Pinyin:	kuài	J-音読み:	カイ
Strokes	12 | 7	Wade-Giles:	k'uai	J-訓読み:	かたまり
HSK	1	Cantonese:	faai3	Korean 音读:	괴
Frequency	793	Minnan:	tè	Korean 训读:	덩어리
Big5	B6F4	Bopomofo:	ㄎㄨㄞˋ	K-eumdok:	goe
Unihan	U+5757	JP-Onyomi:	kai	K-hundok:	deongeori
Kangxi Dictionary	P235	JP-Kunyomi:	katamari	Vietnamese:	cái

VARIANTS | 凷

COMBINATIONS

板塊 - plate, tectonic plates
石塊 - rock
地塊 - land parcel
冰塊 - ice cube

磚塊 - brick or tiles

SAYINGS

鐵板一塊 - someone is so stuck in his own way that he will not ever change, like a stick in the mud

HISTORICAL

甲骨文 (2000BC)	金文 (1000BC)	篆文 (200BC)	隸 (200AD)
		塊	块

FONTS

楷 行 草 宋
块 块 块 块

778BC
Tang Dynasty
Liu Gongquan

778BC
Tang Dynasty
Lu Jianzhi

1051BC
Song Dynasty
Mi Fu

1051BC
Song Dynasty
Su Shi

THE GENIUS OF Chinese Characters

STANDARD	SIMPLIFIED	MEANING
誰	谁	• who: 誰說 • anyone: 誰也會 • what (person): 誰人

正: 丶 亠 亠 言 言 言 訁 訁 訁 訁 誰 誰
誰 誰
简: 丶 讠 讠 讠 讠 讠 讠 讠 谁 谁

ETYMOLOGY

Radical: 言
Speak 言 + 隹 (phonetic): who, an interrogative pronoun that refers to people

DATA

Radical (部首)	149: 言	Pinyin:	shuí	J-音読み:	スイ
Strokes	15 | 10	Wade-Giles:	shei	J-訓読み:	だれ
HSK	1	Cantonese:	sui6	Korean 音读:	수
Frequency	648	Minnan:	chiâ	Korean 训读:	누구, 무엇
Big5	BDD6	Bopomofo:	ㄕㄨㄟˊㄕㄟˊ	K-eumdok:	su
Unihan	U+8C01	JP-Onyomi:	sui	K-hundok:	nugu, mueot
Kangxi Dictionary	P1165	JP-Kunyomi:	dare	Vietnamese:	who

VARIANTS

COMBINATIONS

誰知 - who knows
愛誰誰 - whatever
誰人 - which person

SAYINGS

鹿死誰手 - whoever kills the deer (will be victorious)
莫敢誰何 - nobody dare (stop him)
誰家竈內無烟 - every family has its problems
捨我其誰 - Who but myself can do it?
人非聖賢, 誰能無過 - no one is a saint, who doesn't make mistakes (we all make mistakes)

HISTORICAL

甲骨文 (2000BC)	金文 (1000BC)	篆文 (200BC)	隸 (200AD)

FONTS

楷 行 草 宋

266AD Jing Dynasty Wang Xizhi
778BC Tang Dynasty Liu Gongquan
1280AD Yuan Dynasty Zhao Mengfu
1829AD Ming Dynasty Dong Qichang

171

THE GENIUS OF Chinese Characters

STANDARD	SIMPLIFIED	MEANING
嗎	吗	• (yes/no question particle): 是你嗎 • morphine: 嗎啡

正 丨 冂 口 叮 吓 吁 吁 吁 嗎 嗎 嗎 嗎 嗎
简 丨 冂 口 叮 吗 吗

ETYMOLOGY: Radical: 口 Mouth 口 + 馬(phonetic): scold. Borrowed as a mood word at the end of interrogative sentences.

DATA

Radical (部首)	30: 口	Pinyin:	ma	J-音読み:	バ
Strokes	13 | 6	Wade-Giles:	ma	J-訓読み:	N/A
HSK	1	Cantonese:	ma3	Korean 音读:	마
Frequency	453	Minnan:	mô	Korean 训读:	꾸짖다
Big5	B6DC	Bopomofo:	ㄇㄚˊ/ㄇㄚˇ	K-eumdok:	ma
Unihan	U+5417	JP-Onyomi:	ba	K-hundok:	kkujitda
Kangxi Dictionary	P202	JP-Kunyomi:	N/A	Vietnamese:	bạn

VARIANTS

COMBINATIONS

不是嗎? - isn't that so?
可不是嗎 - exactly

SAYINGS

n/a

HISTORICAL

甲骨文 (2000BC)	(1000BC)	篆文 (200BC)	隸 (200AD)
			吗

FONTS

楷	行	草	宋
吗	吗	吗	吗

THE GENIUS OF Chinese CHARACTERS

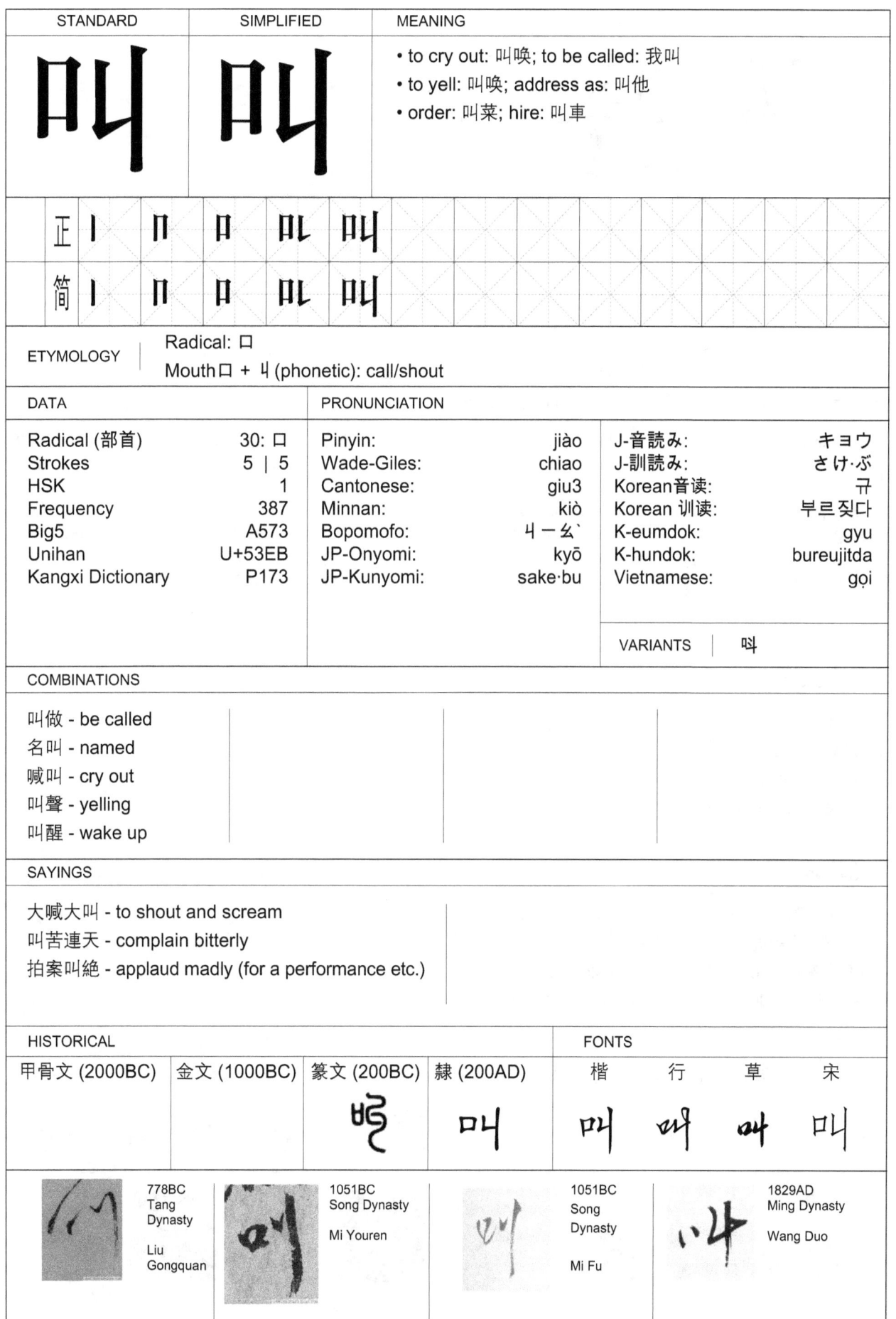

STANDARD	SIMPLIFIED	MEANING
叫	叫	• to cry out: 叫唤; to be called: 我叫 • to yell: 叫唤; address as: 叫他 • order: 叫菜; hire: 叫車

正 丨 冂 口 叫 叫
简 丨 冂 口 叫 叫

ETYMOLOGY
Radical: 口
Mouth 口 + 丩 (phonetic): call/shout

DATA
- Radical (部首): 30: 口
- Strokes: 5 | 5
- HSK: 1
- Frequency: 387
- Big5: A573
- Unihan: U+53EB
- Kangxi Dictionary: P173

PRONUNCIATION
- Pinyin: jiào
- Wade-Giles: chiao
- Cantonese: giu3
- Minnan: kiò
- Bopomofo: ㄐ一ㄠˋ
- JP-Onyomi: kyō
- JP-Kunyomi: sake·bu
- J-音読み: キョウ
- J-訓読み: さけ・ぶ
- Korean 音读: 규
- Korean 训读: 부르짖다
- K-eumdok: gyu
- K-hundok: bureujitda
- Vietnamese: gọi

VARIANTS | 呌

COMBINATIONS
叫做 - be called
名叫 - named
喊叫 - cry out
叫聲 - yelling
叫醒 - wake up

SAYINGS
大喊大叫 - to shout and scream
叫苦連天 - complain bitterly
拍案叫絕 - applaud madly (for a performance etc.)

HISTORICAL

甲骨文 (2000BC)　金文 (1000BC)　篆文 (200BC)　隸 (200AD)

FONTS

楷　行　草　宋

778BC Tang Dynasty Liu Gongquan
1051BC Song Dynasty Mi Youren
1051BC Song Dynasty Mi Fu
1829AD Ming Dynasty Wang Duo

THE GENIUS OF CHINESE CHARACTERS

STANDARD	SIMPLIFIED	MEANING
亮	亮	• bright: 光亮 • transparent: 亮藍 • brightness: 亮度 • clear (voice): 清亮

| 正 | 丶 | 亠 | 广 | 方 | 古 | 声 | 亭 | 亨 | 亮 |
| 簡 | 丶 | 亠 | 广 | 方 | 古 | 声 | 亭 | 亨 | 亮 |

ETYMOLOGY

Radical: 亠

儿(people) replaced 口 under 高(high) : standing on a high place → well-lit → bright/light

DATA

- Radical (部首): 8: 亠
- Strokes: 9 | 9
- HSK: 1
- Frequency: 840
- Big5: AB47
- Unihan: U+4EAE
- Kangxi Dictionary: P89

PRONUNCIATION

- Pinyin: liàng
- Wade-Giles: liang
- Cantonese: leung4
- Minnan: liāng
- Bopomofo: ㄌㄧㄤˋ
- JP-Onyomi: ryō
- JP-Kunyomi: suke
- J-音読み: リョウ
- J-訓読み: すけ
- Korean 音读: 량, 양
- Korean 训读: 밝다, 환하다
- K-eumdok: ryang, yang
- K-hundok: bakda, hwanhada
- Vietnamese: sáng

VARIANTS | 倞

COMBINATIONS

- 漂亮 - pretty
- 月亮 - moon
- 明亮 - bright
- 響亮 - loud and clear
- 發亮 - shine

SAYINGS

- 事後諸葛亮 - good hindsight
- 打開天窗說亮話 - speak frankly
- 高風亮節 - noble character and sterling integrity
- 鮮眉亮眼 - description of a beautiful female

HISTORICAL

甲骨文 (2000BC)	金文 (1000BC)	篆文 (200BC)	隸 (200AD)
			亮

FONTS

楷	行	草	宋
亮	亮	亮	亮

- 778BC Tang Dynasty — Lu Jianzhi
- 778BC Tang Dynasty — Liu Zhengfu
- 1280AD Yuan Dynasty — Zhao Mengfu
- 1829AD Ming Dynasty — Dong Qichang

THE GENIUS OF Chinese Characters

STANDARD	SIMPLIFIED	MEANING
哪	哪	• where: 哪裏 • which: 哪個

正	丨	丨丨	口	叮	吋	吋	吶	哪	哪
简	丨	丨丨	口	叮	吋	吋	吶	哪	哪

ETYMOLOGY — Radical: 口 Mouth口 + 那 (phonetic): mimetic word, the sound of a wizard performing rituals. "Which" is a borrowed meaning.

DATA

Radical (部首)	30: 口
Strokes	9 | 9
HSK	
Frequency	652
Big5	ADFE
Unihan	U+54EA
Kangxi Dictionary	P190

PRONUNCIATION

Pinyin:	nǎ
Wade-Giles:	na
Cantonese:	na4
Minnan:	ná
Bopomofo:	ㄋㄚˇ/ㄋㄨㄛˊ
JP-Onyomi:	da, na
JP-Kunyomi:	N/A

J-音読み:	ダ, ナ
J-訓読み:	N/A
Korean 音读:	나
Korean 训读:	어찌, 어느
K-eumdok:	na
K-hundok:	eojji, eoneu
Vietnamese:	ở đâu

VARIANTS	那, 郍

COMBINATIONS

哪裏 - where?
哪個 - who?
哪怕 - even though
哪些 - which ones?

SAYINGS

n/a

HISTORICAL

甲骨文 (2000BC)	金文 (1000BC)	篆文 (200BC)	隸 (200AD)
			哪

FONTS

楷	行	草	宋
哪	哪	哪	哪

THE GENIUS OF CHINESE CHARACTERS

STANDARD	SIMPLIFIED	MEANING
媽	妈	• mother: 媽媽 • maidservant: 老媽子

正: 丨 𡿨 女 女 𡜁 𡜂 妒 妒 媽 媽 媽 媽 媽
简: 丨 𡿨 女 女 𡜁 妈 妈

ETYMOLOGY
Radical: 女
Women 女 + 馬(phonetic): mother

DATA
		PRONUNCIATION			
Radical (部首)	38: 女	Pinyin:	mā	J-音読み:	ボ, モ
Strokes	13 | 6	Wade-Giles:	ma	J-訓読み:	はは
HSK	1	Cantonese:	ma1	Korean 音读:	마, 모
Frequency	750	Minnan:	má	Korean 训读:	어머니, 할머니
Big5	B6FD	Bopomofo:	ㄇㄚ	K-eumdok:	ma, mo
Unihan	U+5988	JP-Onyomi:	bo, mo	K-hundok:	eomeoni, halmeoni
Kangxi Dictionary	P268	JP-Kunyomi:	haha	Vietnamese:	mẹ

VARIANTS

COMBINATIONS
媽媽 - mother
爸媽 - parents
後媽 - stepmother
大媽 - father's elder brother's wife
舅媽 - maternal uncle's wife
姑媽 - father's elder sister
姨媽 - mother's elder sister

SAYINGS
婆婆媽媽 - overly careful, fastidious

HISTORICAL
甲骨文 (2000BC)	金文 (1000BC)	篆文 (200BC)	隸 (200AD)

FONTS
楷	行	草	宋
妈	妈	妈	妈	妈

THE GENIUS OF Chinese CHARACTERS

STANDARD	SIMPLIFIED	MEANING
爸	爸	• father: 爸爸

| 正 | ノ | 八 | 父 | 父 | 줏 | 爷 | 爷 | 爸 |
| 简 | ノ | 八 | 父 | 父 | 줏 | 爷 | 爷 | 爸 |

ETYMOLOGY
Radical: 父
Father 父 + 巴 (phonetic): father

DATA
- Radical (部首): 88: 父
- Strokes: 8 | 8
- HSK: 1
- Frequency: 1050
- Big5: AAA8
- Unihan: U+7238
- Kangxi Dictionary: P690

PRONUNCIATION
- Pinyin: bà
- Wade-Giles: pa
- Cantonese: ba1
- Minnan: pā
- Bopomofo: ㄅㄚˋ
- JP-Onyomi: ha, ba
- JP-Kunyomi: N/A

- J-音読み: ハ, バ
- J-訓読み: N/A
- Korean 音读: 파
- Korean 训读: 아버지, 아빠
- K-eumdok: pa
- K-hundok: abeoji, appa
- Vietnamese: cha

VARIANTS

COMBINATIONS
- 爸爸 - father
- 老爸 - daddy
- 後爸 - stepfather
- 親爸 - biological father

SAYINGS
n/a

HISTORICAL
甲骨文 (2000BC)	金文 (1000BC)	篆文 (200BC)	隸 (200AD)
			爸

FONTS
楷	行	草	宋
爸	爸	爸	爸

THE GENIUS OF Chinese CHARACTERS

STANDARD	SIMPLIFIED	MEANING
坐	坐	• to sit: 坐下; go to: 坐堂 • ride in: 坐車; a seat: 坐位 • be in labor (woman): 坐蓐 • a shopkeeper: 坐賈

| 正 | ノ | 人 | 𠂉 | 从 | 丛 | 坐 | 坐 |
| 简 | ノ | 人 | 𠂉 | 从 | 丛 | 坐 | 坐 |

ETYMOLOGY
Radical: 土
Two people 人 sitting face to face on a mound 土: sit → be/be in

DATA

		PRONUNCIATION			
Radical (部首)	32: 土	Pinyin:	zuò	J-音読み:	ザ
Strokes	7 | 7	Wade-Giles:	tso	J-訓読み:	すわ·る
HSK	1	Cantonese:	choh5	Korean 音读:	좌
Frequency	611	Minnan:	chē	Korean 训读:	앉다
Big5	A7A4	Bopomofo:	ㄗㄨㄛˋ	K-eumdok:	jwa
Unihan	U+5750	JP-Onyomi:	za	K-hundok:	anda
Kangxi Dictionary	P225	JP-Kunyomi:	suwa·ru	Vietnamese:	ngồi

VARIANTS | 座

COMBINATIONS

坐下 - sit down
乘坐 - ride
坐落 - located
坐車 - to take the car
坐標 - coordinate

SAYINGS

坐立不安 - agitated when sitting or standing/restless
坐不安席 - to sit but to not be able to relax
席地而坐 - to sit on the floor

安坐而食 - to sponge on somebody
坐井觀天 - to view the sky from the bottom of a well
坐失良機 - to sit and waste a good opportunity
坐北朝南 - to face south with the back to the north

HISTORICAL

甲骨文 (2000BC)	金文 (1000BC)	篆文 (200BC)	隸 (200AD)
		坐	坐

FONTS

楷	行	草	宋
坐	坐	坐	坐

266AD Jing Dynasty Wang Xizhi

778BC Tang Dynasty Guo Quan

1280AD Yuan Dynasty Zhao Mengfu

1829AD Ming Dynasty Dong Qichang

THE GENIUS OF CHINESE CHARACTERS

STANDARD	SIMPLIFIED	MEANING
漢	汉	• Chinese (Han) people: 漢人; Han Dynasty: 漢朝 • Chinese chatacters: 漢字; Chinese language: 漢語 • Chinese race: 漢族; a man: 好漢

正: 丶 丶 氵 氵 汜 泔 泔 淖 淖 淖 漢 漢

简: 丶 丶 氵 汊 汉

ETYMOLOGY Radical: 水 Water 水 + a part of "難"(phonetic): the Han river → the Milky way.
漢 was the name of Han dynasty → China → men

DATA

		PRONUNCIATION			
Radical (部首)	85: 水	Pinyin:	hàn	J-音読み:	カン
Strokes	14 | 5	Wade-Giles:	han	J-訓読み:	から
HSK	1	Cantonese:	hon3	Korean 音读:	한
Frequency	711	Minnan:	hàn	Korean 训读:	한수, 한나라
Big5	BA7E	Bopomofo:	ㄏㄢˋ	K-eumdok:	han
Unihan	U+6C49	JP-Onyomi:	kan	K-hundok:	hansu, hannara
Kangxi Dictionary	P464	JP-Kunyomi:	kara	Vietnamese:	người trung quốc

VARIANTS | 漢(J)

COMBINATIONS

漢語 - Chinese language
漢字 - Chinese characters
武漢 - Wuhan city
老漢 - old man

SAYINGS

英雄好漢 - heroes
鉦鉦鐵漢 - a strong and determined man
氣衝霄漢 - dauntless
大男子漢 - he-man

HISTORICAL

甲骨文 (2000BC)	金文 (1000BC)	篆文 (200BC)	隸 (200AD)
	𤁉	𤁉	汉

FONTS

楷 行 草 宋
汉 汉 汉 汉

266AD Jing Dynasty Wang Xizhi
778BC Tang Dynasty Yan Zhenqing
1280AD Yuan Dynasty Zhao Mengfu
1829AD Ming Dynasty Dong Qichang

THE GENIUS OF CHINESE CHARACTERS

STANDARD	SIMPLIFIED	MEANING
飯	饭	• cooked rice: 米飯 • meal: 早飯 • food: 吃飯

Stroke order (正): 丿 亽 今 今 今 食 食 飠 飯 飯 飯
Stroke order (简): 丿 𠂉 饣 饣 饣 饭 饭

ETYMOLOGY
Radical: 食
Food 食 + 反 (phonetic): rice → feed/eat

DATA

		PRONUNCIATION			
Radical (部首)	184: 食	Pinyin:	fàn	J-音読み:	ハン
Strokes	12 | 7	Wade-Giles:	fan	J-訓読み:	めし
HSK	1	Cantonese:	faan6	Korean 音读:	반
Frequency	935	Minnan:	pñg	Korean 训读:	밥
Big5	B6BA	Bopomofo:	ㄈㄢˋ	K-eumdok:	ban
Unihan	U+996D	JP-Onyomi:	han	K-hundok:	bap
Kangxi Dictionary	P1417	JP-Kunyomi:	meshi	Vietnamese:	cơm

VARIANTS

COMBINATIONS

吃飯 - eat
飯店 - restaurant
晚飯 - supper
早飯 - breakfast
午飯 - lunch

飯桌 - dining table

SAYINGS

家常便飯 - a common occurrence
粗茶淡飯 - plain tea and simple food
塵飯塗羹 - dusty rice and dirty broth
施粥捨飯 - to provide alms and rice

大鍋飯 - egalitarianism

HISTORICAL

甲骨文 (2000BC)	金文 (1000BC)	篆文 (200BC)	隸 (200AD)

FONTS
楷　行　草　宋

266AD Jing Dynasty — Wang Xizhi
778BC Tang Dynasty — Liu Gongquan
1280AD Yuan Dynasty — Zhao Mengfu
1829AD Ming Dynasty — Dong Qichang

THE GENIUS OF CHINESE CHARACTERS

STANDARD	SIMPLIFIED	MEANING
衣	衣	• clothes: 衣服; to dress: 以衣 • uniform: 號衣; coating: 糖衣 • placenta: 衣胞

正: 丶 亠 亣 亡 衣 衣
简: 丶 亠 亣 亡 衣 衣

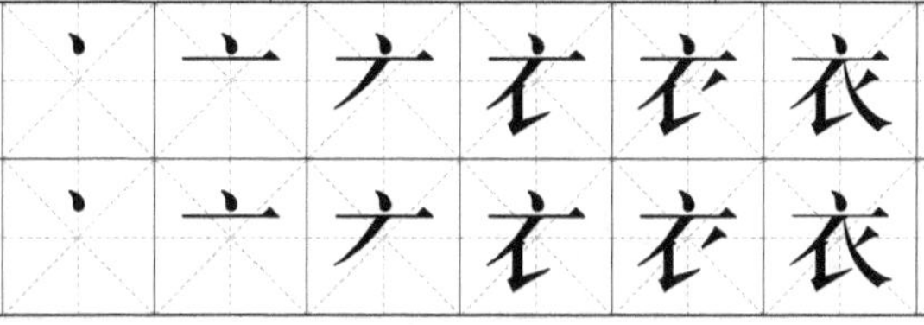

ETYMOLOGY

Radical: 衣

Pictograph: A tiled traditional Chinese robe, clothing = wear clothes

DATA

Radical (部首)	145: 衣
Strokes	6 | 6
HSK	1
Frequency	725
Big5	A6E7
Unihan	U+8863
Kangxi Dictionary	P1111

PRONUNCIATION

Pinyin:	yī
Wade-Giles:	i
Cantonese:	yi1
Minnan:	i
Bopomofo:	ㄧ
JP-Onyomi:	i, e
JP-Kunyomi:	koromo

J-音読み:	イ, エ
J-訓読み:	ころも
Korean 音读:	의
Korean 训读:	옷
K-eumdok:	ui
K-hundok:	ot
Vietnamese:	quần áo

VARIANTS | 衤

COMBINATIONS

大衣 - overcoat
毛衣 - sweater
上衣 - jacket
雨衣 - raincoat
睡衣 - pyjamas

SAYINGS

節衣縮食 - to save on food and clothing
衣冠禽獸 - brute
衣食無憂 - not worried about clothes and food
衣食住行 - people's basic needs

繼承衣鉢 - to take up somebody's mantle
衣食父母 - the people one depends upon for one's livelihood

HISTORICAL

甲骨文 (2000BC)　　金文 (1000BC)　　篆文 (200BC)　　隸 (200AD)

FONTS

楷　行　草　宋

266AD
Jing Dynasty
Wang Xizhi

778BC
Tang Dynasty
Yan Zhenqing

1280AD
Yuan Dynasty
Zhao Mengfu

1829AD
Ming Dynasty
Dong Qichang

THE GENIUS OF CHINESE CHARACTERS

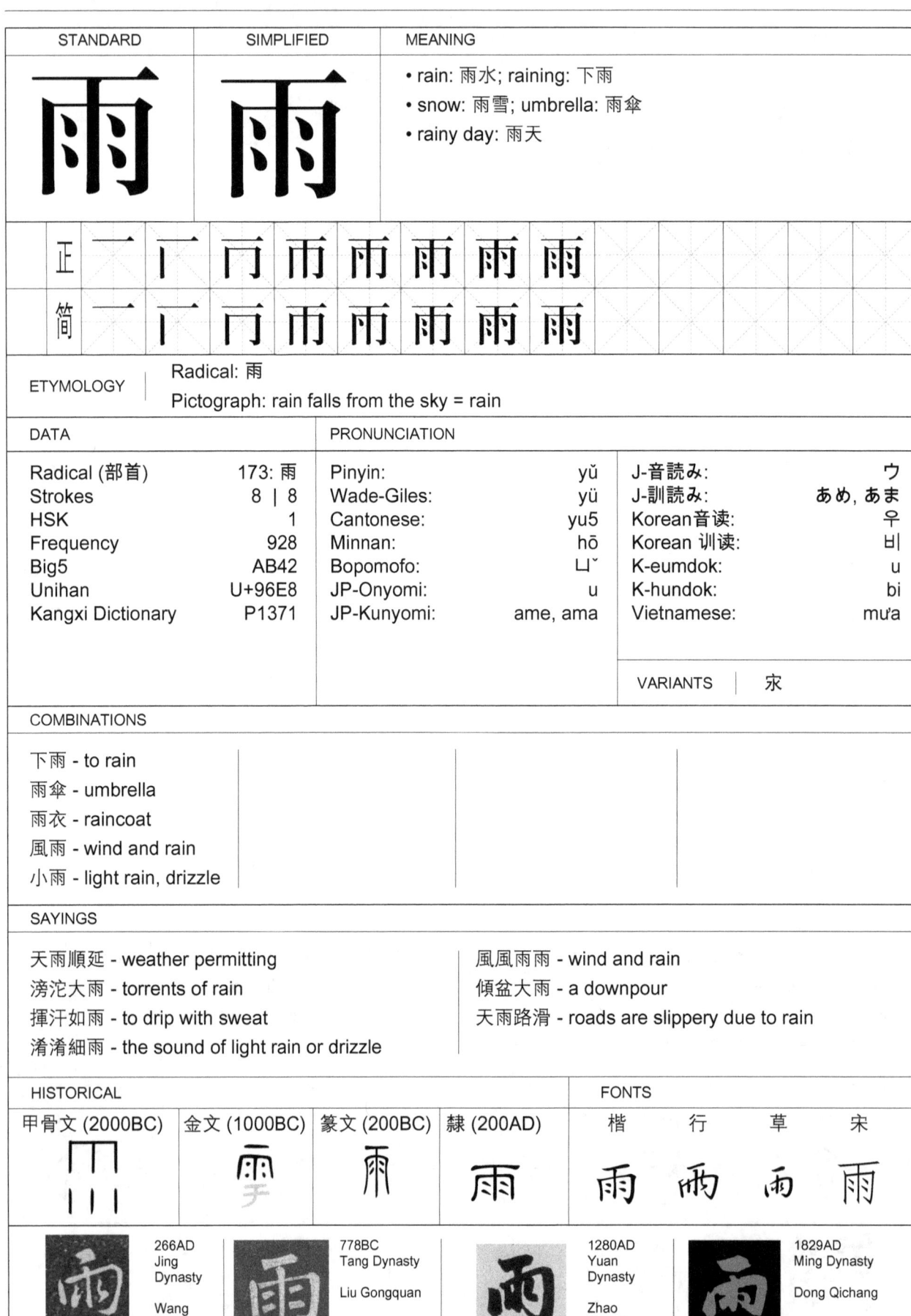

THE GENIUS OF CHINESE CHARACTERS

STANDARD	SIMPLIFIED	MEANING
冷	冷	• cold: 寒冷; unfamiliar: 冷字 • coolheaded: 冷眼; sarcastic: 冷笑 • done in secret: 冷箭

| 正 | ` | 冫 | 冫 | 冷 | 冷 | 冷 | 冷 |
| 简 | ` | 冫 | 冫 | 冷 | 冷 | 冷 | 冷 |

ETYMOLOGY
Radical: 冫
Icicle 冫 + 令 (phonetic): cold

DATA

Radical (部首)	15: 冫
Strokes	7 | 7
HSK	1
Frequency	700
Big5	A74E
Unihan	U+51B7
Kangxi Dictionary	P132

PRONUNCIATION

Pinyin:	lěng
Wade-Giles:	lêng
Cantonese:	laang5
Minnan:	léng
Bopomofo:	ㄌㄥˇ
JP-Onyomi:	rei
JP-Kunyomi:	tsume·tai, sa·meru

J-音読み:	レイ
J-訓読み:	つめ·たい, さ·める
Korean 音读:	랭, 냉
Korean 训读:	차다, 식히다
K-eumdok:	raeng, naeng
K-hundok:	chada, sikida
Vietnamese:	lạnh

VARIANTS

COMBINATIONS

冷静 - sober
冷淡 - cold, uncaring
寒冷 - frigid
冷却 - thaw
冷笑 - sneer

SAYINGS

冷言冷語 - sarcastic comments
冷眼旁觀 - the cool eye of a bystander
捏一把冷汗 - to break out into a cold sweat
忽冷忽熱 - suddenly cold, suddenly hot

心灰意冷 - downhearted and dejected
冷酷無情 - cold hearted

HISTORICAL

甲骨文 (2000BC)	金文 (1000BC)	篆文 (200BC)	隸 (200AD)
		冷	冷

FONTS

楷	行	草	宋
冷	冷	冷	冷

266AD
Jing Dynasty
Wang Xizhi

778BC
Tang Dynasty
Liu Gongquan

1280AD
Yuan Dynasty
Zhao Mengfu

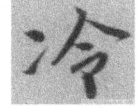
1829AD
Ming Dynasty
Tang Yin

183

THE GENIUS OF CHINESE CHARACTERS

STANDARD	SIMPLIFIED	MEANING
姐	姐	• older sister: 姐姐; elder sister: 大姐 • young lady (miss): 小姐; women: 姐兒

正: ㄑ 女 女 奵 奵 妲 妲 姐
简: ㄑ 女 女 奵 奵 妲 妲 姐

ETYMOLOGY
Radical: 女
Women 女 + 且 (phonetic): mother (dialect words) = sister

DATA

Radical (部首)	38: 女
Strokes	8 | 8
HSK	1
Frequency	830
Big5	A96A
Unihan	U+59D0
Kangxi Dictionary	P258

PRONUNCIATION

Pinyin:	jiě	J-音読み:	ソ, シャ
Wade-Giles:	chieh	J-訓読み:	あね
Cantonese:	je2	Korean 音读:	저
Minnan:	ché	Korean 训读:	누이
Bopomofo:	ㄐㄧㄝˇ	K-eumdok:	jeo
JP-Onyomi:	so, sha	K-hundok:	nui
JP-Kunyomi:	ane	Vietnamese:	em gái

VARIANTS	媎, 姉(J)

COMBINATIONS

小姐 - young lady
大姐 - elder sister
姐妹 - sisters
人魚小姐 - mermaid

SAYINGS

千金小姐 - a young lady with a thousand pieces of gold

HISTORICAL

甲骨文 (2000BC)	金文 (1000BC)	篆文 (200BC)	隸 (200AD)
		姐	姐

FONTS

楷	行	草	宋
姐	姐	姐	姐

THE GENIUS OF CHINESE CHARACTERS

STANDARD	SIMPLIFIED	MEANING
謝	谢	• to thank: 感謝; thanks: 謝謝 • to decline: 辭謝; wither: 花謝

正: 丶 亠 二 三 言 言 言 訁 訒 訒 訒 訒 謝 謝 謝 謝

简: 丶 讠 讠 讠 讠 讠 讠 讠 讠 讠 谢 谢

ETYMOLOGY

Radical: 言

Speak 言 + 射 (phonetic): refuse, apologize = thanks

DATA

Radical (部首)	149: 言	Pinyin:	xiè	J-音読み:	シャ
Strokes	17 | 12	Wade-Giles:	hsieh	J-訓読み:	あやま・る
HSK	1	Cantonese:	je6	Korean 音读:	사
Frequency	897	Minnan:	siā	Korean 训读:	사례하다
Big5	C1C2	Bopomofo:	ㄒ一ㄝˋ	K-eumdok:	sa
Unihan	U+8C22	JP-Onyomi:	sha	K-hundok:	saryehada
Kangxi Dictionary	P1176	JP-Kunyomi:	ayama·ru	Vietnamese:	cảm tạ

PRONUNCIATION

VARIANTS

COMBINATIONS

謝謝 - thanks
謝絕 - politely refuse
多謝 - many thanks
謝意 - gratitude

SAYINGS

暗門謝客 - to close the door to visitors

HISTORICAL

甲骨文 (2000BC) | 金文 (1000BC) | 篆文 (200BC) | 隸 (200AD)

FONTS

楷 行 草 宋

266AD Jing Dynasty Wang Xizhi

778BC Tang Dynasty Liu Gongquan

1280AD Yuan Dynasty Zhao Mengfu

1829AD Ming Dynasty Tang Yin

THE GENIUS OF CHINESE CHARACTERS

STANDARD	SIMPLIFIED	MEANING
		• dish (type of food): 葷菜 • vegetable: 菜蔬 • dull green: 菜青 • famished: 菜色

| 正 | 一 | 十 | 艹 | 艹 | 苎 | 苎 | 莁 | 莁 | 苹 | 苹 | 菜 |
| 简 | 一 | 十 | 艹 | 艹 | 苎 | 苎 | 莁 | 莁 | 苹 | 苹 | 菜 |

ETYMOLOGY

Radical: 艹

Grass 艹 + 采 (phonetic): vegetables = dish/cuisine

DATA

		PRONUNCIATION			
Radical (部首)	140: 艹	Pinyin:	cài	J-音読み:	サイ
Strokes	11 | 11	Wade-Giles:	ts'ai	J-訓読み:	な
HSK	1	Cantonese:	choi3	Korean 音读:	채
Frequency	1266	Minnan:	chhài	Korean 训读:	나물
Big5	B5E6	Bopomofo:	ㄘㄞˋ	K-eumdok:	chae
Unihan	U+83DC	JP-Onyomi:	sai	K-hundok:	namul
Kangxi Dictionary	P1038	JP-Kunyomi:	na	Vietnamese:	món ăn

VARIANTS

COMBINATIONS

蔬菜 - vegetables   點菜 - order food
菜單 - menu
白菜 - Chinese cabbage
青菜 - greens
菠菜 - spinach

SAYINGS

小菜一碟 - a small appetizer, easily done
撿到籃裏就是菜 - all is grist that comes to the mill

HISTORICAL

甲骨文 (2000BC)	金文 (1000BC)	篆文 (200BC)	隸 (200AD)
		菜	菜

FONTS

楷	行	草	宋
菜	菜	菜	菜

266AD
Jing Dynasty
Wang Xizhi

778BC
Tang Dynasty
Ouyang Xun

1280AD
Yuan Dynasty
Zhao Mengfu

1829AD
Ming Dynasty
Tang Yin

THE GENIUS OF Chinese CHARACTERS

STANDARD	SIMPLIFIED	MEANING
		• zero (number): 一百零五 • withered: 凋零 • retail: 零賣 • spare parts: 零件

正	一	二	厂	币	币	币	币	雨	季	雭	寥	零	零
简	一	二	厂	币	币	币	币	雨	季	雭	寥	零	零

ETYMOLOGY Radical: 雨
Rain 雨 + 令 (phonetic): drizzle, fall(rain/snow), withered = fraction

DATA

		PRONUNCIATION			
Radical (部首)	173: 雨	Pinyin:	líng	J-音読み:	レイ
Strokes	13 | 13	Wade-Giles:	ling	J-訓読み:	ゼロ, あま・り
HSK	1	Cantonese:	ling4	Korean 音读:	령,영
Frequency	1342	Minnan:	lân	Korean 训读:	떨어지다
Big5	B973	Bopomofo:	ㄌㄥˊ	K-eumdok:	ryeong, yeong
Unihan	U+96F6	JP-Onyomi:	rei	K-hundok:	tteorojida
Kangxi Dictionary	P1372	JP-Kunyomi:	zero, ama·ri	Vietnamese:	số không

	VARIANTS	靁, 零

COMBINATIONS

零件 - spare parts
零錢 - small change
零售 - sell retail
零食 - snacks
零下 - below zero

SAYINGS

感激涕零 - to shed tears of gratitude
七零八落 - everything broken and in disorder
四海飄零 - drifting aimlessly
零打碎敲 - to do things in bits and pieces

零零星星 - fragmentary

HISTORICAL

甲骨文 (2000BC)	金文 (1000BC)	篆文 (200BC)	隸 (200AD)
		零	零

FONTS

楷	行	草	宋
零	零	零	零

1051BC
Song Dynasty
Su Shi

1051BC
Song Dynasty
Mi Fu

1280AD
Yuan Dynasty
Zhao Mengfu

1829AD
Ming Dynasty
Tang Yin

THE GENIUS OF CHINESE CHARACTERS

STANDARD	SIMPLIFIED	MEANING
睡	睡	• to sleep: 睡覺; nap: 小睡 • doze: 瞌睡; feel sleepy: 想睡

正: 丨 冂 冂 日 目 貝 貯 貯 貯 貯 貯 貯 睡
简: 丨 冂 冂 日 目 貝 貯 貯 貯 貯 貯 貯 睡

ETYMOLOGY

Radical: 目
Eye 目 + fall 垂 (phonetic): sitting and having a nap = sleep

DATA

Radical (部首)	109: 目	Pinyin:	shuì	J-音読み:	スイ
Strokes	13 | 13	Wade-Giles:	shui	J-訓読み:	ねむ·る
HSK	1	Cantonese:	sui6	Korean 音读:	수
Frequency	964	Minnan:	chōe	Korean 训读:	졸음
Big5	BACE	Bopomofo:	ㄕㄨㄟˋ	K-eumdok:	su
Unihan	U+7761	JP-Onyomi:	sui	K-hundok:	joreum
Kangxi Dictionary	P810	JP-Kunyomi:	nemu·ru	Vietnamese:	ngủ

VARIANTS

COMBINATIONS

睡覺 - to sleep
入睡 - go to sleep
睡衣 - pyjamas
午睡 - take a nap after lunch

睡醒 - wake up

SAYINGS

打起瞌睡 - to doze off
席地而睡 - to sleep on the ground
昏昏欲睡 - drowsy

HISTORICAL

甲骨文 (2000BC)	金文 (1000BC)	篆文 (200BC)	隸 (200AD)
		睡	睡

FONTS

楷 行 草 宋
睡 睡 睡 睡

778BC Tang Dynasty Guo Quan

1280AD Yuan Dynasty Zhao Mengfu

1829AD Ming Dynasty Tang Yin

1829AD Ming Dynasty Dong Qichang

THE GENIUS OF CHINESE CHARACTERS

STANDARD	SIMPLIFIED	MEANING
喝	喝	• to drink: 喝水; to applaud: 喝采 • shout: 吆喝; threaten: 喝呼

正	丨	冂	口	口丨	口冂	口口	口日	呵	喝	喝	喝	喝
简	丨	冂	口	口丨	口冂	口口	口日	呵	喝	喝	喝	喝

ETYMOLOGY

Radical: 口

Mouth 口 + 曷 (phonetic): the husky sound when thirsty, thirsty = drink

DATA

Radical (部首)	30: 口
Strokes	12 | 12
HSK	1
Frequency	983
Big5	B3DC
Unihan	U+559D
Kangxi Dictionary	P199

PRONUNCIATION

Pinyin:	hē
Wade-Giles:	hê,ho
Cantonese:	hot3
Minnan:	hoah
Bopomofo:	ㄏㄜ
JP-Onyomi:	katsu
JP-Kunyomi:	shika·ru

J-音読み:	カツ
J-訓読み:	しか・る
Korean 音读:	갈
Korean 训读:	꾸짖다
K-eumdok:	gal
K-hundok:	kkujitda
Vietnamese:	uống

VARIANTS: 喝(J), 哈

COMBINATIONS

- 喝酒 - to drink wine
- 吆喝 - cry out
- 喝茶 - drink tea
- 吃喝 - eat and drink
- 喝醉 - drink until drunk
- 喝湯 - drink soup

SAYINGS

- 吃喝玩樂 - to eat, drink and be merry
- 吃喝嫖賭 - to go dining, whoring and gambling
- 喝西北風 - cold and hungry
- 當頭棒喝 - give timely warning

HISTORICAL

甲骨文 (2000BC)	金文 (1000BC)	篆文 (200BC)	隸 (200AD)
		喝	喝

FONTS

楷	行	草	宋
喝	喝	喝	喝

THE GENIUS OF CHINESE CHARACTERS

STANDARD	SIMPLIFIED	MEANING
茶	茶	• tea: 濃茶 • tea tree: 茶樹 • teacup: 茶杯

| 正 | 一 | 十 | 艹 | 艹 | 艾 | 苶 | 苶 | 茶 | 茶 |
| 简 | 一 | 十 | 艹 | 艹 | 艾 | 苶 | 苶 | 茶 | 茶 |

ETYMOLOGY

Radical: 艹

Grass 艹 + 余 (phonetic): tea

DATA

Radical (部首)	140: 艹
Strokes	9 | 9
HSK	1
Frequency	1272
Big5	AFF9
Unihan	U+8336
Kangxi Dictionary	P1029

PRONUNCIATION

Pinyin:	chá
Wade-Giles:	ch'a
Cantonese:	cha4
Minnan:	tê
Bopomofo:	ㄔㄚˊ
JP-Onyomi:	cha, sa
JP-Kunyomi:	N/A

J-音読み:	チャ, サ
J-訓読み:	N/A
Korean 音读:	차
Korean 训读:	차(茶)
K-eumdok:	cha
K-hundok:	cha(lyam)
Vietnamese:	trà

VARIANTS | 茶

COMBINATIONS

喝茶 - to drink tea
茶葉 - tea leaves
茶杯 - teacup
茶館 - teahouse
茶壺 - teapot

紅茶 - black tea

SAYINGS

粗茶淡飯 - plain tea and simple food
茶餘飯後 - at one's leisure

HISTORICAL

甲骨文 (2000BC)	金文 (1000BC)	篆文 (200BC)	隸 (200AD)
			茶

FONTS

楷	行	草	宋
茶	茶	茶	茶

 266AD Jing Dynasty Wang Xizhi

 778BC Tang Dynasty Liu Gongquan

 1280AD Yuan Dynasty Zhao Mengfu

 1829AD Ming Dynasty Tang Yin

THE GENIUS OF CHINESE CHARACTERS

STANDARD	SIMPLIFIED	MEANING
貓	猫	• cat: 猫 • wild cat: 猫狸 • owl: 猫頭鷹

正: ノ 犭 犭 犭 犷 犷 犷 猎 猎 猫 猫
简: ノ 犭 犭 犭 犷 犷 犷 猎 猎 猫 猫

ETYMOLOGY | Radical: 豸
An animal with an open mouth 豸 + 苗 (phonetic): cat

DATA

Radical (部首)	153: 豸		
Strokes	15 | 11		
HSK	1		
Frequency	1673		
Big5	BFDF		
Unihan	U+732B		
Kangxi Dictionary	P1202		

PRONUNCIATION

Pinyin:	māo	J-音読み:	ビョウ
Wade-Giles:	mao	J-訓読み:	ねこ
Cantonese:	maau1	Korean 音读:	묘
Minnan:	niau	Korean 训读:	고양이
Bopomofo:	ㄇㄠ	K-eumdok:	myo
JP-Onyomi:	byō	K-hundok:	goyangi
JP-Kunyomi:	neko	Vietnamese:	con mèo

VARIANTS | 猫(J)

COMBINATIONS

熊猫 - panda
小猫 - kitten
狸猫 - leopard cat
猫膩 - trick
猫腰 - to bend over

SAYINGS

照猫畫虎 - uninspired imitation

HISTORICAL

甲骨文 (2000BC)	金文 (1000BC)	篆文 (200BC)	隸 (200AD)
		貓	猫

FONTS

楷 行 草 宋
猫 猫 猫 猫

1280AD
Yuan Dynasty
Zhao Mengfu

THE GENIUS OF Chinese Characters

STANDARD	SIMPLIFIED	MEANING
桌	桌	• table: 桌子 • desk: 書桌

正: 丶 丨 广 卢 卢 卣 卓 卓 桌
简: 丶 丨 广 卢 卢 卣 卓 卓 桌

ETYMOLOGY

Radical: 木
Higher 卓 + wood 木 (replaced the "十" under "卓"): table

DATA

Radical (部首)	75: 木	Pinyin:	zhuō	J-音読み:	タク
Strokes	10 | 10	Wade-Giles:	cho	J-訓読み:	すぐ·れる
HSK	1	Cantonese:	cheuk3	Korean 音读:	탁
Frequency	1193	Minnan:	toh	Korean 训读:	높다, 탁자
Big5	AEE0	Bopomofo:	ㄓㄨㄛ	K-eumdok:	t'ak
Unihan	U+684C	JP-Onyomi:	taku	K-hundok:	nopda, takja
Kangxi Dictionary	P525	JP-Kunyomi:	sugu·reru	Vietnamese:	bàn

VARIANTS | 卓, 楺

COMBINATIONS

桌子 - table
桌面 - desktop
餐桌 - dining table
桌燈 - desk lamp

SAYINGS

n/a

HISTORICAL

甲骨文 (2000BC)	金文 (1000BC)	篆文 (200BC)	隸 (200AD)

FONTS

楷 行 草 宋

桌 桌 桌 桌 桌

THE GENIUS OF CHINESE CHARACTERS

STANDARD	SIMPLIFIED	MEANING
狗	狗	• dog: 狗 • wild dogs: 野狗

正 ノ 丿 犭 犭 犭 犭 狗 狗
简 ノ 丿 犭 犭 犭 犭 狗 狗

ETYMOLOGY

Radical: 犭
Dog 犬 + 句 (phonetic): dog

DATA

Radical (部首)	94: 犭
Strokes	8 | 8
HSK	1
Frequency	1281
Big5	AAAF
Unihan	U+72D7
Kangxi Dictionary	P709

PRONUNCIATION

Pinyin:	gǒu
Wade-Giles:	kou
Cantonese:	gau2
Minnan:	káu
Bopomofo:	ㄍㄡˇ
JP-Onyomi:	ku, kō
JP-Kunyomi:	inu

J-音読み:	ク, コウ
J-訓読み:	いぬ
Korean 音读:	구
Korean 训读:	개, 강아지
K-eumdok:	ku
K-hundok:	gae, gangaji
Vietnamese:	chó

VARIANTS | 狗

COMBINATIONS

小狗 - puppy
狼狗 - wolfdog
狗熊 - black bear
狗吠 - bark
狗糧 - dog food

SAYINGS

狗拿耗子 - mind your own business
豬狗不如 - worse than a dog or pig
狗仗人勢 - a dog menaces based on its master's power

人模狗樣 - to pose as something better than oneself
狗血噴頭 - torrent of abuse
金窩銀窩不如自己的狗窩 - there's no place like home

HISTORICAL

甲骨文 (2000BC)	金文 (1000BC)	篆文 (200BC)	隸 (200AD)
		狗	狗

FONTS

楷	行	草	宋
狗	狗	狗	狗

THE GENIUS OF CHINESE CHARACTERS

STANDARD	SIMPLIFIED	MEANING
漂	漂	• to bleach: 漂白 • to drift: 漂流 • elegant: 漂亮 • to float: 漂浮

正 ` ` 氵 氵 氵 氵 沪 沪 沪 沪 漂 漂 漂 漂

简 ` ` 氵 氵 氵 氵 沪 沪 沪 沪 漂 漂 漂 漂

ETYMOLOGY

Radical: 水
Water 水 + 票 (phonetic): floating = wash/vagrancy

DATA

Radical (部首)	85: 水
Strokes	14 | 14
HSK	1
Frequency	1568
Big5	BA7D
Unihan	U+6F02
Kangxi Dictionary	P644

PRONUNCIATION

Pinyin:	piāo
Wade-Giles:	p'iao
Cantonese:	piu3
Minnan:	phiau
Bopomofo:	ㄆㄧㄠˋ/ㄆㄧㄠˇ/ㄆㄧㄠ
JP-Onyomi:	hyō
JP-Kunyomi:	tada·you

J-音読み:	ヒョウ
J-訓読み:	ただ・よう
Korean 音读:	표
Korean 训读:	떠다니다
K-eumdok:	p'yo
K-hundok:	tteodanida
Vietnamese:	trôi dạt

VARIANTS | 飘

COMBINATIONS

漂亮 - beautiful
漂流 - rafting
漂泊 - to drift
漂白 - to bleach
漂洗 - to rinse

漂洋 - to cross the ocean

SAYINGS

n/a

HISTORICAL

甲骨文 (2000BC)	金文 (1000BC)	篆文 (200BC)	隶 (200AD)
		漂	漂

FONTS

楷 行 草 宋
漂 漂 漂 漂

778BC
Tang Dynasty
Lu Jianzhi

1037BC
Song Dynasty
Su Shi

1280AD
Yuan Dynasty
Zhao Mengfu

1743AD
Qing Dynasty
Deng Shiru

THE GENIUS OF CHINESE CHARACTERS

STANDARD	SIMPLIFIED	MEANING
椅	椅	• chair: 椅子 • seat: 座椅

正: 一 十 十 木 木 杧 栌 栌 栌 梼 椅 椅 椅
简: 一 十 十 木 木 杧 栌 栌 栌 梼 椅 椅

ETYMOLOGY
Radical: 木
Wood 木 + 奇 (phonetic): catalpa ovata. 椅 replaced 倚 with the meaning of "chair"

DATA
Radical (部首)	75: 木
Strokes	12 | 12
HSK	1
Frequency	1663
Big5	B4C8
Unihan	U+6905
Kangxi Dictionary	P535

PRONUNCIATION
Pinyin:	yǐ
Wade-Giles:	i
Cantonese:	yi5
Minnan:	í
Bopomofo:	一ˇ
JP-Onyomi:	i
JP-Kunyomi:	N/A

J-音読み:	イ
J-訓読み:	N/A
Korean 音读:	의
Korean 训读:	의자, 걸상
K-eumdok:	ŭi
K-hundok:	uija, geolsang
Vietnamese:	cái ghế

VARIANTS | 倚

COMBINATIONS
椅子 - chair
座椅 - seat
輪椅 - wheelchair
長椅 - bench
睡椅 - couch

SAYINGS
n/a

HISTORICAL
甲骨文 (2000BC)	金文 (1000BC)	篆文 (200BC)	隸 (200AD)
		椅	椅

FONTS
楷	行	草	宋
椅	椅	椅	椅

778BC
Tang Dynasty

Lu Jianzhi

THE GENIUS OF CHINESE CHARACTERS

STANDARD	SIMPLIFIED	MEANING
喂	喂	• interjection to call attention: 喂

正: 丨 冂 口 口' 口冂 口冂 口円 口甲 口罒 喂 喂 喂
简: 丨 冂 口 口' 口冂 口冂 口円 口甲 口罒 喂 喂 喂

ETYMOLOGY
Radical: 口
Mouth 口 + fear 畏: scare/be afraid of, call/say "hello"

DATA
- Radical (部首): 30: 口
- Strokes: 12 | 12
- HSK: 1
- Frequency: 1988
- Big5: B3DE
- Unihan: U+5582
- Kangxi Dictionary: P197

PRONUNCIATION
- Pinyin: wèi
- Wade-Giles: wei
- Cantonese: wai3
- Minnan: oeh
- Bopomofo: ㄨㄟˋ
- JP-Onyomi: i
- JP-Kunyomi: N/A
- J-音読み: イ
- J-訓読み: N/A
- Korean 音读: 위,외
- Korean 训读: 두렵다
- K-eumdok: wi, oe
- K-hundok: duryeopda
- Vietnamese: chào

VARIANTS | 畏

COMBINATIONS
喂 - hello (when answering the phone)

SAYINGS
n/a

HISTORICAL
- 甲骨文 (2000BC)
- 金文 (1000BC)
- 篆文 (200BC)
- 隶 (200AD): 喂

FONTS
楷 行 草 宋
喂 喂 喂 喂

THE GENIUS OF CHINESE CHARACTERS

STANDARD	SIMPLIFIED	MEANING
蘋	苹	• apple: 蘋果 • duckweed: 浮萍

正: 一 十 艹 艹 艹 芷 芷 芷 芷 芦 苦 苹 苹
蓣 蓣 蓣 蓣 蘋 蘋

简: 一 十 艹 艹 艹 艹 芏 苹

ETYMOLOGY
Radical: 艹
Grass 艹 + 頻 (phonetic): duckweed

DATA
- Radical (部首): 140: 艹
- Strokes: 19 | 8
- HSK: 1
- Frequency: 2478
- Big5: C4AB
- Unihan: U+82F9
- Kangxi Dictionary: P1068

PRONUNCIATION
- Pinyin: píng
- Wade-Giles: p'ing
- Cantonese: ping4
- Minnan: pîn
- Bopomofo: ㄆㄧㄥˊ
- JP-Onyomi: hin
- JP-Kunyomi: ukikusa
- J-音読み: ヒン
- J-訓読み: うきくさ
- Korean音读: 빈
- Korean 训读: 네가래
- K-eumdok: pin
- K-hundok: negarae
- Vietnamese: táo

VARIANTS: 萍

COMBINATIONS
蘋果 - apple
蘋果汁 - apple juice
蘋果派 - apple pie

SAYINGS
n/a

HISTORICAL
甲骨文 (2000BC)	金文 (1000BC)	篆文 (200BC)	隸 (200AD)
		苹 (seal)	苹

FONTS
楷 行 草 宋
苹 苹 苹 苹

- 1037BC Song Dynasty — Mi Fu
- 1037BC Song Dynasty — Su Shi
- 1280AD Yuan Dynasty — Zhao Mengfu
- 1829AD Ming Dynasty — Huang Daozhou

THE GENIUS OF CHINESE CHARACTERS

STANDARD	SIMPLIFIED	MEANING
爲	为	• for: 爲了; because of: 因爲 • take...to be: 以…爲例; to become: 成爲 • act: 行爲; as: 作爲

正	一	一	丆	丏	产	严	爲	爲	爲	爲	爲
简	丶	ソ	为	为							

ETYMOLOGY Radical: 火 The relevant oracle bone form is 爫 hand + 象 elephant, driving elephants to work = made/do

DATA

Radical (部首)	86: 火		
Strokes	9 | 4		
HSK	2		
Frequency	18		
Big5	ACB0		
Unihan	U+4E3A		
Kangxi Dictionary			

PRONUNCIATION

Pinyin:	wéi	J-音読み:	イ	
Wade-Giles:	wei	J-訓読み:	な·す,ため	
Cantonese:	wai4	Korean 音读:	위	
Minnan:	ûi	Korean 训读:	하다	
Bopomofo:	ㄨㄟˊ/ㄨㄟ	K-eumdok:	wi	
JP-Onyomi:	i	K-hundok:	hada	
JP-Kunyomi:	na·su, tame	Vietnamese:	cho	

VARIANTS

COMBINATIONS

因爲 - because	更爲 - even more
認爲 - to believe	
爲了 - in order to	
成爲 - to become	
行爲 - behavior	

SAYINGS

習以爲常 - to be accustomed to	言爲心聲 - one's words reflect one's thinking
所作所爲 - a person's actions and conduct	反敗爲勝 - to turn defeat into victory
不爲所動 - to remain unmoved	化敵爲友 - to convert an enemy into a friend
無能爲力 - incapable of action	引以爲榮 - to regard it as an honor

HISTORICAL

甲骨文 (2000BC)	金文 (1000BC)	篆文 (200BC)	隸 (200AD)

FONTS

楷　行　草　宋

266AD Jing Dynasty Wang Xizhi	778BC Tang Dynasty Liu Gongquan	1280AD Yuan Dynasty Zhao Mengfu	1829AD Ming Dynasty Dong Qichang

THE GENIUS OF CHINESE CHARACTERS

STANDARD	SIMPLIFIED	MEANING
到	到	• to arrive: 到來 • to (a place): 到達 • until (a time): 到

正 一 乙 云 至 至 至 到 到
简 一 乙 云 至 至 至 到 到

ETYMOLOGY
Radical: 刀
Arrive 至 + knife 刀 (phonetic): arrive

DATA

Radical (部首)	18: 刀	Pinyin:	dào	J-音読み:	トウ
Strokes	8 | 8	Wade-Giles:	tao	J-訓読み:	いた·る
HSK	2	Cantonese:	do3	Korean 音读:	도
Frequency	22	Minnan:	kàu	Korean 训读:	이르다
Big5	A8EC	Bopomofo:	ㄉㄠˋ	K-eumdok:	to
Unihan	U+5230	JP-Onyomi:	tō	K-hundok:	ireuda
Kangxi Dictionary	P138	JP-Kunyomi:	ita·ru	Vietnamese:	đến

VARIANTS | 倒

COMBINATIONS

看到 - to see, saw
感到 - to feel, felt
得到 - to get, got
想到 - to think of
受到 - to receive

回到 - to return to
達到 - to reach
來到 - to come

SAYINGS

功到自然成 - effort will undoubtedly lead to success
馬到成功 - to acheive instant success
一天到晚 - all day long

大限到來 - to die
新來乍到 - newly arrived
水到渠成 - where water flows a channel will form
面面俱到 - to take care of everything

HISTORICAL

甲骨文 (2000BC) | 金文 (1000BC) | 篆文 (200BC) | 隸 (200AD)

FONTS

楷 行 草 宋

778BC Tang Dynasty Guo Quan
778BC Tang Dynasty Yan Zhenqing
1280AD Yuan Dynasty Zhao Mengfu
1829AD Ming Dynasty Dong Qichang

THE GENIUS OF CHINESE CHARACTERS

STANDARD	SIMPLIFIED	MEANING
以	以	• therefore: 所以 • Israel: 以色列

正 レ レ 以 以
简 レ レ 以 以

ETYMOLOGY
Radical: 人
People 人 working with plough: use = via

DATA

		PRONUNCIATION			
Radical (部首)	9: 人	Pinyin:	yǐ	J-音読み:	イ
Strokes	4 | 4	Wade-Giles:	i	J-訓読み:	もっ·て
HSK	2	Cantonese:	yi5	Korean 音读:	이
Frequency	23	Minnan:	í	Korean 训读:	~로, ~써
Big5	A548	Bopomofo:	ㄧˇ	K-eumdok:	i
Unihan	U+4EE5	JP-Onyomi:	i	K-hundok:	~ro, ~sseo
Kangxi Dictionary	P94	JP-Kunyomi:	mot·te	Vietnamese:	đến

VARIANTS | 㠯, 以(J)

COMBINATIONS

可以 - can
所以 - therefore
以及 - as well as
以來 - since
以爲 - to believe

以上 - the above
以下 - the following
以外 - except for

SAYINGS

開始以前 - before the beginning
予以照顧 - to ask somebody to carefully consider a request
自以爲是 - to believe one is always right

以史爲鑒 - to learn from history
引以爲憾 - to consider regrettable
虛席以待 - to reserve a seat for somebody
難以自已 - cannot control oneself

HISTORICAL

甲骨文 (2000BC)	金文 (1000BC)	篆文 (200BC)	隸 (200AD)

FONTS

楷 行 草 宋

266AD Jing Dynasty — Wang Xizhi
778BC Tang Dynasty — Liu Gongquan
1280AD Yuan Dynasty — Zhao Mengfu
1829AD Ming Dynasty — Dong Qichang

THE GENIUS OF CHINESE CHARACTERS

STANDARD	SIMPLIFIED	MEANING
行	行	• a row: 一行; to go: 行走 • profession: 同行; to walk: 步行 • behavior: 行爲; conduct: 進行 • to travel: 旅行; OK: 可行

正 ノ ク 彳 行 行 行
简 ノ ク 彳 行 行 行

ETYMOLOGY
Radical: 行
Pictograph: a diagram of an intersection of roads, road = walk

DATA

Radical (部首)	144: 行	Pinyin: háng	J-音読み: ギョウ, コウ
Strokes	6 | 6	Wade-Giles: hang	J-訓読み: い·く, おこな·う
HSK	2	Cantonese: hong4	Korean音读: 행
Frequency	53	Minnan: hêng	Korean 训读: 다니다, 가다
Big5	A6E6	Bopomofo: ㄒㄧㄥˊ/ㄏㄤˊ	K-eumdok: haeng
Unihan	U+884C	JP-Onyomi: gyō, kou	K-hundok: danida, gada
Kangxi Dictionary	P1108	JP-Kunyomi: i·ku, okona·u	Vietnamese: hàng

VARIANTS

COMBINATIONS

進行 - to advance
舉行 - to hold
行動 - operation
行爲 - action
行政 - administrative

銀行 - bank
行業 - profession

SAYINGS

隨行就市 - fluctuate in line with market conditions
尋行數墨 - smooth the sentence
一目十行 - read rapidly
字裏行間 - between the lines

HISTORICAL

甲骨文 (2000BC)	金文 (1000BC)	篆文 (200BC)	隸 (200AD)

FONTS

楷 行 草 宋

266AD Jing Dynasty Wang Xizhi
778BC Tang Dynasty Liu Gongquan
1280AD Yuan Dynasty Zhao Mengfu
1829AD Ming Dynasty Dong Qichang

THE GENIUS OF CHINESE CHARACTERS

STANDARD	SIMPLIFIED	MEANING
就	就	• to approach: 就 • only: 就 • emphasis: 就 • near: 就

正	丶	亠	广	亣	亩	亨	亨	京	京	尌	就	就
简	丶	亠	广	亣	亩	亨	亨	京	京	尌	就	就

ETYMOLOGY

Radical: 尤
High place 京 + 尤 (phonetic): climb to a high place = approach/engage in

DATA

		PRONUNCIATION			
Radical (部首)	43: 尤	Pinyin:	jiù	J-音読み:	シュウ, ジュ
Strokes	12 | 12	Wade-Giles:	chiu	J-訓読み:	つ・く
HSK	2	Cantonese:	jau6	Korean 音读:	취
Frequency	27	Minnan:	chiū	Korean 训读:	나아가다, 이루다
Big5	B44E	Bopomofo:	ㄐㄧㄡˋ	K-eumdok:	ch'wi
Unihan	U+5C31	JP-Onyomi:	shū, ju	K-hundok:	naagada, iruda
Kangxi Dictionary	P299	JP-Kunyomi:	tsu·ku	Vietnamese:	trên

VARIANTS

COMBINATIONS

就是 - even
就要 - will
就業 - getting a job
成就 - accomplishment
就算 - granted that

就讀 - to go to school

SAYINGS

陳力就列 - to put in effort to secure a position
將錯就錯 - continuing to make error after error
一切就緒 - everything in its place and ready
功成名就 - to win success and recognition

按部就班 - to work according to order
因陋就簡 - crude but simple method

HISTORICAL

甲骨文 (2000BC)	金文 (1000BC)	篆文 (200BC)	隸 (200AD)

FONTS

楷 行 草 宋

266AD Jing Dynasty Wang Xizhi

778BC Tang Dynasty Liu Gongquan

1280AD Yuan Dynasty Zhao Mengfu

1829AD Ming Dynasty Dong Qichang

THE GENIUS OF Chinese Characters

STANDARD	SIMPLIFIED	MEANING
新	新	• new: 新; newly: 新近 • Singapore: 新加坡; fresh: 新的 • modern: 新式的; recent: 最新的

| 正 | 丶 | 亠 | 亠 | 立 | 立 | 辛 | 辛 | 亲 | 新 | 新 | 新 | 新 |
| 简 | 丶 | 亠 | 亠 | 立 | 立 | 辛 | 辛 | 亲 | 新 | 新 | 新 | 新 |

ETYMOLOGY

Radical: 斤
亲 (phonetic) + axe 斤: cut down trees with axe. "New" is a borrowed meaning

DATA

Radical (部首)   69: 斤
Strokes   13 | 13
HSK   2
Frequency   161
Big5   B773
Unihan   U+65B0
Kangxi Dictionary P480

PRONUNCIATION

Pinyin: xīn
Wade-Giles: hsin
Cantonese: san1
Minnan: sin
Bopomofo: ㄒㄧㄣ
JP-Onyomi: shin
JP-Kunyomi: atara·shī, nī

J-音読み: シン
J-訓読み: あたら·しい, にい
Korean 音读: 신
Korean 训读: 새로운
K-eumdok: shin
K-hundok: saeroun
Vietnamese: mới

VARIANTS | 薪

COMBINATIONS

新聞 - news
創新 - innovation
重新 - again
最新 - latest
新型 - new type

新鮮 - fresh
出新 - newborn

SAYINGS

面目一新 - a complete change
耳目一新 - something new to see and hear
清新自然 - as fresh and clean as nature
萬象更新 - nature takes on a new look

萬古張新 - to remain forever new
日新月異 - daily renewal/monthly change
標新立异 - start something new and different

HISTORICAL

甲骨文 (2000BC) | 金文 (1000BC) | 篆文 (200BC) | 隸 (200AD)

FONTS

楷   行   草   宋
新   新   新   新

266AD
Jing Dynasty
Wang Xizhi

778BC
Tang Dynasty
Liu Gongquan

1280AD
Yuan Dynasty
Zhao Mengfu

1829AD
Ming Dynasty
Dong Qichang

THE GENIUS OF CHINESE CHARACTERS

STANDARD	SIMPLIFIED	MEANING
經	经	• pass through: 經過 • scripture: 宗教經文 • to undergo: 經歷; classic: 經典的 • through: 透過

ETYMOLOGY
Radical: 糸
Silk 糸 + 巠 (phonetic): meridian, weaving/the north-south road = govern/pass through

DATA

Radical (部首)	120: 糸
Strokes	13 | 8
HSK	2
Frequency	62
Big5	B867
Unihan	U+7ECF
Kangxi Dictionary	P925

PRONUNCIATION

Pinyin:	jīng	J-音読み:	ケイ, キョウ
Wade-Giles:	ching	J-訓読み:	へ·る, た·つ
Cantonese:	ging1	Korean 音读:	경
Minnan:	keng	Korean 训读:	지나다
Bopomofo:	ㄐㄧㄥ	K-eumdok:	kyŏng
JP-Onyomi:	kei, kyō	K-hundok:	jinada
JP-Kunyomi:	he·ru, ta·tsu	Vietnamese:	xuyên qua

VARIANTS | 巠

COMBINATIONS

經濟 - economy
已經 - already
經過 - to pass through
經驗 - experience
經營 - operate

經理 - manager
經常 - frequently
經貿 - trade
神經 - nerve

SAYINGS

滿腹經綸 - full of wisdom
經年累月 - for years
正經八百 - prim and proper
飽經憂患 - having experienced hardship

過去經驗 - past experience
一本正經 - very serious
苦心經營 - to build up an enterprise through painstaking efforts

HISTORICAL

甲骨文 (2000BC)	金文 (1000BC)	篆文 (200BC)	隸 (200AD)
	巠	經	经

FONTS

楷 行 草 宋
经 经 经 经

266AD Jing Dynasty Wang Xizhi
778BC Tang Dynasty Liu Gongquan
1280AD Yuan Dynasty Zhao Mengfu
1829AD Ming Dynasty Dong Qichang

THE GENIUS OF CHINESE CHARACTERS

STANDARD	SIMPLIFIED	MEANING
也	也	• also: 也 • too: 也

正 乛 乜 也
简 乛 乜 也

ETYMOLOGY | Radical: 乙 Pictograph: a long snake. The role of mood particle at the end of a sentence is borrowed

DATA

Radical (部首)	5: 乙
Strokes	3 | 3
HSK	2
Frequency	31
Big5	A45D
Unihan	U+4E5F
Kangxi Dictionary	P84

PRONUNCIATION

Pinyin:	yě
Wade-Giles:	yeh
Cantonese:	ya5
Minnan:	ā
Bopomofo:	ㄧㄝˇ
JP-Onyomi:	ya
JP-Kunyomi:	ka, nari

J-音読み:	ヤ
J-訓読み:	か, なり
Korean 音读:	야
Korean 训读:	어조사(語助辭)
K-eumdok:	ya
K-hundok:	eojosa(bwajyuldut),
Vietnamese:	và cũng

VARIANTS | 㐆, 迆

COMBINATIONS

也不 - neither
也許 - perhaps
也罷 - never mind
再也 - any more

SAYINGS

空空如也 - as empty as anything
來而不往非禮也 - it is impolite not to reciprocate

HISTORICAL

甲骨文 (2000BC)	金文 (1000BC)	篆文 (200BC)	隸 (200AD)

FONTS

楷　行　草　宋

266AD Jing Dynasty Wang Xizhi
778BC Tang Dynasty Liu Gongquan
1280AD Yuan Dynasty Zhao Mengfu
1829AD Ming Dynasty Dong Qichang

THE GENIUS OF CHINESE CHARACTERS

STANDARD	SIMPLIFIED	MEANING
場	场	• field: 牧場 • place: 場所 • market: 市場

正	一	十	土	圤	护	坏	坦	埸	塌	場	場
简	一	十	土	圬	场	场					

ETYMOLOGY

Radical: 土
Soil 土 + 昜 (phonetic): the flat place where people pray to their ancestors = field

DATA

Radical (部首)	32: 土	Pinyin:	chǎng	J-音読み:	ジョウ
Strokes	12 | 6	Wade-Giles:	ch'ang	J-訓読み:	ば
HSK	2	Cantonese:	cheung4	Korean 音读:	장
Frequency	249	Minnan:	tiûⁿ	Korean 训读:	마당
Big5	B3F5	Bopomofo:	ㄔㄤˇ	K-eumdok:	chang
Unihan	U+573A	JP-Onyomi:	jō	K-hundok:	madang
Kangxi Dictionary	P234	JP-Kunyomi:	ba	Vietnamese:	cánh đồng

VARIANTS

COMBINATIONS

市場 - marketplace
立場 - position
現場 - the scene
機場 - airport
場所 - location

場面 - scene

SAYINGS

市場調查 - market research
派上用場 - to put to good use
憑票入場 - admission by ticket only
救場如救火 - the show must go on

HISTORICAL

甲骨文 (2000BC)	金文 (1000BC)	篆文 (200BC)	隸 (200AD)
		場	场

FONTS

楷	行	草	宋
场	场	场	场

266AD Jing Dynasty Wang Xizhi

778BC Tang Dynasty Liu Gongquan

1280AD Yuan Dynasty Zhao Mengfu

1829AD Ming Dynasty Tang Yin

THE GENIUS OF CHINESE CHARACTERS

STANDARD	SIMPLIFIED	MEANING
第	第	• prefix for ordinal numbers: 第

正	ノ	ト	ケ	竹	竹	竹	竺	竿	笃	第	第
简	ノ	ト	ケ	竹	竹	竹	竺	竿	笃	第	第

ETYMOLOGY

Radical: 竹
Bamboo 竹 + 弟 (phonetic). order = level/sequence

DATA

Radical (部首)	118: 竹
Strokes	11 | 11
HSK	2
Frequency	114
Big5	B2C4
Unihan	U+7B2C
Kangxi Dictionary	P881

PRONUNCIATION

Pinyin:	dì	J-音読み:	ダイ, テイ
Wade-Giles:	ti	J-訓読み:	つい·で
Cantonese:	dai6	Korean音读:	제
Minnan:	tē	Korean 训读:	차례
Bopomofo:	ㄉㄧˋ	K-eumdok:	che
JP-Onyomi:	dai, tei	K-hundok:	charye
JP-Kunyomi:	tsui·de	Vietnamese:	đầu tiên

VARIANTS	弟

COMBINATIONS

第一 - first
品第 - grade
故第 - former residence
次第 - order

SAYINGS

第二個人 - the second person
第一時間 - in the first moments
闔第光臨 - the whole family is invited

HISTORICAL

甲骨文 (2000BC)	金文 (1000BC)	篆文 (200BC)	隸 (200AD)
		第	第

FONTS

楷	行	草	宋
第	第	第	第

266AD Jing Dynasty Wang Xizhi

778BC Tang Dynasty Liu Gongquan

1280AD Yuan Dynasty Zhao Mengfu

1829AD Ming Dynasty Tang Yin

THE GENIUS OF CHINESE CHARACTERS

STANDARD	SIMPLIFIED	MEANING
過	过	• to pass: 路過 • to pass (time): 過去 • pass through: 經過 • to live: 過活

正: 丨 冂 冋 冋 咼 咼 咼 冎 過 過 過
简: 一 寸 寸 寸 过 过

ETYMOLOGY

Radical: 辵
Walk 辵 + 咼 (phonetic): pass through, visit/excessively

DATA

Radical (部首)	162: 辵		
Strokes	11 | 6		
HSK	2		
Frequency	46		
Big5	B94C		
Unihan	U+8FC7		
Kangxi Dictionary	P1261		

PRONUNCIATION

Pinyin:	guò	J-音読み:	力
Wade-Giles:	kuo	J-訓読み:	すぎ·る, あやま·ち
Cantonese:	gwoh3	Korean 音读:	과
Minnan:	kòe	Korean 训读:	예전
Bopomofo:	ㄍㄨㄛˋ	K-eumdok:	kwa
JP-Onyomi:	ka	K-hundok:	yejeon
JP-Kunyomi:	su·giru, ayama·chi	Vietnamese:	quá khứ

VARIANTS

COMBINATIONS

過去 - the past   超過 - to surpass
不過 - but, only   見過 - have seen
通過 - to pass through   過多 - too many
經過 - to pass by   過來 - come here
過程 - process

SAYINGS

改過從善 - to correct faults   富不過三代 - wealth never survives three
蒙混過關 - to get away with it   generations
聞過則喜 - to accept criticism gladly   得過且過 - satisfied to just get by
過時不候 - being late is not acceptable   知過必改 - realizing one's faults

HISTORICAL

甲骨文 (2000BC)	金文 (1000BC)	篆文 (200BC)	隸 (200AD)

FONTS

楷 行 草 宋

过 过 过 过

266AD
Jing Dynasty
Wang Xizhi

778BC
Tang Dynasty
Yan Zhenqing

1280AD
Yuan Dynasty
Zhao Mengfu

1829AD
Ming Dynasty
Dong Qichang

THE GENIUS OF Chinese Characters

STANDARD	SIMPLIFIED	MEANING
自	自	• self: 自我; oneself: 自己 • since: 自從… • personal: 親自的

正: ′ 丨 冂 冃 自 自
简: ′ 丨 冂 冃 自 自

ETYMOLOGY

Radical: 自
Pictograph: nose = oneself

DATA

		PRONUNCIATION			
Radical (部首)	132: 自	Pinyin:	zì	J-音読み:	ジ, シ
Strokes	6 | 6	Wade-Giles:	tzu	J-訓読み:	みずか・ら
HSK	2	Cantonese:	ji6	Korean 音读:	자
Frequency	43	Minnan:	chū	Korean 训读:	스스로
Big5	A6DB	Bopomofo:	ㄗˋ	K-eumdok:	cha
Unihan	U+81EA	JP-Onyomi:	ji, shi	K-hundok:	seuseuro
Kangxi Dictionary	P1000	JP-Kunyomi:	mizuka·ra	Vietnamese:	tự

VARIANTS

COMBINATIONS

自己 - oneself   自主 - independent
自然 - nature   各自 - each
自由 - freedom
自治 - autonomy
自身 - itself

SAYINGS

自由自在 - free and without restraints   心静自然凉 - a calm heart keeps you cool
沾沾自喜 - to be complacent   自命不凡 - egotistical
自始至終 - from start to finish
自言自語 - talk to oneself

HISTORICAL

甲骨文 (2000BC)   金文 (1000BC)   篆文 (200BC)   隸 (200AD)

FONTS

楷   行   草   宋

266AD
Jing Dynasty
Wang Xizhi

778BC
Tang Dynasty
Yan Zhenqing

1280AD
Yuan Dynasty
Zhao Mengfu

1829AD
Ming Dynasty
Dong Qichang

THE GENIUS OF CHINESE CHARACTERS

STANDARD	SIMPLIFIED	MEANING
得	得	• to obtain: 獲得; gain: 得到 • must: 得; proud: 得意的 • a sentence particle used after a verb to show effect: 得

| 正 | ′ | ⺈ | 彳 | 彳 | 彳ㇿ | 彳日 | 彳日 | 得 | 得 | 得 | 得 |
| 简 | ′ | ⺈ | 彳 | 彳 | 彳ㇿ | 彳日 | 彳日 | 得 | 得 | 得 | 得 |

ETYMOLOGY
Radical: 彳
Pick up 寸 shells 貝 (now 目, denotes money) on the road 彳: gain = satisfy/can

DATA
Radical (部首) — 60: 彳
Strokes — 11 | 11
HSK — 2
Frequency — 39
Big5 — B16F
Unihan — U+5F97
Kangxi Dictionary — P367

PRONUNCIATION
Pinyin: dé
Wade-Giles: tê
Cantonese: dak1
Minnan: tit
Bopomofo: ㄉㄜˊ
JP-Onyomi: toku
JP-Kunyomi: e·ru

J-音読み: トク
J-訓読み: え·る
Korean 音读: 득
Korean 训读: 얻다
K-eumdok: tŭk
K-hundok: eotda
Vietnamese: được

VARIANTS | 㝵

COMBINATIONS
覺得 - to think, to feel
得到 - to get
取得 - to acquire
得了 - all right
獲得 - to obtain

記得 - to remember
顯得 - to seem
變得 - to become

SAYINGS
迫不得已 - to have no alternative
洋洋得意 - immensely pleased with oneself
悠然自得 - carefree
患得患失 - to worry about gains and losses

得道多助 - a just cause enjoys abundant support
自鳴得意 - to think highly of oneself
多勞多得 - he who works more earns more
怡然自得 - happy and content

HISTORICAL
甲骨文 (2000BC) | 金文 (1000BC) | 篆文 (200BC) | 隸 (200AD)

FONTS
楷　行　草　宋

266AD Jing Dynasty — Wang Xizhi
778BC Tang Dynasty — Yan Zhenqing
1280AD Yuan Dynasty — Zhao Mengfu
1829AD Ming Dynasty — Dong Qichang

THE GENIUS OF CHINESE CHARACTERS

STANDARD	SIMPLIFIED	MEANING
報	报	• to report: 報告 • newspaper: 報紙 • revenge: 報復

Stroke order (Standard): 一 十 土 耂 耂 幸 幸 幸 幸' 報 報 報
Stroke order (Simplified): 一 丁 扌 扌 扩 护 报 报

ETYMOLOGY
Radical: 土
Grasp the prisoner in chains 幸 by hands 又: judgment, report, reply/inform = news

DATA
- Radical (部首): 32: 土
- Strokes: 12 | 7
- HSK: 2
- Frequency: 234
- Big5: B3F8
- Unihan: U+62A5
- Kangxi Dictionary: P234

PRONUNCIATION
- Pinyin: bào
- Wade-Giles: pao
- Cantonese: bo3
- Minnan: pò
- Bopomofo: ㄅㄠˋ
- JP-Onyomi: hō
- JP-Kunyomi: muku·iru
- J-音読み: ホウ
- J-訓読み: むく·いる
- Korean 音读: 보
- Korean 训读: 갚다
- K-eumdok: po
- K-hundok: gapda
- Vietnamese: báo cáo

VARIANTS

COMBINATIONS
- 報道 - to report
- 報告 - to inform
- 報紙 - newspaper
- 報導 - news coverage
- 公報 - announcement
- 預報 - forecast
- 情報 - information-gathering

SAYINGS
- 報仇雪恨 - avenge oneself
- 打擊報復 - retaliate
- 惡有惡報 - evil has its retribution
- 恩將仇報 - repay kindness with ingratitude
- 善有善報 - one good turn deserves another
- 通風報信 - divulge secret information
- 投桃報李 - return a favor with a favor
- 以德報德 - responding to kindness with kindness

HISTORICAL
- 甲骨文 (2000BC)
- 金文 (1000BC)
- 篆文 (200BC)
- 隸 (200AD)

FONTS
楷 行 草 宋

- 266AD Jing Dynasty Wang Xizhi
- 778BC Tang Dynasty Yan Zhenqing
- 1280AD Yuan Dynasty Zhao Mengfu
- 1829AD Ming Dynasty Dong Qichang

THE GENIUS OF CHINESE CHARACTERS

STANDARD	SIMPLIFIED	MEANING
進	进	• to enter: 進入 • advance: 前進 • to come in: 進到 • make progress: 進步

| 正 | ノ | 亻 | 亻 | 亻 | 亻 | 隹 | 隹 | 隹 | 進 | 進 |
| 简 | 一 | 二 | 丅 | 井 | 艹 | 讲 | 进 | | | |

ETYMOLOGY Radical: 辶 The feet 辶 of a short-tailed bird 隹 can only walk forward: go forward = improve/make progress/enter

DATA

Radical (部首)	162: 辶
Strokes	11 | 7
HSK	2
Frequency	81
Big5	B669
Unihan	U+8FDB
Kangxi Dictionary	P1259

PRONUNCIATION

Pinyin:	jìn
Wade-Giles:	chin
Cantonese:	jun3
Minnan:	chìn
Bopomofo:	ㄐㄧㄣˋ
JP-Onyomi:	shin
JP-Kunyomi:	susu·mu

J-音読み:	シン
J-訓読み:	すす・む
Korean 音读:	진
Korean 训读:	나아가다
K-eumdok:	chin
K-hundok:	naagada
Vietnamese:	vào

VARIANTS

COMBINATIONS

進入 - to enter
進行 - to advance
促進 - to promote
先進 - advanced
進來 - to come in

進去 - to go in
進步 - progress
進程 - process

SAYINGS

倍道而進 - make progress
進寸退尺 - advance and retreat
進銳退速 - forward and backward
進退維谷 - a dilemma

進退無門 - there is no way to get in and out
不驚進士 - no one can be a champion
竿頭日進 - make rapid progress
兼程前進 - advance at the double

HISTORICAL

甲骨文 (2000BC)	金文 (1000BC)	篆文 (200BC)	隸 (200AD)

FONTS

楷　行　草　宋

进　进　进　进

266AD
Jing Dynasty
Wang Xizhi

778BC
Tang Dynasty
Yan Zhenqing

1280AD
Yuan Dynasty
Zhao Mengfu

1829AD
Ming Dynasty
Dong Qichang

THE GENIUS OF Chinese CHARACTERS

STANDARD	SIMPLIFIED	MEANING
動	动	• to move: 移動; to act: 表現; to use: 使用 • to change: 改變; action: 行爲; happen: 發生 • movement: 動作; eat or drink: 吃/喝 • get moving: 動起來; stir: 攪拌 • touch (one's heart): 觸動（內心）

正	一	二	广	亓	亓	旨	盲	重	重	動	動
简	一	二	云	云	刼	动					

ETYMOLOGY

Radical: 力
Power 力 + 重 (phonetic): take action = move/act

DATA

		PRONUNCIATION			
Radical (部首)	19: 力	Pinyin:	dòng	J-音読み:	ドウ
Strokes	11 | 6	Wade-Giles:	tung	J-訓読み:	うご・く/き
HSK	2	Cantonese:	dung6	Korean 音读:	동
Frequency	73	Minnan:	tōng	Korean 训读:	움직이다
Big5	B0CA	Bopomofo:	ㄉㄨㄥˋ	K-eumdok:	tong
Unihan	U+52A8	JP-Onyomi:	dō	K-hundok:	umjigida
Kangxi Dictionary	P148	JP-Kunyomi:	ugo·ku/ki	Vietnamese:	di chuyển

VARIANTS

COMBINATIONS

活動 - activity	激動 - emotionally moved
行動 - action	
推動 - to push	動力 - power
運動 - to exercise	動員 - to mobilize
動作 - movement	

SAYINGS

感天動地 - deeply affecting　　　　　　　轟動一時 - to cause a sensation
不爲所動 - to remain unmoved　　　　　　震天動地 - to shake heaven and earth
按兵不動 - to hold back the troops and stay put　天搖地動 - earth shattering
大動干戈 - to go to war　　　　　　　　　待時而動 - wait for a suitable time before acting

HISTORICAL

甲骨文 (2000BC)	金文 (1000BC)	篆文 (200BC)	隸 (200AD)
	𠂉	勳	动

FONTS

楷　　行　　草　　宋
动　　动　　动　　动

266AD
Jing Dynasty
Wang Xizhi

778BC
Tang Dynasty
Yan Zhenqing

1280AD
Yuan Dynasty
Zhao Mengfu

1829AD
Ming Dynasty
Dong Qichang

THE GENIUS OF CHINESE CHARACTERS

STANDARD	SIMPLIFIED	MEANING
還	还	• still: 静止; to pay back: 還錢; to return: 返回 • yet: 還沒有; also: 也; surname: 別名; (not) yet: 沒有 • besides: 除了; else: 其他; in addition: 除了 • more: 更多的

正: 一 丁 丆 罒 罒 罒 罒 罒 罒 罒 罒 睘 睘
睘 睘 還

简: 一 丆 不 不 不 还 还

ETYMOLOGY

Radical: 辵
Walk 辵 + circular 睘 (a part of 環 phonetic): return = circular/look back

DATA

Radical (部首)	162: 辵
Strokes	16 | 7
HSK	2
Frequency	80
Big5	C1D9
Unihan	U+8FD8
Kangxi Dictionary	P1266

PRONUNCIATION

Pinyin:	hái	J-音読み:	カン
Wade-Giles:	hai	J-訓読み:	かえ・る
Cantonese:	waan4	Korean 音读:	환
Minnan:	hân	Korean 训读:	돌아오다
Bopomofo:	ㄏㄨㄢˊ/ㄏㄞˊ	K-eumdok:	hwan
JP-Onyomi:	kan	K-hundok:	doraoda
JP-Kunyomi:	kae·ru	Vietnamese:	cũng thế

VARIANTS

COMBINATIONS

往還 - to go back and forth
生還 - return alive
還報 - retributive
還價 - to haggle
還口 - to talk back
還禮 - to return courtesy
還手 - to strike back

SAYINGS

返本還原 - return to the source
討價還價 - to haggle back and forth
勒逼還債 - press for payment of debts
那還用説 - that goes without saying
解鈴還須 - whoever starts trouble should end it

HISTORICAL

甲骨文 (2000BC)	金文 (1000BC)	篆文 (200BC)	隸 (200AD)

FONTS

楷 行 草 宋

266AD Jing Dynasty — Wang Xizhi
778BC Tang Dynasty — Liu Gongquan
1280AD Yuan Dynasty — Zhao Mengfu
1829AD Ming Dynasty — Dong Qichang

THE GENIUS OF CHINESE CHARACTERS

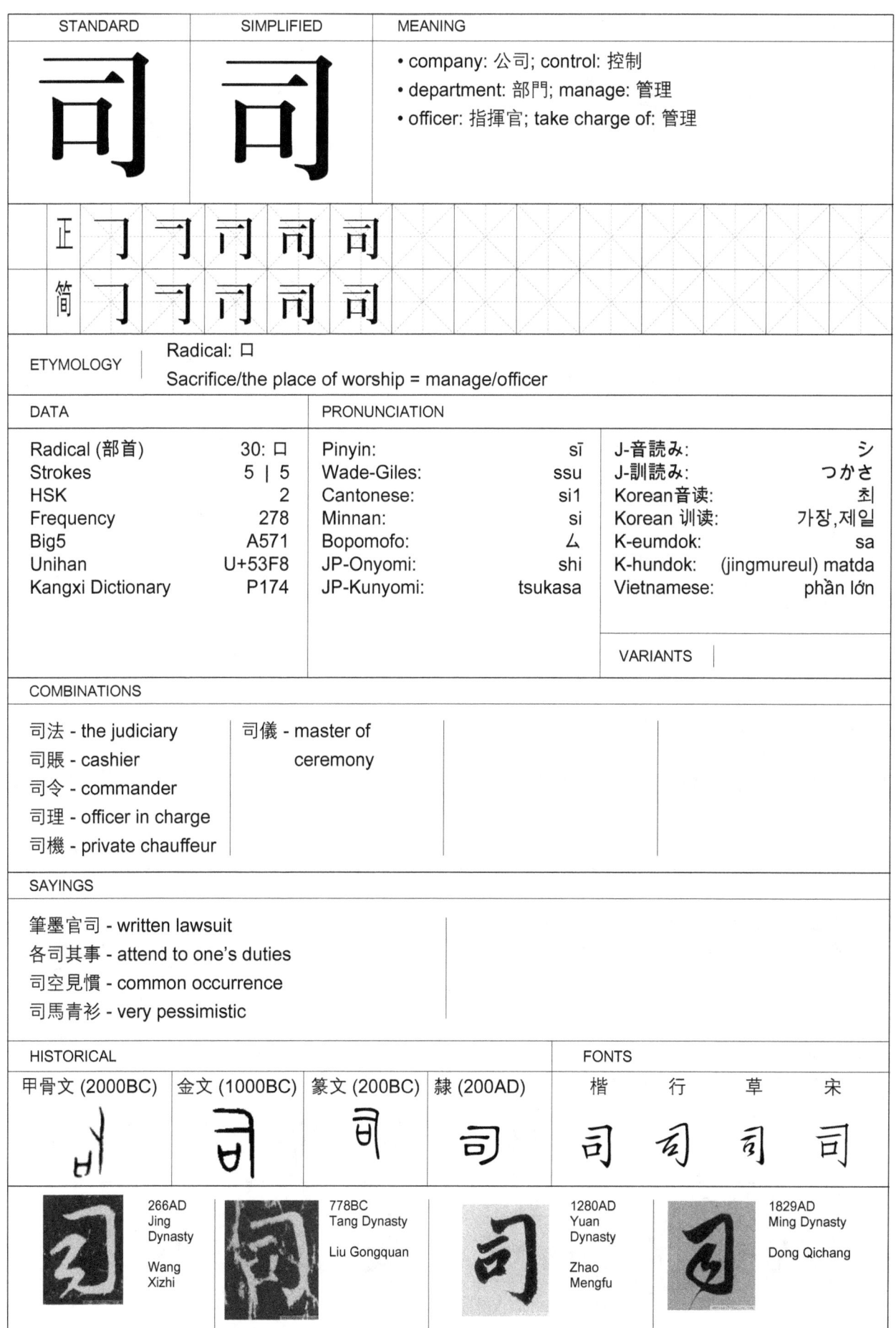

STANDARD	SIMPLIFIED	MEANING
司	司	• company: 公司; control: 控制 • department: 部門; manage: 管理 • officer: 指揮官; take charge of: 管理

正: 丁 コ 司 司 司
简: 丁 コ 司 司 司

ETYMOLOGY
Radical: 口
Sacrifice/the place of worship = manage/officer

DATA
- Radical (部首): 30: 口
- Strokes: 5 | 5
- HSK: 2
- Frequency: 278
- Big5: A571
- Unihan: U+53F8
- Kangxi Dictionary: P174

PRONUNCIATION
- Pinyin: sī
- Wade-Giles: ssu
- Cantonese: si1
- Minnan: si
- Bopomofo: ㄙ
- JP-Onyomi: shi
- JP-Kunyomi: tsukasa
- J-音読み: シ
- J-訓読み: つかさ
- Korean 音读: 최
- Korean 训读: 가장,제일
- K-eumdok: sa
- K-hundok: (jingmureul) matda
- Vietnamese: phần lớn

VARIANTS

COMBINATIONS
- 司法 - the judiciary
- 司賬 - cashier
- 司令 - commander
- 司理 - officer in charge
- 司機 - private chauffeur
- 司儀 - master of ceremony

SAYINGS
- 筆墨官司 - written lawsuit
- 各司其事 - attend to one's duties
- 司空見慣 - common occurrence
- 司馬青衫 - very pessimistic

HISTORICAL

甲骨文 (2000BC)	金文 (1000BC)	篆文 (200BC)	隸 (200AD)

FONTS
楷　行　草　宋

- 266AD Jing Dynasty — Wang Xizhi
- 778BC Tang Dynasty — Liu Gongquan
- 1280AD Yuan Dynasty — Zhao Mengfu
- 1829AD Ming Dynasty — Dong Qichang

THE GENIUS OF CHINESE CHARACTERS

STANDARD	SIMPLIFIED	MEANING
最	最	• most: 最; (the) most: 最多 • -est: 最; exceedingly: 尤其 • extremely: 極其地 • more than anything 比任何都要多 (最)

正: 丨 冂 冂 日 旦 早 昂 冔 冔 昴 最 最
简: 丨 冂 冂 日 旦 早 昂 冔 冔 昴 最 最

ETYMOLOGY Radical: 冂 Forward 月 (part of 冒 cover) cut off enemy's ears 耳 with hands 又: render meritorious service = most/exceedingly

DATA
- Radical (部首): 13: 冂
- Strokes: 12 | 12
- HSK: 2
- Frequency: 139
- Big5: B3CC
- Unihan: U+6700
- Kangxi Dictionary: P503

PRONUNCIATION
- Pinyin: zuì
- Wade-Giles: tsui
- Cantonese: jui3
- Minnan: chòe
- Bopomofo: ㄗㄨㄟˋ
- JP-Onyomi: sai
- JP-Kunyomi: motto·mo
- J-音読み: サイ
- J-訓読み: もっと·も
- Korean 音读: 최
- Korean 训读: 가장,제일
- K-eumdok: ch'oe
- K-hundok: gajang, jeil
- Vietnamese: phần lớn

VARIANTS

COMBINATIONS
- 最小 - minimum
- 最高 - tallest
- 最要緊 - most important
- 最先 - earliest
- 最佳 - finest
- 最便宜 - cheapest
- 最美 - most beautiful

SAYINGS
- 爲善最樂 - doing good is most pleasurable
- 不耻最後 - being last is not shameful

HISTORICAL

甲骨文 (2000BC)	金文 (1000BC)	篆文 (200BC)	隸 (200AD)
		冣	最

FONTS
楷 行 草 宋
最 最 最 最

266AD Jing Dynasty — Wang Xizhi

778BC Tang Dynasty — Yan Zhenqing

1280AD Yuan Dynasty — Zhao Mengfu

1829AD Ming Dynasty — Dong Qichang

THE GENIUS OF CHINESE CHARACTERS

STANDARD	SIMPLIFIED	MEANING
所	所	• place: 地方; actually: 真正地 • firm: 公司; location: 地點 • numerary adjunct: 數量輔助

正: 丶 厂 斤 斤 斤 盯 所 所
简: 丶 厂 斤 斤 斤 盯 所 所

ETYMOLOGY

Radical: 斤
Axe 斤 + 戶 (phonetic): the sound of lumber. The meaning of "place" was borrowed

DATA

Radical (部首)	63: 戶
Strokes	8 | 8
HSK	2
Frequency	54
Big5	A9D2
Unihan	U+6240
Kangxi Dictionary	P415

PRONUNCIATION

Pinyin:	suǒ
Wade-Giles:	so
Cantonese:	soh2
Minnan:	só
Bopomofo:	ㄙㄨㄛˇ
JP-Onyomi:	sho
JP-Kunyomi:	tokoro
J-音読み:	ショ
J-訓読み:	ところ
Korean 音读:	소
Korean 训读:	바
K-eumdok:	so
K-hundok:	ba
Vietnamese:	địa điểm

VARIANTS

COMBINATIONS

厕所 - toilet
診所 - clinic
派出所 - police station
所識 - an acquaintance
所爲 - reason

所司 - one's duties
所謂 - so-called

SAYINGS

隨心所欲 - at one's own will
不知所措 - at a loss
強人所難 - force one's hand
匪夷所思 - unthinkable cases

眾所周知 - as everyone knows
千夫所指 - be universally condemned
暢所欲言 - speak up freely
各得其所 - everything gets its just rewards

HISTORICAL

甲骨文 (2000BC)	金文 (1000BC)	篆文 (200BC)	隸 (200AD)
	斦	斦	所

FONTS

楷 行 草 宋
所 所 所 所

266AD Jing Dynasty Wang Xizhi

778BC Tang Dynasty Liu Gongquan

1280AD Yuan Dynasty Zhao Mengfu

1829AD Ming Dynasty Dong Qichang

THE GENIUS OF CHINESE CHARACTERS

STANDARD	SIMPLIFIED	MEANING
但	但	• but: 但是; however: 然而 • only: 僅僅; still: 仍然 • yet: 還沒有; merely: 僅僅

正 ノ 亻 仁 佀 但 但 但
简 ノ 亻 仁 佀 但 但 但

ETYMOLOGY Radical: 人 People 人 + 旦 (phonetic): topless. But/however/provided that/just are borrowed meanings

DATA

Radical (部首)	9: 人		
Strokes	7 | 7		
HSK	2		
Frequency	95		
Big5	A6FD		
Unihan	U+4F46		
Kangxi Dictionary	P970		

PRONUNCIATION

Pinyin:	dàn	J-音読み:	タン, ダン
Wade-Giles:	tan	J-訓読み:	ただ·し
Cantonese:	daan6	Korean音读:	단
Minnan:	nā	Korean 训读:	다만, 오직
Bopomofo:	ㄉㄢˋ	K-eumdok:	tan
JP-Onyomi:	tan, dan	K-hundok:	daman, ojik
JP-Kunyomi:	tada·shi	Vietnamese:	nhưng

VARIANTS

COMBINATIONS

但是 - but
但祇 - only
但凡 - all
但使 - only if
但願 - hope

但須 - only want
但望 - only hope

SAYINGS

不求有功, 但求無過 - ask for no merits, but pray there be no faults

HISTORICAL

甲骨文 (2000BC)	金文 (1000BC)	篆文 (200BC)	隸 (200AD)
		但	但

FONTS

楷　行　草　宋
但　但　但　但

| 266AD
Jing Dynasty
Wang Xizhi | 778BC
Tang Dynasty
Liu Gongquan | 1280AD
Yuan Dynasty
Zhao Mengfu | 1829AD
Ming Dynasty
Dong Qichang |

THE GENIUS OF CHINESE CHARACTERS

STANDARD	SIMPLIFIED	MEANING
長	长	• long: 長; chief: 主要地; elder: 年長的; to grow: 成長 • head: 領導; length: 長度; to develop: 發展 • constantly: 不變的; forever: 永遠; Director: 領導 • always: 一直; excel in: 擅長; leader: 領導 • strong point: 主要的觀點

正　一　厂　厂　F　E　E　E　長　長

簡　丿　亠　匕　长

ETYMOLOGY　Radical: 長 Pictograph: a long-haired old man with a cane, elder, far/long /grow = often

DATA

Radical (部首)	168: 長			
Strokes	8 | 4			
HSK	2			
Frequency	109			
Big5	AAF8			
Unihan	U+957F			
Kangxi Dictionary	P1328			

PRONUNCIATION

Pinyin:	zhǎng
Wade-Giles:	ch'ang
Cantonese:	cheung4
Minnan:	chhiâng
Bopomofo:	ㄔㄤˊ/ㄓㄤˇ
JP-Onyomi:	chō
JP-Kunyomi:	naga·i

J-音読み:	チョウ
J-訓読み:	なが·い
Korean 音读:	장
Korean 训读:	길다
K-eumdok:	chang
K-hundok:	gilda
Vietnamese:	dài

VARIANTS

COMBINATIONS

長頸鹿 - giraffe　　　長城 - the Great Wall
長大 - grow up　　　長空 - the sky
長價 - rise in price　　長逝 - to pass away
長風 - swift wind
長兄 - eldest brother

SAYINGS

揠苗助長 - haste makes waste　　身無長物 - have no valuable things
草長鶯飛 - describing an ideal environment　博采眾長 - draw upon the strengths of others
傲不可長 - avoid arrogance　　　乘風破浪 - to be ambitious and unafraid of
鞭長莫及 - beyond the reach　　　　　　　　setbacks

HISTORICAL

甲骨文 (2000BC)	金文 (1000BC)	篆文 (200BC)	隸 (200AD)

FONTS

楷　行　草　宋

 266AD Jing Dynasty Wang Xizhi

 778BC Tang Dynasty Liu Gongquan

 1280AD Yuan Dynasty Zhao Mengfu

 1829AD Ming Dynasty Dong Qichang

THE GENIUS OF CHINESE CHARACTERS

STANDARD	SIMPLIFIED	MEANING
員	员	• member: 成員; employee: 職員 • person: 個人; personnel: 全體人員 • staff member: 職工

Stroke order (正): 丨 冂 口 尸 吕 吕 冒 冒 員 員
Stroke order (简): 丨 冂 口 尸 吕 员 员

ETYMOLOGY

Radical: 口 A cauldron 鼎 (now is simplified as 贝) with a circle 口 shown above the rim: circle, unit of quantity = member

DATA

		PRONUNCIATION			
Radical (部首)	30: 口	Pinyin:	yuán	J-音読み:	イン
Strokes	10 | 7	Wade-Giles:	yüen	J-訓読み:	かず
HSK	2	Cantonese:	yuen4	Korean 音读:	원
Frequency	200	Minnan:	ôan	Korean 训读:	인원
Big5	ADFB	Bopomofo:	ㄩㄢˊ	K-eumdok:	wǒn
Unihan	U+5458	JP-Onyomi:	in	K-hundok:	inwon
Kangxi Dictionary	P189	JP-Kunyomi:	˙kazu	Vietnamese:	hội viên

VARIANTS

COMBINATIONS

職員 - staff member   機員 - mechanic
駕駛員 - pilot   會員 - society member
打字員 - typist   球員 - ballplayer
參議員 - senator
運動員 - athlete

SAYINGS

反面教員 - negative example

HISTORICAL

甲骨文 (2000BC)	金文 (1000BC)	篆文 (200BC)	隸 (200AD)

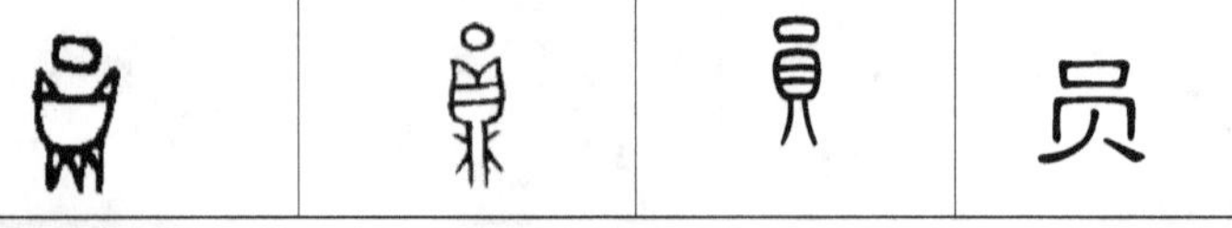

FONTS

楷　行　草　宋

266AD Jing Dynasty Wang Xizhi
778BC Tang Dynasty Liu Gongquan 
1280AD Yuan Dynasty Zhao Mengfu 
1829AD Ming Dynasty Wang Duo

THE GENIUS OF CHINESE CHARACTERS

STANDARD	SIMPLIFIED	MEANING
次	次	• second(ary): 次要的; next: 下一個; order: 順序 • sequence: 次序; measure word: 計量單位 • nth: 計量單位; number (of times): 次數 • inferior: 高級; times: 次數; to help: 幫助 • nimble: 聰明的; surname 別名; time 時間

| 正 | 丶 | 冫 | 冫 | 汁 | 汐 | 次 |
| 简 | 丶 | 冫 | 冫 | 汁 | 汐 | 次 |

ETYMOLOGY — Radical: 欠 Second 二 (now 冫, phonetic) + people open his mouth 欠 (lack of breath): the second-class = number (of times)

DATA

		PRONUNCIATION			
Radical (部首)	76: 欠	Pinyin:	cì	J-音読み:	ジ, シ
Strokes	6 | 6	Wade-Giles:	tz'u	J-訓読み:	つぎ, つ・ぐ
HSK	2	Cantonese:	chi3	Korean 音读:	차
Frequency	183	Minnan:	chhù	Korean 训读:	다음, 둘째
Big5	A6B8	Bopomofo:	ㄘˋ	K-eumdok:	ch'a
Unihan	U+6B21	JP-Onyomi:	ji,shi	K-hundok:	daeum, duljjae
Kangxi Dictionary	P565	JP-Kunyomi:	tsugi, tsu·gu	Vietnamese:	thời đại

VARIANTS

COMBINATIONS

多次 - many times　　　　次長 - vice-minister
舟次 - during voyage　　　次數 - number of times
次之 - next to it
次等 - second-rate
次第 - order

SAYINGS

不可造次 - do not hurry blindly　　　　語無倫次 - allophasis/incoherence
造次顛沛 - destitute and homeless　　　不次之遷/超階越次 - exceptional promotion
鱗次櫛比 - row upon row　　　　　　　　鮑魚之次 - a bad environment
三番五次 - again and again

HISTORICAL

甲骨文 (2000BC)	金文 (1000BC)	篆文 (200BC)	隸 (200AD)	FONTS 楷 行 草 宋

 266AD Jing Dynasty Wang Xizhi

 778BC Tang Dynasty Liu Gongquan

 1280AD Yuan Dynasty Zhao Mengfu

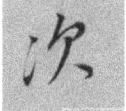 1829AD Ming Dynasty Dong Qichang

THE GENIUS OF CHINESE CHARACTERS

STANDARD	SIMPLIFIED	MEANING
體	体	• body: 身體; form: 體 • style: 體例; system: 體系 • group: 集體; unit: 個體

正: 丨 冂 冎 冎 咼 骨 骨 骨 骨 骨 骨 骨 骨
骨豊 骨豊 骨豊 骨豐 骨豐 體 體 體 體

简: 丿 亻 仁 什 仆 休 体

ETYMOLOGY

Radical: 欠
Bone 骨 + 豊 (phonetic): entire body = feel/limb/essence

DATA

Radical (部首)	188: 骨
Strokes	22 | 7
HSK	2
Frequency	149
Big5	C5E9
Unihan	U+4F53
Kangxi Dictionary	P1451

PRONUNCIATION

Pinyin:	tǐ
Wade-Giles:	t'i
Cantonese:	tai2
Minnan:	thé
Bopomofo:	ㄊㄧˇ
JP-Onyomi:	tai, tei
JP-Kunyomi:	karada

J-音読み:	タイ, テイ
J-訓読み:	からだ
Korean 音读:	체
Korean 训读:	몸, 신체
K-eumdok:	ch'e
K-hundok:	mom, sinche
Vietnamese:	thân hình

VARIANTS | 体(J)

COMBINATIONS

- 液體 - fluid
- 本體 - essence
- 體沉 - heavy
- 體罰 - corporal punishment
- 體操 - physical exercise
- 體用 - substance and function
- 體魄 - a person's physique

SAYINGS

- 遍體鱗傷 - be a mass of bruises
- 不成體統 - have no manners, ill-mannered
- 不識大體 - cannot think about the bigger picture
- 量體裁衣 - act according to actual circumstances
- 身體力行 - set an example
- 魂不附體 - be scared out of wits

HISTORICAL

(2000BC)	金文 (1000BC)	篆文 (200BC)	隸 (200AD)
	豊	體	体

FONTS

楷	行	草	宋
体	体	体	体

- 266AD Jing Dynasty, Wang Xizhi
- 778BC Tang Dynasty, Liu Gongquan
- 1280AD Yuan Dynasty, Zhao Mengfu
- 1829AD Ming Dynasty, Dong Qichang

THE GENIUS OF Chinese CHARACTERS

STANDARD	SIMPLIFIED	MEANING
等	等	• grade: 等差; rank: 等級; and so on: 等等 • await: 等待; class: 等; equal to: 等于 • et cetera: 等等

ETYMOLOGY

Radical: 竹
The bamboo slips 竹 in the office 寺 are neat and tidy: neat/consistent, type/class/rank

DATA

Radical (部首)	118: 竹
Strokes	12 | 12
HSK	2
Frequency	158
Big5	B5A5
Unihan	U+7B49
Kangxi Dictionary	P882

PRONUNCIATION

Pinyin:	děng
Wade-Giles:	têng
Cantonese:	dang2
Minnan:	téng
Bopomofo:	ㄉㄥˇ
JP-Onyomi:	tō
JP-Kunyomi:	hito·shī
J-音読み:	トウ
J-訓読み:	ひと・しい
Korean 音读:	등
Korean 训读:	무리, 부류
K-eumdok:	tŭng
K-hundok:	muri, buryu
Vietnamese:	chờ đợi

VARIANTS | 䓁

COMBINATIONS

同等 - same class
等人 - wait for someone
相等 - equal
等等 - and so forth
等級 - grade

等式 - equality
等著瞧 - wait and see

SAYINGS

等量齊觀 - to equate different things
高人一等 - superior to others
罪加一等 - doubly guilty
三六九等 - various grades and ranks

著作等身 - a prolific writer
等米下鍋 - in straitened circumstances
同休等戚 - share joys and sorrows
等閒視之 - regard as unimportant

HISTORICAL

甲骨文 (2000BC)	金文 (1000BC)	篆文 (200BC)	隸 (200AD)

266AD Jing Dynasty Wang Xizhi
778BC Tang Dynasty Liu Gongquan
1280AD Yuan Dynasty Zhao Mengfu
1829AD Ming Dynasty Dong Qichang

FONTS

楷 行 草 宋

THE GENIUS OF CHINESE CHARACTERS

STANDARD	SIMPLIFIED	MEANING
著	着	• to wear: 帶著; to wear (clothes): 穿著 • catch: 接著; suffer: 著; to touch: 著 • to write: 著; along with: 隨著

正 ` ⺍ 艹 苎 兰 䒑 芊 差 着 着 着
简 ` ⺍ 艹 苎 兰 䒑 芊 差 着 着 着

ETYMOLOGY: Radical: 目 Bamboo 竹 (now ⺮) + 者 (phonetic): chopsticks. The meanings of "write"/"book" were borrowed from 書

DATA

Radical (部首)	109: 目
Strokes	11 | 11
HSK	2
Frequency	41
Big5	B5DB
Unihan	U+7740
Kangxi Dictionary	P1044

PRONUNCIATION

Pinyin:	zhe
Wade-Giles:	chao
Cantonese:	jeuk6
Minnan:	tiòh
Bopomofo:	ㄓㄛˊ/ㄓㄨˋ
JP-Onyomi:	cho
JP-Kunyomi:	ichijiru·shī

J-音読み:	チョ
J-訓読み:	いちじる·しい
Korean 音读:	저
Korean 训读:	뜰
K-eumdok:	chŏ
K-hundok:	tteul
Vietnamese:	viết

VARIANTS	著

COMBINATIONS

著述 - author's works
著棋 - play chess
著花 - blossoms
著色 - to apply color

SAYINGS

不著邊際 - irrelevant
大處著墨 - concentrate on major problems
歪打正著 - hit the mark by a fluke
吃不了兜著走 - to bear all consequences

一著不慎滿盤皆輸 - one careless move loses the whole game
急驚風撞著慢郎中 - an urgent case receiving slow treatment

HISTORICAL

甲骨文 (2000BC)	金文 (1000BC)	篆文 (200BC)	隸 (200AD)

FONTS

楷	行	草	宋
着	着	着	着

THE GENIUS OF CHINESE CHARACTERS

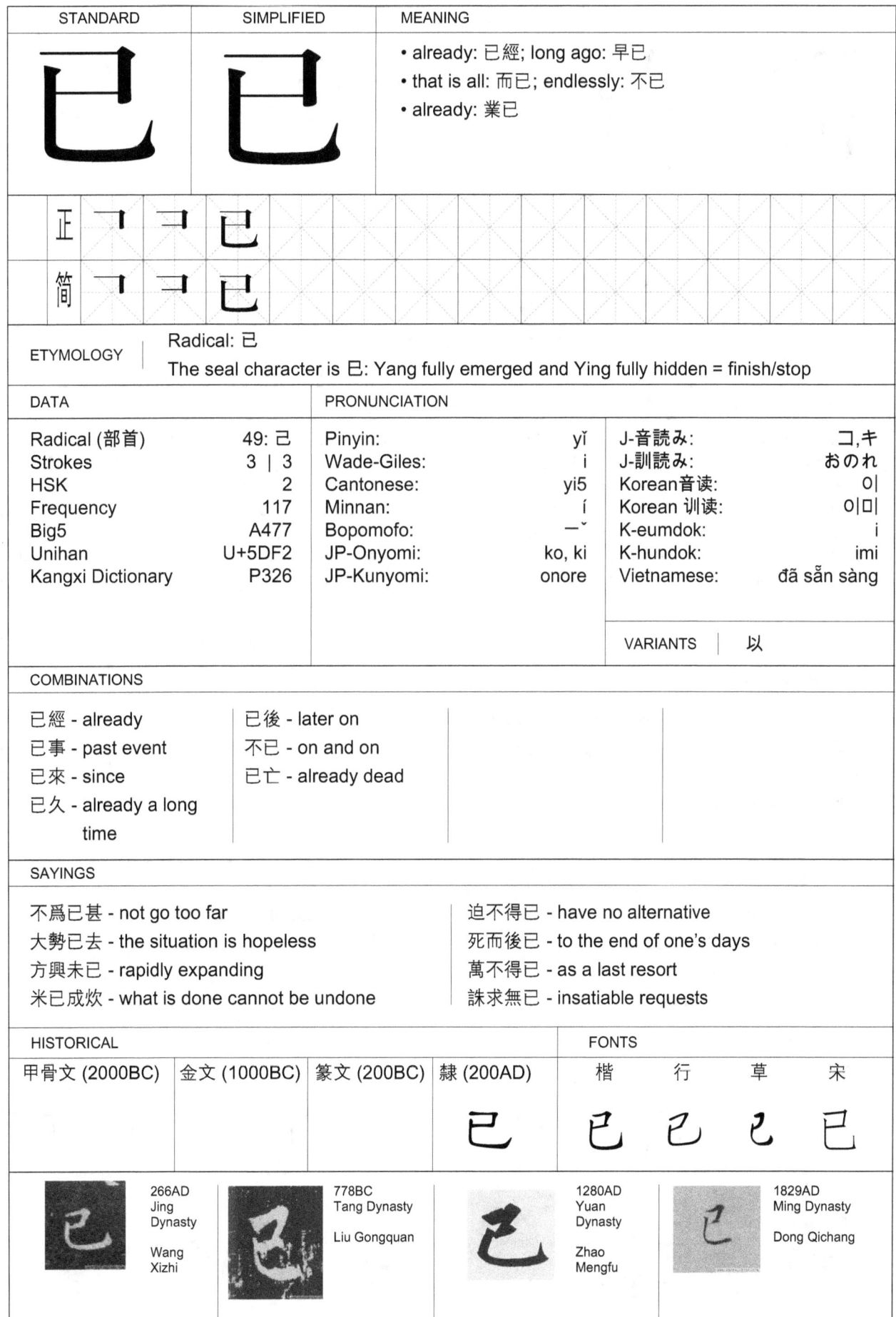

STANDARD	SIMPLIFIED	MEANING
已	已	• already: 已經; long ago: 早已 • that is all: 而已; endlessly: 不已 • already: 業已

正 フ 己 已
简 フ 己 已

ETYMOLOGY

Radical: 已

The seal character is 巳: Yang fully emerged and Ying fully hidden = finish/stop

DATA

Radical (部首)	49: 己
Strokes	3 | 3
HSK	2
Frequency	117
Big5	A477
Unihan	U+5DF2
Kangxi Dictionary	P326

PRONUNCIATION

Pinyin:	yǐ
Wade-Giles:	i
Cantonese:	yi5
Minnan:	í
Bopomofo:	ˇ
JP-Onyomi:	ko, ki
JP-Kunyomi:	onore
J-音読み:	コ, キ
J-訓読み:	おのれ
Korean 音读:	이
Korean 训读:	이미
K-eumdok:	i
K-hundok:	imi
Vietnamese:	đã sẵn sàng

VARIANTS | 以

COMBINATIONS

已經 - already
已事 - past event
已來 - since
已久 - already a long time

已後 - later on
不已 - on and on
已亡 - already dead

SAYINGS

不爲已甚 - not go too far
大勢已去 - the situation is hopeless
方興未已 - rapidly expanding
米已成炊 - what is done cannot be undone

迫不得已 - have no alternative
死而後已 - to the end of one's days
萬不得已 - as a last resort
誅求無已 - insatiable requests

HISTORICAL

甲骨文 (2000BC)	金文 (1000BC)	篆文 (200BC)	隸 (200AD)

FONTS

楷 行 草 宋

已 已 已 已 已

266AD Jing Dynasty Wang Xizhi

778BC Tang Dynasty Liu Gongquan

1280AD Yuan Dynasty Zhao Mengfu

1829AD Ming Dynasty Dong Qichang

THE GENIUS OF CHINESE CHARACTERS

STANDARD	SIMPLIFIED	MEANING
間	间	• among: 之間; between: 中間 • space: 空間; period, time 期間

正: 丨 ㄱ ㄧ 尸 尸 門 門 門 門 問 間 間
简: 丶 丨 门 门 问 问 间

ETYMOLOGY: Radical: 日 The sun 日 shone through the crack between two sides of a gate 門: between/among = space/time

DATA

		PRONUNCIATION			
Radical (部首)	169: 門	Pinyin:	jiān	J-音読み:	カン, ケン
Strokes	12 | 7	Wade-Giles:	chien	J-訓読み:	あいだ, ま
HSK	2	Cantonese:	gaan3	Korean 音读:	간
Frequency	135	Minnan:	keng	Korean 训读:	사이
Big5	B6A1	Bopomofo:	ㄐㄧㄢ	K-eumdok:	kan
Unihan	U+95F4	JP-Onyomi:	kan, ken	K-hundok:	sai
Kangxi Dictionary	P1333	JP-Kunyomi:	aida, ma	Vietnamese:	giữa

VARIANTS

COMBINATIONS

田間 - the fields
中間 - midpoint
間隙 - space
其間 - in the interval
少間 - in a little while

間諜 - a secret agent
間隔 - intermission

SAYINGS

黃金時間 - prime time
間不容髮 - extremely critical
親密無間 - closely united
人間地獄 - a hell on earth

人間天堂 - an earthly paradise
瞬息之間 - in the twinkling of an eye
天上人間 - immeausrably vast difference
挑撥離間 - alienate one person from another

HISTORICAL | FONTS

甲骨文 (2000BC) | 金文 (1000BC) | 篆文 (200BC) | 隸 (200AD) | 楷 行 草 宋

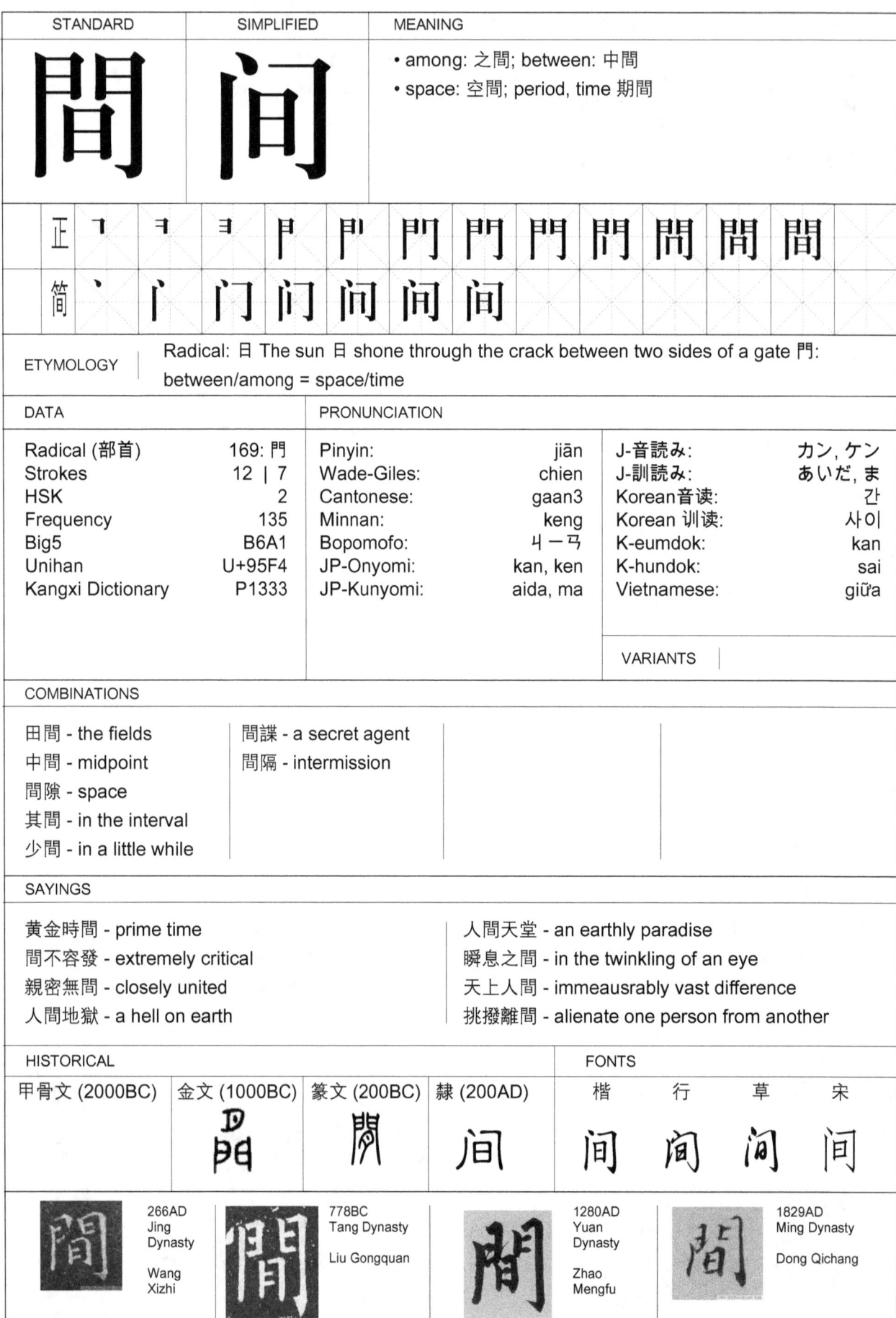

266AD Jing Dynasty Wang Xizhi
778BC Tang Dynasty Liu Gongquan
1280AD Yuan Dynasty Zhao Mengfu
1829AD Ming Dynasty Dong Qichang

THE GENIUS OF CHINESE CHARACTERS

STANDARD	SIMPLIFIED	MEANING
比	比	• compare: 比較; competition: 比賽 • compare: 相比; contrast: 對比

正 一 ヒ 上 比
简 一 ヒ 上 比

ETYMOLOGY Radical: 比
One person immediately behind the other: adjacent/consistent = compare/near

DATA

		PRONUNCIATION			
Radical (部首)	81: 比	Pinyin:	bǐ	J-音読み:	ヒ, ビ
Strokes	4 | 4	Wade-Giles:	pi	J-訓読み:	くら·べる
HSK	2	Cantonese:	bei2	Korean 音读:	비
Frequency	199	Minnan:	pí	Korean 训读:	견주다, 비교하다
Big5	A4F1	Bopomofo:	ㄅㄧˇ	K-eumdok:	pi
Unihan	U+6BD4	JP-Onyomi:	hi,bi	K-hundok:	gyeonjuda, bigyohada
Kangxi Dictionary	P590	JP-Kunyomi:	kura·beru	Vietnamese:	tỉ lệ

VARIANTS 匕, 夶

COMBINATIONS

比來 - recently (lit.)
比如 - for example
比方 - for instance
比賽 - contest
比喻 - a metaphor

比及 - by the time (lit.)
可比 - be just like, comparable

SAYINGS

比比皆是 - in abundance
比肩接踵 - jostle each other
比手劃脚 - mime
比翼雙飛 - happy couple

今非昔比 - things are no longer as they were
鱗次櫛比 - row upon row of
朋比爲奸 - join in plotting treason
壽比南山 - longevity

HISTORICAL

甲骨文 (2000BC)	金文 (1000BC)	篆文 (200BC)	隸 (200AD)

FONTS

楷 行 草 宋

| 266AD Jing Dynasty Wang Xizhi | 778BC Tang Dynasty Liu Gongquan | 1280AD Yuan Dynasty Zhao Mengfu | 1829AD Ming Dynasty Dong Qichang |

THE GENIUS OF CHINESE CHARACTERS

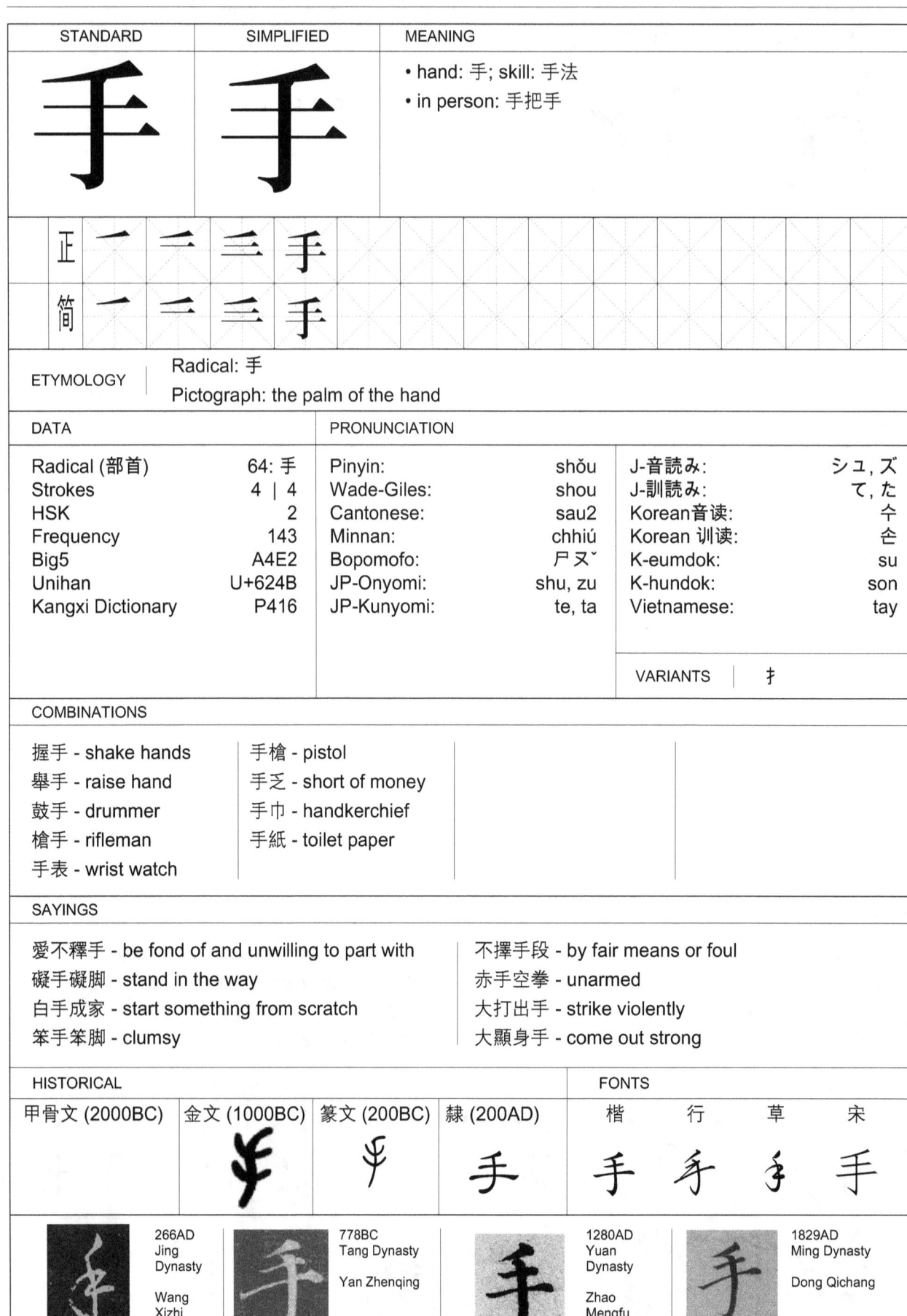

STANDARD	SIMPLIFIED	MEANING
手	手	• hand: 手; skill: 手法 • in person: 手把手

正 一 二 三 手
简 一 二 三 手

ETYMOLOGY
Radical: 手
Pictograph: the palm of the hand

DATA

Radical (部首)	64: 手		
Strokes	4 | 4		
HSK	2		
Frequency	143		
Big5	A4E2		
Unihan	U+624B		
Kangxi Dictionary	P416		

PRONUNCIATION

Pinyin:	shǒu	J-音読み:	シュ, ズ
Wade-Giles:	shou	J-訓読み:	て, た
Cantonese:	sau2	Korean 音读:	수
Minnan:	chhiú	Korean 训读:	손
Bopomofo:	ㄕㄡˇ	K-eumdok:	su
JP-Onyomi:	shu, zu	K-hundok:	son
JP-Kunyomi:	te, ta	Vietnamese:	tay

VARIANTS | 扌

COMBINATIONS

握手 - shake hands
舉手 - raise hand
鼓手 - drummer
槍手 - rifleman
手表 - wrist watch

手槍 - pistol
手乏 - short of money
手巾 - handkerchief
手紙 - toilet paper

SAYINGS

愛不釋手 - be fond of and unwilling to part with
礙手礙脚 - stand in the way
白手成家 - start something from scratch
笨手笨脚 - clumsy

不擇手段 - by fair means or foul
赤手空拳 - unarmed
大打出手 - strike violently
大顯身手 - come out strong

HISTORICAL

甲骨文 (2000BC)	金文 (1000BC)	篆文 (200BC)	隸 (200AD)
	手	手	手

FONTS

楷 行 草 宋
手 手 手 手

266AD
Jing Dynasty
Wang Xizhi

778BC
Tang Dynasty
Yan Zhenqing

1280AD
Yuan Dynasty
Zhao Mengfu

1829AD
Ming Dynasty
Dong Qichang

THE GENIUS OF CHINESE CHARACTERS

STANDARD	SIMPLIFIED	MEANING
表	表	• surface layer: 表層 • state clearly: 表白 • convey: 表達 • statistical table: 表報

正 一 ニ 三 丰 圭 尹 尹 表 表
简 一 ニ 三 丰 圭 尹 尹 表 表

ETYMOLOGY

Radical: 毛

Clothing 衣 + hair/fur 毛: A fur coat worn over clothes, exterior/surface = display/express

DATA

Radical (部首)	145: 衣
Strokes	8 | 8
HSK	2
Frequency	177
Big5	AAED
Unihan	U+8868
Kangxi Dictionary	P1111

PRONUNCIATION

Pinyin:	biǎo
Wade-Giles:	piao
Cantonese:	biu2
Minnan:	piáu
Bopomofo:	ㄅㄧㄠˇ
JP-Onyomi:	hyō
JP-Kunyomi:	omote, arawa·su

J-音読み:	ヒョウ
J-訓読み:	おもて, あらわ·す
Korean 音读:	표
Korean 训读:	겉, 거죽, 겉면
K-eumdok:	p'yo
K-hundok:	geot, geojuk, geonmyeon
Vietnamese:	bàn

VARIANTS	錶

COMBINATIONS

圖表 - chart
表情 - expression
表明 - demonstrate
表相 - external appearance

表示 - show
表率 - model
表決 - decide by vote
表彰 - commend

SAYINGS

表裏不一 - two-faced
表裏如一 - be the same outside and inside
表面文章 - ostentation
出人意表 - exceeding all expectations

萬世師表 - the teacher for all ages
虛有其表 - appear better than it is
由表及裏 - from the surface to the center
自我表現 - self-expression

HISTORICAL

甲骨文 (2000BC)	金文 (1000BC)	篆文 (200BC)	隸 (200AD)
		褱	表

FONTS

楷 行 草 宋
表 表 表 表

266AD
Jing Dynasty
Wang Xizhi

778BC
Tang Dynasty
Liu Gongquan

1280AD
Yuan Dynasty
Zhao Mengfu

1829AD
Ming Dynasty
Dong Qichang

THE GENIUS OF CHINESE CHARACTERS

STANDARD	SIMPLIFIED	MEANING
兩	两	• two, both, ounce: 兩 • twice: 兩倍

正 一 丆 厂 币 帀 兩 兩 兩
简 一 丆 厂 万 丙 两 两

ETYMOLOGY — Radical: 入
One 一 + two identical things placed side by side 网: double/a pair of, unit of weight

DATA

Radical (部首)	11: 入
Strokes	8 | 7
HSK	2
Frequency	133
Big5	A8E2
Unihan	U+4E24
Kangxi Dictionary	P126

PRONUNCIATION

Pinyin:	liǎng
Wade-Giles:	liang
Cantonese:	leung5
Minnan:	nńg
Bopomofo:	ㄌㄧㄤˇ
JP-Onyomi:	ryō
JP-Kunyomi:	futa·tsu

J-音読み:	リョウ
J-訓読み:	ふた·つ
Korean 音读:	량, 양
Korean 训读:	두, 둘, 쌍
K-eumdok:	ryang, yang
K-hundok:	du, dul, ssang
Vietnamese:	hai

VARIANTS | 両(J), 网

COMBINATIONS

兩個人 - two persons
兩相好 - two lovers
兩夫妻 - man and wife
兩造 - both parties to a law suit
兩院制 - bicameral system
兩面 - both sides

SAYINGS

兩面三刀 - be two-faced
兩小無猜 - innocence of childhood friends
三長兩短 - unexpected misfortune
三天兩頭 - every other day or so
三言兩語 - with just a few words
誓不兩立 - to be irreconcilable
一刀兩斷 - make a clean break with
一舉兩得 - kill two birds with one stone

HISTORICAL

甲骨文 (2000BC)	金文 (1000BC)	篆文 (200BC)	隸 (200AD)
	兩	兩	兩

266AD Jing Dynasty Wang Xizhi
778BC Tang Dynasty Yan Zhenqing
1280AD Yuan Dynasty Zhao Mengfu
1829AD Ming Dynasty Dong Qichang

FONTS

楷	行	草	宋
兩	两	两	两

THE GENIUS OF CHINESE CHARACTERS

STANDARD	SIMPLIFIED	MEANING
意	意	• idea: 意見; meaning: 意思 • expectation: 意表; Italy: 意大利 • zucchini: 意大利青瓜

正: 丶 亠 立 产 产 产 音 音 音 音 意 意 意
简: 丶 亠 立 产 产 产 音 音 音 音 意 意 意

ETYMOLOGY
Radical: 心
Heart 心 + sound 音: heartfelt wishes = meaning/desire/guess

DATA

		PRONUNCIATION			
Radical (部首)	61: 心	Pinyin:	yì	J-音読み:	イ
Strokes	13 | 13	Wade-Giles:	i	J-訓読み:	おも·う
HSK	2	Cantonese:	yi3	Korean 音读:	의
Frequency	104	Minnan:	ì	Korean 训读:	뜻, 의미
Big5	B74E	Bopomofo:	ㄧˋ	K-eumdok:	ŭi
Unihan	U+610F	JP-Onyomi:	i	K-hundok:	tteut, uimi
Kangxi Dictionary	P394	JP-Kunyomi:	omo·u	Vietnamese:	ý nghĩa

VARIANTS | 噫

COMBINATIONS

心意 - desire
失意 - disappointed
主意 - a mind set
善意 - good intentions
意見 - opinion

意圖 - intention
意義 - meaning

SAYINGS

不懷好意 - harbor evil designs
不以爲意 - not take it seriously
差强人意 - just passable
稱心如意 - as one wishes

誠心誠意 - honestly
出乎意料 - beyond expectations
得意忘形 - get dizzy with success
得意洋洋 - cheerful and confident

HISTORICAL

甲骨文 (2000BC)	金文 (1000BC)	篆文 (200BC)	隸 (200AD)	FONTS
		意	意	楷 行 草 宋 意 意 意 意

266AD
Jing Dynasty
Wang Xizhi

778BC
Tang Dynasty
Yan Zhenqing

1280AD
Yuan Dynasty
Zhao Mengfu

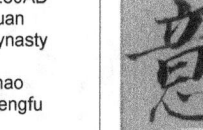
1829AD
Ming Dynasty
Dong Qichang

THE GENIUS OF CHINESE CHARACTERS

STANDARD	SIMPLIFIED	MEANING
務	务	• serve: 服務; assignment: 任務 • business: 業務; obligation: 義務

正: 一 ⼆ 予 予 矛 矛 矛 務 務
简: 丿 ク 久 冬 务

ETYMOLOGY: Radical: 力 Power 力 + try hard 敄 (phonetic): tend to, the most important thing/business = must

DATA

Radical (部首)	19: 力	Pinyin:	wù
Strokes	10 | 5	Wade-Giles:	wu
HSK	2	Cantonese:	mo6
Frequency	245	Minnan:	bū
Big5	B0C8	Bopomofo:	ㄨˋ
Unihan	U+52A1	JP-Onyomi:	mu
Kangxi Dictionary	P148	JP-Kunyomi:	tsuto·meru

J-音読み:	ム
J-訓読み:	つと·める
Korean 音读:	무
Korean 训读:	힘쓰다
K-eumdok:	mu
K-hundok:	himsseuda
Vietnamese:	kinh doanh

VARIANTS

COMBINATIONS

職務 - duties
債務 - debts
務求 - strive to
務醫 - be a doctor
校務 - school affairs

務必 - must
務實 - try to be practical
政務 - political business

SAYINGS

不急之務 - matter of no great urgency
不識時務 - behind the times
不務空名 - not to seek empty fame
不務正業 - not live by honest work

除惡務盡 - exterminate evils once and for all
當務之急 - a task of top priority

HISTORICAL

甲骨文 (2000BC) | 金文 (1000BC) | 篆文 (200BC) | 隸 (200AD)

FONTS

楷 行 草 宋

266AD Jing Dynasty Wang Xizhi
778BC Tang Dynasty Liu Goongquan
1280AD Yuan Dynasty Zhao Mengfu
1829AD Ming Dynasty Dong Qichang

THE GENIUS OF CHINESE CHARACTERS

STANDARD	SIMPLIFIED	MEANING
正	正	• right, proper: 正確; in process of: 正在 • genuine: 真正; formal: 正式

正 一 丁 下 正 正
简 一 丁 下 正 正

ETYMOLOGY

Radical: 止
Move 止 (footsteps) to the target location: conquer, correct, justice = main

DATA

Radical (部首)	77: 止		
Strokes	5 | 5		
HSK	2		
Frequency	129		
Big5	A5BF		
Unihan	U+6B63		
Kangxi Dictionary	P574		

PRONUNCIATION

Pinyin:	zhèng
Wade-Giles:	chêng
Cantonese:	jing3
Minnan:	chiàⁿ
Bopomofo:	ㄓㄥˋ
JP-Onyomi:	sei, shō
JP-Kunyomi:	tada·shī, masa

J-音読み:	セイ, ショウ
J-訓読み:	ただ·しい, まさ
Korean 音读:	정
Korean 训读:	바르다
K-eumdok:	chŏng
K-hundok:	bareuda
Vietnamese:	tích cực

VARIANTS	政, 正

COMBINATIONS

正直 - upright	正犯 - main culprit
新正 - New Year	正命 - natural death
改正 - to correct	正午 - high noon
修正 - revise	
正門 - main door	

SAYINGS

不務正業 - ignore onés proper occupation	就地正法 - carry out a death sentence on the spot
風華正茂 - be in one's prime	壽終正寢 - die a natural death
撥亂反正 - bring order out of chaos	歪打正著 - score a lucky hit
名正言順 - be right and proper	言歸正傳 - get down to business

HISTORICAL

甲骨文 (2000BC)	金文 (1000BC)	篆文 (200BC)	隸 (200AD)

FONTS

楷　行　草　宋

266AD Jing Dynasty Wang Xizhi

778BC Tang Dynasty Yan Zhenqing

1280AD Yuan Dynasty Zhao Mengfu

1829AD Ming Dynasty Dong Qichang

THE GENIUS OF CHINESE CHARACTERS

STANDARD	SIMPLIFIED	MEANING
房	房	• house, building: 房子 • room: 房間 • kitchen: 厨房 • housing: 房屋

| 正 | 丶 | 亠 | 二 | 户 | 戶 | 戶 | 房 | 房 |
| 简 | 丶 | 亠 | 二 | 户 | 户 | 户 | 房 | 房 |

ETYMOLOGY

Radical: 戶
Door 戶 + 方 (phonetic): houses on either side, house = branches of a family

DATA

Radical (部首)　　　　63: 戶
Strokes　　　　　　　　8 | 8
HSK　　　　　　　　　　2
Frequency　　　　　　512
Big5　　　　　　　　　A9D0
Unihan　　　　　　　　U+623F
Kangxi Dictionary　　P415

PRONUNCIATION

Pinyin:　　　　fáng
Wade-Giles:　　fang
Cantonese:　　fong4
Minnan:　　　　pâng
Bopomofo:　　　ㄈㄤˊ
JP-Onyomi:　　　bō
JP-Kunyomi:　　fusa

J-音読み:　　ボウ
J-訓読み:　　ふさ
Korean 音读: 방
Korean 训读: 방
K-eumdok:　　pang
K-hundok:　　bang
Vietnamese:　phòng

VARIANTS

COMBINATIONS

房客 - tenant
藥房 - pharmacy
房東 - landlord
房產 - real estate
門房 - gatekeeper

賬房 - treasurer
房捐 - house tax
平房 - one-storied house

SAYINGS

文房四寶 - the "scholar's four jewels", the brush pen, the ink stick, the ink bowl, and paper

HISTORICAL

甲骨文 (2000BC)　　金文 (1000BC)　　篆文 (200BC)　　隸 (200AD)

FONTS

楷　行　草　宋
房　房　房　房

266AD Jing Dynasty Wang Xizhi

778BC Tang Dynasty Guo Quan

1280AD Yuan Dynasty Zhao Mengfu

1829AD Ming Dynasty Dong Qichang

THE GENIUS OF CHINESE CHARACTERS

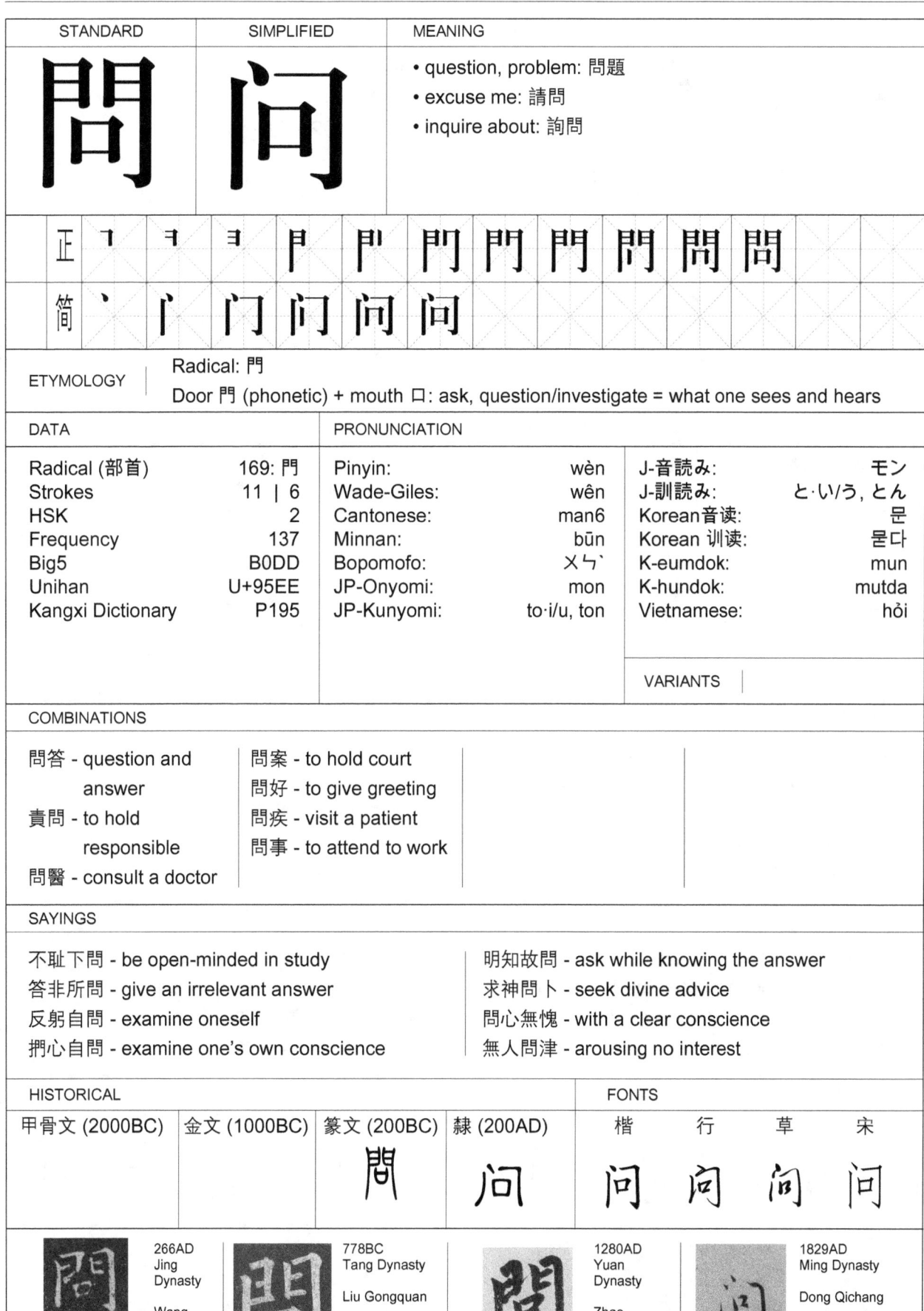

STANDARD	SIMPLIFIED	MEANING
問	问	• question, problem: 問題 • excuse me: 請問 • inquire about: 詢問

正: 丨 ㄱ ㅋ 戶 戶 門 門 門 問 問 問
简: ゛ 丨 门 问 问 问

ETYMOLOGY
Radical: 門
Door 門 (phonetic) + mouth 口: ask, question/investigate = what one sees and hears

DATA

Radical (部首)	169: 門	Pinyin:	wèn
Strokes	11 | 6	Wade-Giles:	wên
HSK	2	Cantonese:	man6
Frequency	137	Minnan:	būn
Big5	B0DD	Bopomofo:	ㄨㄣˋ
Unihan	U+95EE	JP-Onyomi:	mon
Kangxi Dictionary	P195	JP-Kunyomi:	to·i/u, ton

PRONUNCIATION

J-音読み:	モン
J-訓読み:	と・い/う, とん
Korean 音读:	문
Korean 训读:	묻다
K-eumdok:	mun
K-hundok:	mutda
Vietnamese:	hỏi

VARIANTS

COMBINATIONS

問答 - question and answer
責問 - to hold responsible
問醫 - consult a doctor
問案 - to hold court
問好 - to give greeting
問疾 - visit a patient
問事 - to attend to work

SAYINGS

不恥下問 - be open-minded in study
答非所問 - give an irrelevant answer
反躬自問 - examine oneself
捫心自問 - examine one's own conscience
明知故問 - ask while knowing the answer
求神問卜 - seek divine advice
問心無愧 - with a clear conscience
無人問津 - arousing no interest

HISTORICAL

甲骨文 (2000BC) | 金文 (1000BC) | 篆文 (200BC) | 隸 (200AD)

FONTS

楷 行 草 宋

266AD Jing Dynasty Wang Xizhi
778BC Tang Dynasty Liu Gongquan
1280AD Yuan Dynasty Zhao Mengfu
1829AD Ming Dynasty Dong Qichang

THE GENIUS OF CHINESE CHARACTERS

STANDARD	SIMPLIFIED	MEANING
門	门	• door: 門; entrance: 門口 • go out: 出門; gate: 大門 • department 部門; specialized: 專門

正: 丨 ㄱ ㅋ ㅌ 巴 門 門 門
简: 丶 丆 门

ETYMOLOGY
Radical: 門
A two-sided door 戶: gate, by way of = category/class

DATA
Radical (部首)	169: 門
Strokes	8 | 3
HSK	2
Frequency	185
Big5	AAF9
Unihan	U+95E8
Kangxi Dictionary	P1329

PRONUNCIATION
Pinyin:	mén
Wade-Giles:	mên
Cantonese:	moon4
Minnan:	bûn
Bopomofo:	ㄇㄣˊ
JP-Onyomi:	mon
JP-Kunyomi:	kado, to
J-音読み:	モン
J-訓読み:	かど, と
Korean 音读:	문
Korean 训读:	문
K-eumdok:	mun
K-hundok:	mun
Vietnamese:	cửa

VARIANTS

COMBINATIONS
- 房門 - door
- 門丁 - gatekeeper
- 門口 - doorway
- 門票 - admission ticket
- 門限 - threshold
- 門牙 - incisor (front teeth)

SAYINGS
- 班門弄斧 - be conceited
- 閉門思過 - ponder over one's mistakes in solitude
- 杜門謝客 - live in complete seclusion
- 分門別類 - classify according to subjects
- 關門大吉 - close down for good
- 開門見山 - come straight to the point
- 門當戶對 - equal in social status
- 門可羅雀 - a deserted house

HISTORICAL / FONTS

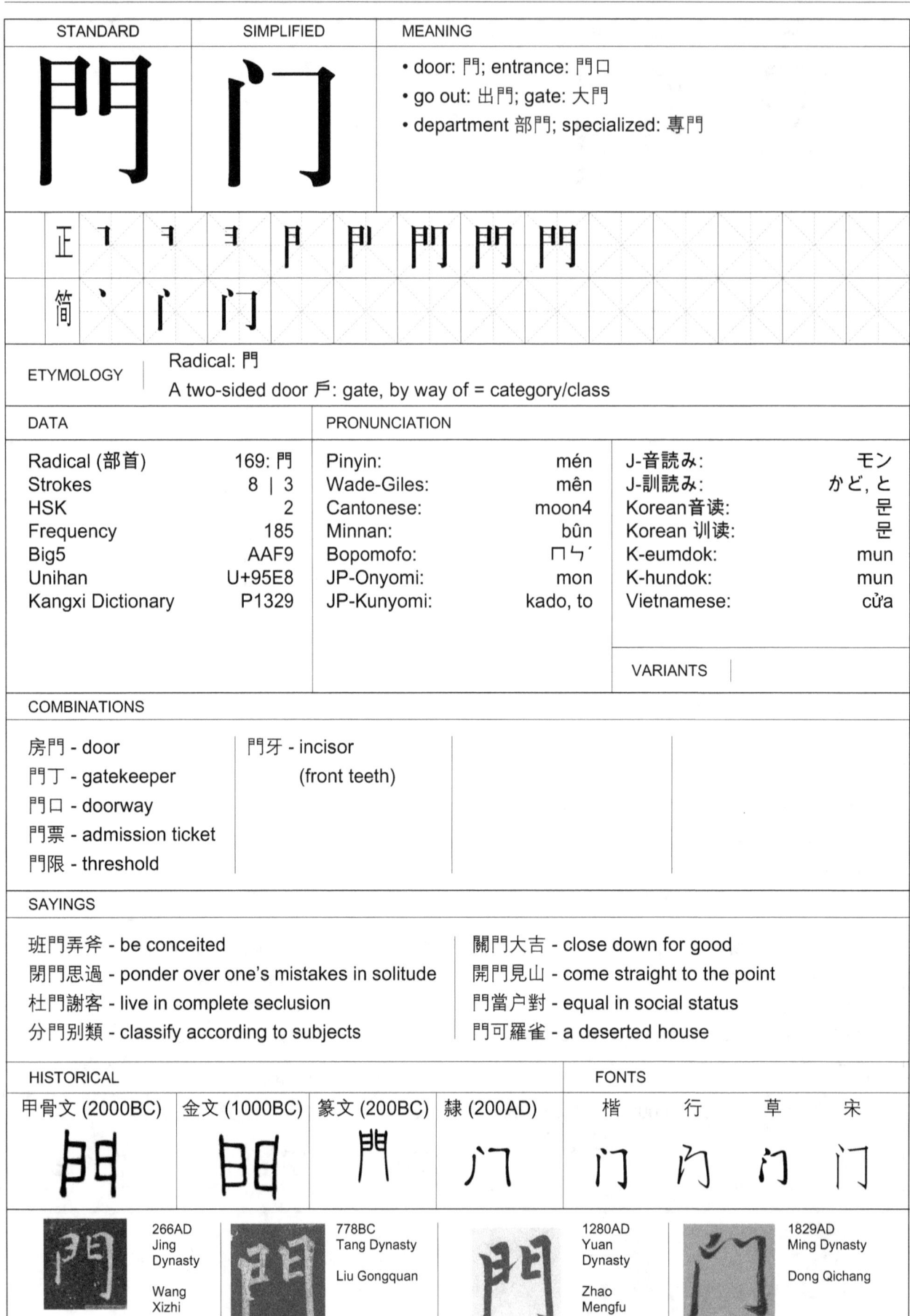

甲骨文 (2000BC) | 金文 (1000BC) | 篆文 (200BC) | 隸 (200AD) | 楷 行 草 宋

266AD Jing Dynasty, Wang Xizhi
778BC Tang Dynasty, Liu Gongquan
1280AD Yuan Dynasty, Zhao Mengfu
1829AD Ming Dynasty, Dong Qichang

THE GENIUS OF CHINESE CHARACTERS

STANDARD	SIMPLIFIED	MEANING
球	球	• ball: 球; the globe: 地球 • whole world: 全球; soccer: 足球 • tennis: 網球; basketball: 籃球 • team: 球隊

正: 一 二 チ 王 玉 玎 玏 玌 球 球 球
简: 一 二 チ 王 玉 玎 玏 玌 球 球 球

ETYMOLOGY
Radical: 玉
Jade 玉 + 求 (phonetic): good jade. The meaning of "ball" was borrowed

DATA

		PRONUNCIATION			
Radical (部首)	96: 玉	Pinyin:	qiú	J-音読み:	キュウ
Strokes	11 | 11	Wade-Giles:	ch'iu	J-訓読み:	たま
HSK	2	Cantonese:	kau4	Korean 音读:	구
Frequency	628	Minnan:	kiû	Korean 训读:	공
Big5	B279	Bopomofo:	ㄑㄧㄡˊ	K-eumdok:	ku
Unihan	U+7403	JP-Onyomi:	kyū	K-hundok:	gong
Kangxi Dictionary	P732	JP-Kunyomi:	tama	Vietnamese:	trái bóng

VARIANTS | 毬, 璆

COMBINATIONS

排球 - volleyball
籃球 - basketball
球徑 - circumference
球拍 - a racket
球竿 - hockey stick

星球 - a star
滾球 - dribble
鉛球 - shot put

SAYINGS

n/a

HISTORICAL

甲骨文 (2000BC)	金文 (1000BC)	篆文 (200BC)	隸 (200AD)

FONTS

楷 行 草 宋

1829AD Ming Dynasty Dong Qichang
1829AD Ming Dynasty Wang Chong
1829AD Ming Dynasty Wang Duo

THE GENIUS OF CHINESE CHARACTERS

STANDARD	SIMPLIFIED	MEANING
題	题	• question, problem: 問題 • subject: 主題 • topic of conversation: 話題 • title: 題目

Stroke order (Standard 正): 丨 冂 日 日 旦 早 早 昰 是 是 是 題 題 題 題 題 題 題

Stroke order (Simplified 简): 丨 冂 日 日 旦 早 早 昰 是 是 是 题 题 题

ETYMOLOGY

Radical: 頁
Head 頁 + 是 (phonetic): forehead, top = headline/title

DATA

Radical (部首): 181: 頁
Strokes: 18 | 15
HSK: 2
Frequency: 218
Big5: C344
Unihan: U+9898
Kangxi Dictionary: P1406

PRONUNCIATION

Pinyin: tí
Wade-Giles: t'i
Cantonese: tai4
Minnan: tê
Bopomofo: ㄊㄧˊ
JP-Onyomi: dai, tei
JP-Kunyomi: hitai

J-音読み: ダイ, テイ
J-訓読み: ひたい
Korean 音读: 제
Korean 训读: 제목
K-eumdok: che
K-hundok: jemok
Vietnamese: câu hỏi

VARIANTS

COMBINATIONS

問題 - question
主題 - subject
命題 - proposition
題材 - subject matter
標題 - headline

難題 - problem
試題 - test question

SAYINGS

借題發揮 - make an issue of
離題萬裏 - be too far afield
文不對題 - be off the point
小題大作 - make a mountain out of a molehill

HISTORICAL

甲骨文 (2000BC) | 金文 (1000BC) | 篆文 (200BC) | 隸 (200AD)

266AD Jing Dynasty — Wang Xizhi
778BC Tang Dynasty — Yan Zhenqing
1280AD Yuan Dynasty — Zhao Mengfu
1829AD Ming Dynasty — Dong Qichang

FONTS

楷 行 草 宋
題 題 題 題

THE GENIUS OF CHINESE CHARACTERS

STANDARD	SIMPLIFIED	MEANING
教	教	• teach: 教 • religion: 宗教 • teaching: 教學 • classroom: 教室

正	一	十	土	耂	耂	孝	孝	孝	孝	勎	教
简	一	十	土	耂	耂	孝	孝	孝	孝	勎	教

ETYMOLOGY — Radical: 攴 Hold the whip 攴 (now 攵) to urge the students 子 to learn knowledge 爻: teach, train, ask/let

DATA

Radical (部首)	66: 攴
Strokes	11 | 11
HSK	2
Frequency	191
Big5	B1D0
Unihan	U+6559
Kangxi Dictionary	

PRONUNCIATION

Pinyin:	jiāo
Wade-Giles:	chiao
Cantonese:	gaau3
Minnan:	kàu
Bopomofo:	ㄐㄧㄠˋ
JP-Onyomi:	kyō
JP-Kunyomi:	oshi·eru

J-音読み:	キョウ
J-訓読み:	おし・える
Korean 音读:	교
Korean 训读:	가르치다
K-eumdok:	kyo
K-hundok:	gareuchida
Vietnamese:	dạy

VARIANTS

COMBINATIONS

教育 - education
教學 - to teach
教師 - teacher
教授 - professor
教材 - teaching material

宗教 - religion
佛教 - Buddhism
文教 - cultural education
請教 - consult
傳教 - preach

SAYINGS

不屑教誨 - to be impervious to persuasion
教學相長 - teaching benefits student and teacher alike
孺子可教 - the boy is worth teaching

三教九流 - different classes in society
言傳身教 - teach by precept and example
移樽就教 - transfer to education

HISTORICAL

甲骨文 (2000BC)	金文 (1000BC)	篆文 (200BC)	隸 (200AD)
		𢼄	教

FONTS

楷	行	草	宋
教	教	教	教

266AD
Jing Dynasty
Wang Xizhi

778BC
Tang Dynasty
Liu Gongquan

1280AD
Yuan Dynasty
Zhao Mengfu

1829AD
Ming Dynasty
Dong Qichang

THE GENIUS OF CHINESE CHARACTERS

STANDARD	SIMPLIFIED	MEANING
路	路	• road: 道路; highway: 公路 • route: 路綫; on the road: 上路 • surname: 路

Stroke order (正): 丨 冂 口 甲 甲 卩 足 趵 趵 跤 路 路 路
Stroke order (简): 丨 冂 口 甲 甲 卩 足 趵 趵 跤 路 路 路

ETYMOLOGY

Radical: 足
Foot 腳 + 各 (phonetic): road, rule/law/principle

DATA

Radical (部首)	157: 足
Strokes	13 | 13
HSK	2
Frequency	305
Big5	B8F4
Unihan	U+8DEF
Kangxi Dictionary	P1225

PRONUNCIATION

Pinyin:	lù
Wade-Giles:	lu
Cantonese:	lo6
Minnan:	lō
Bopomofo:	ㄌㄨˋ
JP-Onyomi:	ro
JP-Kunyomi:	ji, michi
J-音読み:	ロ
J-訓読み:	じ, みち
Korean 音读:	낙
Korean 训读:	길, 통행, 도로
K-eumdok:	nik
K-hundok:	gil, tonghaeng, doro
Vietnamese:	đường

VARIANTS

COMBINATIONS

- 路綫 - route
- 路上 - on the way
- 路過 - to pass by
- 路燈 - street lamp
- 網路 - network
- 公路 - highway
- 綫路 - circuit
- 一路 - all the way

SAYINGS

- 半路出家 - switch to a new profession
- 筚路褴褛 - endure great hardships in pioneer work
- 必由之路 - the only way
- 广开才路 - open all avenues for people of talent
- 绝路逢生 - be alive in desperation
- 路不拾遗 - a peaceful and prosperous time
- 穷途末路 - reach the end of the rope

HISTORICAL

甲骨文 (2000BC)	金文 (1000BC)	篆文 (200BC)	隸 (200AD)
		踛	路

FONTS

楷	行	草	宋
路	路	路	路

266AD Jing Dynasty Wang Xizhi
778BC Tang Dynasty Ouyang Xun
1280AD Yuan Dynasty Zhao Mengfu
1829AD Ming Dynasty Dong Qichang

THE GENIUS OF Chinese Characters

STANDARD	SIMPLIFIED	MEANING
告	告	• to tell: 告訴 • report: 報告 • advertisement: 廣告 • warn: 警告

| 正 | 丿 | 丄 | 牛 | 生 | 告 | 告 | 告 |
| 简 | 丿 | 丄 | 牛 | 生 | 告 | 告 | 告 |

ETYMOLOGY

Radical: 牛
Cow 牛 + mouth 口: using cows as sacrifices to pray to ancestors, tell = announce

DATA

		PRONUNCIATION			
Radical (部首)	30: 口	Pinyin:	gào	J-音読み:	コク
Strokes	7 | 7	Wade-Giles:	kao	J-訓読み:	つ・げる
HSK	2	Cantonese:	go3	Korean 音读:	고
Frequency	310	Minnan:	kò	Korean 训读:	고하다, 알리다
Big5	A769	Bopomofo:	ㄍㄠˋ	K-eumdok:	ko
Unihan	U+544A	JP-Onyomi:	koku	K-hundok:	gohada, allida
Kangxi Dictionary		JP-Kunyomi:	tsu·geru	Vietnamese:	kiện

VARIANTS	告, 誥

COMBINATIONS

告別 - to bid farewell	告示 - announcement
廣告 - advertisement	
公告 - public notice	
被告 - defendant	
通告 - announce	

SAYINGS

安民告示 - notice to reassure the public
不可告人 - ulterior
大功告成 - be accomplished
乞哀告憐 - beg for mercy

無可奉告 - have nothing to say
諄諄告誡 - tirelessly counsel
自告奮勇 - offer oneself

HISTORICAL

| 甲骨文 (2000BC) | 金文 (1000BC) | 篆文 (200BC) | 隸 (200AD) |

FONTS

楷 行 草 宋

266AD Jing Dynasty Wang Xizhi

778BC Tang Dynasty Yan Zhenqing

1280AD Yuan Dynasty Zhao Mengfu

1829AD Ming Dynasty Dong Qichang

THE GENIUS OF CHINESE CHARACTERS

STANDARD	SIMPLIFIED	MEANING
件	件	• a unit of anything: 一件大事 • all items: 件件

正 ノ 亻 亻 仁 仵 件
简 ノ 亻 亻 仁 仵 件

ETYMOLOGY
Radical: 人
People 人 + cow 牛: cut the cow into pieces, part = a piece of

DATA
- Radical (部首): 11: 入
- Strokes: 6 | 6
- HSK: 2
- Frequency: 250
- Big5: A5F3
- Unihan: U+4EF6
- Kangxi Dictionary: P94

PRONUNCIATION
- Pinyin: jiàn
- Wade-Giles: chien
- Cantonese: gin6
- Minnan: kiāⁿ
- Bopomofo: ㄐㄧㄢˋ
- JP-Onyomi: ken
- JP-Kunyomi: kudari

- J-音読み: ケン
- J-訓読み: くだり
- Korean 音读: 건
- Korean 训读: 물건
- K-eumdok: kun
- K-hundok: mulgeon
- Vietnamese: cái

VARIANTS | 侔

COMBINATIONS
- 條件 - condition
- 案件 - case
- 事件 - incident
- 文件 - document
- 郵件 - mail
- 部件 - parts
- 要件 - important criteria
- 元件 - component

SAYINGS
n/a

HISTORICAL
- 甲骨文 (2000BC)
- 金文 (1000BC)
- 篆文 (200BC): 件
- 隸 (200AD): 件

FONTS
楷 行 草 宋
件 件 件 件

266AD
Jing Dynasty
Wang Xizhi

THE GENIUS OF CHINESE CHARACTERS

STANDARD	SIMPLIFIED	MEANING
運	运	• luck: 氣運; Games (olympic): 運動 • to revolve: 運轉; to transport: 運送 • to exercise skill; fortune: 幸運

正: 丶 冖 冖 冖 𠃌 冝 冒 宣 軍 軍 運 運
簡: 一 二 云 云 㕍 运 运

ETYMOLOGY
Radical: 辵
Move 辵 + 军 (phonetic): transport/migrate, move/turn = fate/use

DATA

		PRONUNCIATION			
Radical (部首)	162: 辵	Pinyin:	yùn	J-音読み:	ウン
Strokes	12 | 7	Wade-Giles:	yün	J-訓読み:	はこ·ぶ
HSK	2	Cantonese:	wan6	Korean 音读:	운
Frequency	345	Minnan:	ūn	Korean 训读:	옮기다
Big5	B942	Bopomofo:	ㄩㄣˋ	K-eumdok:	woon
Unihan	U+8FD0	JP-Onyomi:	un	K-hundok:	un
Kangxi Dictionary	P1261	JP-Kunyomi:	hako·bu	Vietnamese:	may mắn

VARIANTS

COMBINATIONS

運用 - put to use
運轉 - revolve
運行 - moving
運動 - sport, political movement

運動員 - athlete
營運 - run a business
運河 - canal

SAYINGS

財運亨通 - wishing you prosperity
官運亨通 - wishing someone success in officialdom
匠心獨運 - show one's own ingenuity
時來運轉 - catch a break

時運不濟 - have bad luck
應運而生 - emerge as the times require
運籌帷幄 - map out a strategy
運用自如 - handle very skillfully

HISTORICAL

甲骨文 (2000BC)	金文 (1000BC)	篆文 (200BC)	隸 (200AD)
		運	运

FONTS

楷　行　草　宋
运　运　运　运

266AD
Jing Dynasty
Wang Xizhi

778BC
Tang Dynasty
Liu Gongquan

1280AD
Yuan Dynasty
Zhao Mengfu

1829AD
Ming Dynasty
Dong Qichang

THE GENIUS OF CHINESE CHARACTERS

STANDARD	SIMPLIFIED	MEANING
給	给	• to provide: 供給 • to give: 給他 • to pay: 給錢 • sufficient: 自給

正: 乛 幺 幺 幺 幺 糸 糸 糽 紣 紣 給 給
简: 乛 幺 幺 纟 纠 纠 纠 给 给

ETYMOLOGY

Radical: 糸
Silk 糸 + 合 (phonetic): abundant/rich = offer/provide

DATA

		PRONUNCIATION			
Radical (部首)	120: 糸	Pinyin:	gěi	J-音読み:	キュウ
Strokes	12 | 9	Wade-Giles:	kei	J-訓読み:	たま·う
HSK	2	Cantonese:	kap1	Korean 音读:	급
Frequency	180	Minnan:	kip	Korean 训读:	주다
Big5	B5B9	Bopomofo:	ㄍㄟ	K-eumdok:	kehp
Unihan	U+7ED9	JP-Onyomi:	kyū	K-hundok:	juda
Kangxi Dictionary	P923	JP-Kunyomi:	tama·u	Vietnamese:	đưa cho

VARIANTS | 給(J)

COMBINATIONS

賣給 - sell to
交給 - hand over
自給 - support ones self
分給 - divide

SAYINGS

家給人足 - all live in plenty
日不暇給 - hard pressed for time
自給自足 - self-sufficient

HISTORICAL

甲骨文 (2000BC)	金文 (1000BC)	篆文 (200BC)	隸 (200AD)
		給	給

FONTS

楷	行	草	宋
给	给	给	给

266AD Jing Dynasty Wang Xizhi

778BC Tang Dynasty Liu Gongquan

1280AD Yuan Dynasty Zhao Mengfu

1829AD Ming Dynasty Dong Qichang

THE GENIUS OF Chinese Characters

STANDARD	SIMPLIFIED	MEANING
常	常	• always: 常常; frequently: 時常 • normally: 正常; usually: 日常 • often: 經常; common: 平常

正 ｜ 丶 ｜ 丷 ｜ 丷 ｜ 丷 ｜ 兴 ｜ 兴 ｜ 常 ｜ 常 ｜ 常 ｜ 常 ｜ 常

简 ｜ 丶 ｜ 丷 ｜ 丷 ｜ 丷 ｜ 兴 ｜ 兴 ｜ 常 ｜ 常 ｜ 常 ｜ 常 ｜ 常

ETYMOLOGY

Radical: 巾
Cloth 布 + 尚 (phonetic): skirt

DATA

Radical (部首)	50: 巾	Pinyin:	cháng	J-音読み:	ジョウ
Strokes	11 | 11	Wade-Giles:	ch'ang	J-訓読み:	つね, とこ
HSK	2	Cantonese:	seung4	Korean 音读:	상
Frequency	187	Minnan:	siông	Korean 训读:	떳떳하다
Big5	B160	Bopomofo:	ㄔㄤˊ	K-eumdok:	sang
Unihan	U+5E38	JP-Onyomi:	jō	K-hundok:	tteottteotada
Kangxi Dictionary	P333	JP-Kunyomi:	tsune, toko	Vietnamese:	thường xuyên

VARIANTS | 裳, 恖

COMBINATIONS

日常 - Daily
正常 - normal
异常 - unexpected
不正常 - abnormal
常見 - often seen

常年 - year-long
非常 - very

SAYINGS

變化無常 - constantly changing
打破常規 - break precedent
翻覆無常 - wavering
反覆無常 - caprice

非同尋常 - unusual, exceptional
老生常談 - cut and dried
人之常情 - it's only human
習以爲常 - be accustomed to

HISTORICAL

甲骨文 (2000BC) | 金文 (1000BC) | 篆文 (200BC) 常 | 隸 (200AD) 常

FONTS

楷 行 草 宋
常 常 常 常

266AD
Jing Dynasty
Wang Xizhi

778BC
Tang Dynasty
Liu Gongquan

1280AD
Yuan Dynasty
Zhao Mengfu

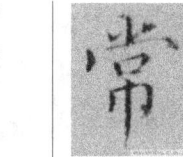
1829AD
Ming Dynasty
Dong Qichang

THE GENIUS OF Chinese CHARACTERS

STANDARD	SIMPLIFIED	MEANING
每	每	• each: 每人 • every: 每天

正	ノ	丶	仁	勹	每	每	每	
简	ノ	丶	仁	勹	每	每	每	

ETYMOLOGY
Radical: 母
The grasses are lush. The meanings of each/every/often are borrowed

DATA

		PRONUNCIATION				
Radical (部首)	80: 母	Pinyin:	měi	J-音読み:	マイ,バイ
Strokes	7 | 7	Wade-Giles:	mei	J-訓読み:	つね
HSK	2	Cantonese:	mooi5	Korean 音读:	매
Frequency	359	Minnan:	múi	Korean 训读:	매양, 늘
Big5	A843	Bopomofo:	ㄇㄟ	K-eumdok:	mae
Unihan	U+6BCF	JP-Onyomi:	mai,bai	K-hundok:	maeyang, neul
Kangxi Dictionary	P589	JP-Kunyomi:	tsune	Vietnamese:	mỗi

VARIANTS	毎

COMBINATIONS

每次 - every time
每月 - every month
每人 - per person
每個人 - every person
每周 - every week

每天 - everyday

SAYINGS
n/a

HISTORICAL

甲骨文 (2000BC)	金文 (1000BC)	篆文 (200BC)	隸 (200AD)
		𣫭	每

FONTS

楷	行	草	宋
每	每	每	每

266AD
Jing Dynasty
Wang Xizhi

778BC
Tang Dynasty
Yan Zhenqing

1280AD
Yuan Dynasty
Zhao Mengfu

1829AD
Ming Dynasty
Dong Qichang

THE GENIUS OF CHINESE CHARACTERS

STANDARD	SIMPLIFIED	MEANING
樂	乐	• music: 樂器 • pleasure: 快樂 ; to enjoy: 樂善 • glad to: 樂助; a melody: 樂曲 • a paradise: 樂國; happy to: 樂于

正: 丨 ㄏ 白 白 白 ㄠ白 纩 纩 纩 樂 樂 樂 樂

樂 樂

简: 一 ㄁ 乐 乐 乐

ETYMOLOGY — Radical: 木
A musical instrument made of silk 糸 and wood 木, 白 is register: music = happy

DATA
- Radical (部首): 75: 木
- Strokes: 15 | 5
- HSK: 2
- Frequency: 619
- Big5: BCD6
- Unihan: U+4E50
- Kangxi Dictionary: P548

PRONUNCIATION
- Pinyin: lè|yuè
- Wade-Giles: lê|yueh
- Cantonese: lok6|ngok6
- Minnan: lók
- Bopomofo: ㄌㄜˋ/ㄩㄝˋ
- JP-Onyomi: gaku, raku
- JP-Kunyomi: tano·shī

- J-音読み: ガク, ラク
- J-訓読み: たの・しい
- Korean 音读: 낙
- Korean 训读: 노래, 음악
- K-eumdok: nock
- K-hundok: norae, eumak
- Vietnamese: vui vẻ

VARIANTS: 楽(J)

COMBINATIONS
- 樂器 - musical instrument
- 樂隊 - band
- 樂園 - paradise
- 樂見 - to view optimistically
- 娛樂 - entertainment
- 音樂會 - concert
- 音樂家 - musician
- 聲樂 - vocal music

SAYINGS
- 安居樂業 - live and work in peace
- 安貧樂道 - bow to one's fate
- 吃喝玩樂 - eat, drink and be merry
- 及時行樂 - make merry while one can
- 津津樂道 - take delight in talking about
- 樂極生悲 - after joy comes sadness
- 天倫之樂 - the happiness of a family union

HISTORICAL
甲骨文 (2000BC)	金文 (1000BC)	篆文 (200BC)	隸 (200AD)

FONTS
楷 行 草 宋
乐 乐 乐 乐

266AD Jing Dynasty
Wang Xizhi

778BC Tang Dynasty
Liu Gongquan

1280AD Yuan Dynasty
Zhao Mengfu

1829AD Ming Dynasty
Dong Qichang

THE GENIUS OF CHINESE CHARACTERS

STANDARD	SIMPLIFIED	MEANING
身	身	• body: 身體 • self: 修身 • be pregnant: 有身 • incarnation: 前身 • at hand: 身邊; person: 人身

正 ' ｲ ｲ 勹 勺 身 身 身
简 ' ｲ ｲ 勹 勺 身 身 身

ETYMOLOGY
Radical: 身
Pictograph: a person with big belly = body/trunk

DATA

		PRONUNCIATION			
Radical (部首)	158: 身	Pinyin:	shēn	J-音読み:	シン
Strokes	7 | 7	Wade-Giles:	chüan	J-訓読み:	み
HSK	2	Cantonese:	san1	Korean 音读:	건
Frequency	164	Minnan:	sin	Korean 训读:	몸, 신체
Big5	A8AD	Bopomofo:	ㄕㄣ	K-eumdok:	kun
Unihan	U+8EAB	JP-Onyomi:	shin	K-hundok:	mom, sinche
Kangxi Dictionary	P1237	JP-Kunyomi:	mi	Vietnamese:	thân hình

VARIANTS

COMBINATIONS

身邊 - by one's side   自身 - itself   下半身 - lower half of body
身心 - body and mind   全身 - whole body   起身 - stand up
身分證 - ID   轉身 - (person) to turn around
身高 - height   終身 - lifelong
身影 - shadow

SAYINGS

安身立命 - live in peace   感同身受 - appreciate it as a personal experience
赤身裸體 - stripped naked   功成身退 - retire after having made one's mark
粉身碎骨 - be smashed to pieces   潔身自好 - keep one's integrity
奮不顧身 - defy personal danger   立身處世 - get on in the world

HISTORICAL

甲骨文 (2000BC)	金文 (1000BC)	篆文 (200BC)	隸 (200AD)

FONTS

楷　行　草　宋

266AD
Jing Dynasty
Wang Xizhi

778BC
Tang Dynasty
Liu Gongquan

1280AD
Yuan Dynasty
Zhao Mengfu

1829AD
Ming Dynasty
Dong Qichang

THE GENIUS OF CHINESE CHARACTERS

STANDARD	SIMPLIFIED	MEANING
別	别	• other: 別人 • distinction: 區別 • to leave: 告別 • to pin up: 別上 • to classify: 類別

正 丨 冂 口 号 另 別 別
简 丨 冂 口 号 另 别 别

ETYMOLOGY
Radical: 刀
The original shape was 分 - leave/depart

DATA
- Radical (部首): 18: 刀
- Strokes: 7 | 7
- HSK: 2
- Frequency: 222
- Big5: A74F
- Unihan: U+522B
- Kangxi Dictionary: P138

PRONUNCIATION
- Pinyin: bié
- Wade-Giles: pieh
- Cantonese: bit6
- Minnan: piåt
- Bopomofo: ㄅㄧㄝˊ
- JP-Onyomi: betsu
- JP-Kunyomi: waka·reru
- J-音読み: ベツ
- J-訓読み: わか・れる
- Korean 音读: 별
- Korean 训读: 나누다
- K-eumdok: byeol
- K-hundok: nanuda
- Vietnamese: đừng

VARIANTS

COMBINATIONS
特別 - special
個別 - individual
別名 - pseudonym
別國 - other country
別處 - elsewhere

別提 - don't mention it
別館 - annex

SAYINGS
n/a

HISTORICAL

甲骨文 (2000BC)	金文 (1000BC)	篆文 (200BC)	隸 (200AD)
		𠛰	別

FONTS
楷　行　草　宋
別　別　別　別

266AD Jing Dynasty Wang Xizhi
778BC Tang Dynasty Yan Zhenqing
1280AD Yuan Dynasty Zhao Mengfu
1829AD Ming Dynasty Dong Qichang

THE GENIUS OF CHINESE CHARACTERS

STANDARD	SIMPLIFIED	MEANING
張	张	• nervous: 緊張 • a flat piece: 一張紙 • open up: 开张 • stretch: 張開 • to set up: 開張; to boast: 誇張

正: フ　フ　弓　弓ˊ　弓ᐟ　弓ᐟ　弭　弭　弭　張　張
简: フ　フ　弓　弓ˊ　弓ˊ　张　张

ETYMOLOGY

Radical: 弓
Bow 弓 + long 長 (phonetic): string the bow, draw a bow = open up/expand

DATA

Radical (部首) — 57: 弓
Strokes — 11 | 7
HSK — 2
Frequency — 318
Big5 — B169
Unihan — U+5F20
Kangxi Dictionary — P259

PRONUNCIATION

Pinyin: zhāng
Wade-Giles: chang
Cantonese: jeung1
Minnan: tiuⁿ
Bopomofo: ㄓㄤ
JP-Onyomi: chō
JP-Kunyomi: ha·ru/ri

J-音読み: チョウ
J-訓読み: は·る/り
Korean 音读: 장
Korean 训读: 베풀다
K-eumdok: jang
K-hundok: bepulda
Vietnamese: trương

VARIANTS

COMBINATIONS

張貼 - to post
緊張 - nervous
主張 - proposition
慌張 - to scurry
舒張 - to dilate

張揚 - to publicize

SAYINGS

大張旗鼓 - on a grand scale
東張西望 - gaze around
飯來張口 - eat a ready-cooked meal
荒荒張張 - covered with confusion, confused

明目張膽 - to be brazen
剖張伴厲 - keep up appearances and be wasteful
哮張一什 - be arrogant for a time
張大其詞 - exaggerate

HISTORICAL

甲骨文 (2000BC) | 金文 (1000BC) | 篆文 (200BC) | 隸 (200AD)

FONTS

楷　行　草　宋

266AD Jing Dynasty Wang Xizhi
778BC Tang Dynasty Liu Gongquan
1280AD Yuan Dynasty Zhao Mengfu
1829AD Ming Dynasty Dong Qichang

RADICALS
部首

Radical No.	Radical	Variant
1	一	
2	丨	
3	丶	
4	丿	乀 乁
5	乙	乚 乛
6	亅	
7	二	
8	亠	
9	人	亻
10	儿	
11	入	
12	八	丷
13	冂	
14	冖	
15	冫	
16	几	
17	凵	
18	刀	刂
19	力	
20	勹	
21	匕	
22	匚	
23	匸	
24	十	
25	卜	
26	卩	
27	厂	
28	厶	
29	又	
30	口	

Radical No.	Radical	Variant
31	囗	
32	土	
33	士	
34	夂	
35	夊	
36	夕	
37	大	
38	女	
39	子	
40	宀	
41	寸	
42	小	
43	尢	尣
44	尸	
45	屮	
46	山	
47	川	巛 巜
48	工	
49	己	
50	巾	
51	干	
52	幺	
53	广	
54	廴	
55	廾	
56	弋	
57	弓	
58	彐	彑
59	彡	
60	彳	

THE GENIUS OF CHINESE CHARACTERS

Radical No.	Radical	Variant
61	心	忄
62	戈	
63	戶	
64	手	扌
65	支	
66	攴	攵
67	文	
68	斗	
69	斤	
70	方	
71	无	
72	日	
73	曰	
74	月	
75	木	
76	欠	
77	止	
78	歹	
79	殳	
80	母	毋
81	比	
82	毛	
83	氏	
84	气	
85	水	氵
86	火	灬
87	爪	爫
88	父	
89	爻	
90	爿	
91	片	
92	牙	
93	牛	牜
94	犭	犬
95	玄	
96	玉	王
97	瓜	
98	瓦	
99	甘	

Radical No.	Radical	Variant
100	生	
101	用	
102	田	
103	疋	
104	疒	
105	癶	
106	白	
107	皮	
108	皿	
109	目	
110	矛	
111	矢	
112	石	
113	示	礻
114	禸	
115	禾	
116	穴	
117	立	
118	竹	
119	米	
120	纟	（糸）
121	缶	
122	网	罒
123	羊	
124	羽	
125	老	
126	而	
127	耒	
128	耳	
129	聿	
130	肉	
131	臣	
132	自	
133	至	
134	臼	
135	舌	
136	舛	
137	舟	
138	艮	

THE GENIUS OF CHINESE CHARACTERS

Radical No.	Radical	Variant
139	色	
140	虍	
141	虎	
142	虫	
143	血	
144	行	
145	衣	衤
146	西	襾
147	见	(見)
148	角	
149	讠	(言)
150	谷	
151	豆	
152	豕	
153	豸	
154	贝	(貝)
155	赤	
156	走	
157	足	
158	身	
159	车	(車)
160	辛	
161	辰	
162	辶	
163	邑	阝
164	酉	
165	釆	
166	里	
167	钅	金
168	长	(長)
169	门	(門)
170	阜	阝
171	隶	
172	隹	
173	雨	
174	青	
175	非	
176	面	
177	革	

Radical No.	Radical	Variant
178	韦	(韋)
179	韭	
180	音	
181	页	(頁)
182	风	(風)
183	飞	(飛)
184	饣	飠 食
185	首	
186	香	
187	马	(馬)
188	骨	
189	高	
190	髟	
191	鬥	
192	鬯	
193	鬲	
194	鬼	
195	鱼	(魚)
196	鸟	(鳥)
197	卤	
198	鹿	
199	麦	(麥)
200	麻	
201	黄	
202	黍	
203	黑	
204	黹	
205	黾	(黽)
206	鼎	
207	鼓	
208	鼠	
209	鼻	
210	齐	(齊)
211	齿	(齒)
212	龙	(龍)
213	龟	(龜)
214	龠	

THE GENIUS OF CHINESE CHARACTERS

INFORMATION SOURCES

The information used to compile this collection comes from a wide variety of sources. Of course, errors remain amongst all of this data, for which we apologize in advance and welcome any guidance to correct them for the next edition.

The sources used include the following:

Lin Yutang's Chinese-English Dictionary of Modern Usage 林語堂《當代漢英詞典》
    (http://humanum.arts.cuhk.edu.hk/Lexis/Lindict/)
Liang Shih-Chiu - A New Practical Chinese English Dictionary
海词汉语 - 汉语词典 (hanyu.dict.cn)
成语词典 (chengyu.98523.com)
汉语词典 (cidian.911cha.com)
HanziCraft (https://hanzicraft.com/character/)
https://hanziyuan.net/
http://ip194097.ntcu.edu.tw/q/q.asp
Wiktionary (https://zh.wiktionary.org)
NAVER Hanja Dictionary (hanja.dict.naver.com)
Arch Chinese (https://www.archchinese.com/arch_chinese_radicals.html)
http://rtega.be/index.php?subpage=39
https://lingua.mtsu.edu/chinese-computing/statistics/char/list
https://www.archchinese.com/arch_chinese_radicals.html
國學大師 (http://www.guoxuedashi.com/)
http://nihongo.monash.edu/Etymological_Dictionary_of_Han_Chinese_Characters.pdf
http://chinese-characters.org/
JapanDict (https://www.japandict.com/kanji)

www.chinanow.com